Algorithmic Short Se
Python

Refine your algorithmic trading edge, consistently generate investment ideas, and build a robust long/short product

Laurent Bernut

BIRMINGHAM—MUMBAI

Algorithmic Short Selling with Python

Producer: Dr. Shailesh Jain
Acquisition Editor – Peer Reviews: Saby Dsilva
Project Editor: Rianna Rodrigues
Development Editor: Edward Doxey
Copy Editor: Safis Editing
Technical Editor: Aditya Sawant
Proofreader: Safis Editing
Indexer: Manju Arasan
Presentation Designer: Pranit Padwal

First published: September 2021

Production reference: 2291221

Published by Packt Publishing Ltd.
Livery Place
35 Livery Street
Birmingham
B3 2PB, UK.

ISBN 978-1-80181-519-2

www.packt.com

Foreword

Since 1996 I have actively and publicly advised investors in the use and execution of a long/short trading strategy well known as trend following. Long/short. That's two words. But amazingly, after all these years, too many investors and traders miss out on the short side of what I do. They see the word *short*. They perhaps even know what it means, but they stay fixated on the long side. Bull markets drive the emotional, visceral side of us human beings, and people can't get enough of the idea that they could be on board with the next Apple, Tesla, Amazon, or Bitcoin at some cheap price. In theory, instant riches as the next one goes to the moon!

This lack of focus on the short side is rather odd. We all saw *The Big Short*. Michael Burry shot to massive fame through that spectacular short trade. We all admired his call during that chaotic period of time. So we all know that epic up moves often have epic down moves. Moonshots don't stay at the moon. They can crash to hell. Do your quick boom bust market history. Scan the charts. My views are not breaking new ground. But where is *The Big Short II*? Was Burry just lucky on that one particular short trade? Doubtful, but I'm not sure, and nor are you, I imagine. That said, I want repeatability. I want a strategy that can survive for decades.

My life first intersected with a dedicated short seller in 2012 (not too long after Burry's infamous trade), when Laurent Bernut, a short trader based in Tokyo, reached out to me with a speaking opportunity in Tokyo. I took that opportunity and it quickly expanded into a speaking tour across Asia. Twenty cities, ten countries, and I was hooked on Asia. I have lived there since. Cheers to Laurent for being a part of chaos theory! Now, you might not think that this professional relationship was a match. I was coming at trading from a systematic trend following perspective and Laurent was coming at trading through a systematic short perspective. The key word though is *systematic*. And a systematic approach is aimed at one thing: repeatability.

Let me go off on a tangent for a moment. When legendary trading author Jack Schwager recently came on my podcast to promote his new book, it was a no brainer for me to have him on. Now, even though Jack knows I have a trend following bias, he also knows I have an open mind. I knew that when he wrote about a series of unknown traders, he had vetted them and their strategies thoroughly. The common denominator, just like with Laurent and I, was a fixation on systematic and repeatable strategies.

This brings me back to Laurent's new book, *Algorithmic Short Selling with Python*. In it, Laurent conveys a determined passion for the short side that has driven him for over a decade. He sees the opportunity, and knows the value in a systematic short side bias. His book, the one you're reading right now, brings excruciating detail and the transparency traders will need to excel on the short side as well as the long side.

From choosing to enter or exit a position, to managing risk and position size, to visualizing and managing a whole portfolio, Laurent breaks down the process and psychology behind developing an effective long/short trading strategy. He also includes versatile source code in Python, which can be implemented on any stock, in any market, with the sole intention of limiting loss, and yielding above average returns. That's all you can ask for from a teacher. Show me all you know. Give it to me straight and hold nothing back.

Now it's up to you to take Laurent's hard work and go apply it.

Michael Covel

Author of *Trend Following* and *TurtleTrader*

Contributors

About the author

Laurent Bernut has 2 decades of experience in alternative investment space. After the US CPA, he compiled financial statements in Japanese and English for a Tokyo Stock Exchange-listed corporation. After serving as an analyst in two Tokyo-based hedge funds, he joined Fidelity Investments Japan as a dedicated quantitative short-seller. Laurent has built numerous portfolio management systems and developed several quantitative models across various platforms. He currently writes and runs algorithmic strategies and is an undisputed authority on short selling on Quora, where he was nominated top writer for 2017, 2018, and 2019.

John McLaughlin, your authentic mentorship manifested this book. Michael Covel, thank you my friend. Grand merci to my editors Ed Doxey and Sofien Kaabar, and to Dr. Shailesh Jain, who believed in this project. Scott Phillips, I love you. Sincere gratitude to Franklin Parker, Douglas Marsh, Andrew Swanscott from the Better System Trader podcast, Alex Ribeiro Castro, Nitesh Khandelwal, and Wazir Kahar. Thank you also to Victor Haghani. Last, but first in my heart, thank you to Jules and Alizee for your loving inspiration.

About the reviewer

Sofien Kaabar is an institutional market strategist with a focus on technical and quantitative strategies. Having graduated from SKEMA business school in Paris and with a background in trading and research, he is currently focused on trading automation and strategies.

I would like to thank my family, especially my parents, who are always on the front line for me and my two sisters, as well as my fiancée, Charline, who tolerates my excessive working time.

Table of Contents

Preface

"There is nothing more powerful than an idea whose time has come."

– Victor Hugo

Market participants always want industries to become more efficient: "cut the middle man," "cost-reduction," "rationalization." We are finally getting a taste of our own medicine. Markets average long-term returns of 8% per annum. Yet, roughly 60% of professional fund managers underperform their benchmark, year in year out. 90% of retail investors blow up. The way we trade has clearly not been working. Despite all the bravado, the emperors of money have been parading naked. We collectively need to evolve if we want to survive this market Darwinism. Evolution does not take prisoners.

Global warming is a reality in the financial services. The glacier of actively managed money is melting. Mutual funds face intense pressure from exchange traded funds to lower fees. Fortunately, there has been a solution right under our noses all along, a *terra incognita* where mankind has never set foot.

If we were to stack all books about investing, trading, markets, on top of each other, trips to the moon would be a sad ecological reality. Yet, if we were to line up books about short selling side by side on a dinner table, there would still be enough room for a bottle of Côte-Rôtie, a divine northern Rhône valley Shiraz-Viognier wine, and a few glasses. Short selling is the key to raising and maintaining assets under management. When the markets tank, those who still stand up, stand out. Money may temporarily flow (and ebb) to those who shine in bull markets, but it will always gravitate towards those who perform in down markets. Investors may forget unimpressive returns, yet they will not forgive drawdowns.

Short selling commands premium fees. Suppose you add a short book to your endangered long-only mutual fund. From that day on, you can command premium management fees and even demand steep performance fees. You will enjoy more freedom in your mandate to trade exotic instruments, freedom to keep a higher cash balance, freedom to selectively disclose your positions. And the price of freedom is to learn to sell short.

Who this book is for

This book is written by a practitioner for practitioners. It is for advanced to expert market participants. Even if you have never coded a line in Python, this book is still for you. It was originally written without the source code. This later addition is meant to help readers implement the concepts in real life. If you are an experienced coder but new to the markets, you will pick up concepts that will help you on your journey. You may however want to supplement your market education with further reading.

Even if you choose never to sell short, this book is still for you. The tools and techniques developed for the short side are built to withstand extreme conditions. If you can survive the arid environment of the short side, imagine how you will thrive on the long side. If you are in the long/short business, the question is not whether you should read this book or not. The real question is can you afford to *not* read this book. You may disagree with some ideas, but they will provoke thoughts and spark conversation. The ideas we originally resist are the ones that makes us grow, so welcome to the space beyond your comfort zone.

What this book covers

Part I, The Inner Game: Demystifying Short Selling

Chapter 1, The Stock Market Game, discusses a few questions: "Is the stock market an art or a science? What if it was just a game? How do you win an infinite complex random game?" This chapters sets the context of the rest of the book.

Chapter 2, 10 Classic Myths About Short Selling, dispels enduring myths about short selling. The most important question is: "do you want to retire on numbers or stories?" If the former, then short sellers are your pension's best friend.

Chapter 3, Take a Walk on the Wild Short Side, explains the arc of the long side mindset on the short side and its predictable failure. This chapter describes the three endemic challenges of the short side: market dynamics, scarcity mentality, and information asymmetry.

Part II, The Outer Game: Developing a Robust Trading Edge

Chapter 4, Long/Short Methodologies: Absolute and Relative, addresses idea generation. You will be able to consistently generate as many if not more ideas on the short side than on the long side.

Chapter 5, Regime Definition, explains several regime definition methodologies to reclassify stocks as bullish, bearish, or inconclusive.

Chapter 6, The Trading Edge is a Number, and Here is the Formula, aims to demystify the mythical, mystical, magical trading edge. Regardless of the asset class and timeframes, there are only two strategies. We explain the pros and cons of each one.

Chapter 7, Improve Your Trading Edge, outlines seven ways to improve the distribution of returns and build a robust trading edge.

Chapter 8, Position Sizing: Money is Made in the Money Management Module, proves that money is made in the money management module. We introduce a game changing approach to equity curve trading.

Chapter 9, Risk is a Number, introduces four risk metrics that unapologetically measure robustness. Short sellers are exceptional risk managers.

Part III, The Long/Short Game: Building a Long/Short Product

Chapter 10, Refining the Investment Universe, explains some common pitfalls to avoid, and investors' desires to address, in order to help distill a large population of stocks into an investable universe. This chapter paves the way to the final part of the book.

Chapter 11, The Long/Short Toolbox, dives into the four most important levers to manage a long/short portfolio. Now that we know what clients want, we look at the tools available to achieve those objectives.

Chapter 12, Signals and Execution, brings together concepts covered in previous chapters, and goes through signal processing, execution, and other vital components when constructing a long/short investment product.

Chapter 13, Portfolio Management System, looks at one of the most underrated tools in your arsenal. Now that you have added a relative short book, whatever tools you have been using so far are in dire need of a radical upgrade. This chapter goes over topics which will help when designing your own Portfolio Management System.

Appendix, Stock Screening, provides a stock screener tool that will address idea generation, the most pressing issue for market participants, and allow you to put everything you have learned into practice.

To get the most out of this book

Sometimes we win, sometimes we learn. The best disposition to get the maximum out of this book is to have lost money on the markets. This will put you in an open state of mind!

Intermediate knowledge of Python, specifically the use of `numpy`, `pandas`, and `matplotlib` will suffice. We will also use some non-standard Python libraries; `yfinance` and `scipy`. High school level competence in algebra and statistics is also necessary.

Download the example code files

The code bundle for the book is also hosted on GitHub at `https://github.com/PacktPublishing/Algorithmic-Short-Selling-with-Python`. We also have other code bundles from our rich catalog of books and videos available at `https://github.com/PacktPublishing/`. Check them out!

Download the color images

We also provide a PDF file that has color images of the screenshots/diagrams used in this book. You can download it here: `https://static.packt-cdn.com/downloads/9781801815192_ColorImages.pdf`.

Conventions used

There are a number of text conventions used throughout this book.

`CodeInText`: Indicates code words in text, database table names, folder names, filenames, file extensions, pathnames, dummy URLs, user input, and Twitter handles. For example; "From the `rolling_profits` and `rolling_losses` functions, calculate `profit_ratio`."

A block of code is set as follows:

```
# Import Libraries
import pandas as pd
import numpy as np
import yfinance as yf
%matplotlib inline
import matplotlib.pyplot as plt
```

Any command-line input or output is written as follows:

```
3.52
```

Bold: Indicates a new term, an important word, or words that you see on the screen, for example, in menus or dialog boxes, also appear in the text like this. For example: "Did the price beat the **volume at weighted average price (VWAP)** or not?"

Warnings or important notes appear like this.

Tips and tricks appear like this.

Get in touch

Feedback from our readers is always welcome.

General feedback: Email feedback@packtpub.com, and mention the book's title in the subject of your message. If you have questions about any aspect of this book, please email us at questions@packtpub.com.

Errata: Although we have taken every care to ensure the accuracy of our content, mistakes do happen. If you have found a mistake in this book we would be grateful if you would report this to us. Please visit, http://www.packtpub.com/submit-errata, selecting your book, clicking on the Errata Submission Form link, and entering the details.

Piracy: If you come across any illegal copies of our works in any form on the Internet, we would be grateful if you would provide us with the location address or website name. Please contact us at copyright@packtpub.com with a link to the material.

If you are interested in becoming an author: If there is a topic that you have expertise in and you are interested in either writing or contributing to a book, please visit http://authors.packtpub.com.

Share your thoughts

Once you've read *Algorithmic Short Selling with Python*, we'd love to hear your thoughts! Scan the QR code below to go straight to the Amazon review page for this book and share your feedback.

https://packt.link/r/1801815194

Your review is important to us and the tech community and will help us make sure we're delivering excellent quality content.

1

The Stock Market Game

"Infinite games have infinite time horizons. And because there is no finish line, no practical end to the game, there is no such thing as "winning" an infinite game. In an infinite game, the objective is to keep playing, to perpetuate the game."

– Simon Sinek

The financial services industry is facing a severe existential crisis. The only things melting faster than the polar ice caps are assets under active management. Evolution does not take prisoners. If active managers do not want to go join the bluefin tuna on the list of endangered species, then maybe learning to sell short would be an invaluable skill to add to their arsenal. As the global financial crisis of 2007-2008 showed us, it's crucial for market participants to be capable of generating profits not only in bull but also in bear markets. To that end, this book will cover the ins and outs of short selling, and develop algorithmic strategies to maximize its effectiveness, with the end goal of creating a robust investment product that will set you apart from your market competitors.

This chapter sets the stage for the book. At some point in your career, you have probably wondered whether the market was more of a science or an art form. What if the market was a perpetual unsolvable puzzle? How do you win an infinite, complex, random game?

We will cover the following topics:

- Is the stock market art or science?
- How do you win this complex, infinite, random game?
- Playing the short selling game

Is the stock market art or science?

"When bankers get together for dinner, they discuss art. When artists get together for dinner, they discuss money."

– Oscar Wilde

Once upon a time, Lorenzo de Medici praised Michelangelo for the quality of his craftsmanship. *Il Divino* replied to *il Magnifico*, "it appears as art only to those who have not worked hard enough to see the craft."

Every market participant has wondered whether the stock market was more of an art than science. The assumption behind art is the notion of innate talent. Some naturals are born gifted. Some aren't, and I am one of those. If talent is innate, then we mere mortals have to resign ourselves that we simply do not have it. However, talent is often an excuse for laziness. Michael Jordan was not a natural. He was thrown out of his basketball team, so he trained and would not go home until he landed 100 free throws. Landed 98? Oops. Do it again. This way, skills can be developed. The output might look like effortless grace. Yet, it takes craft, hard work, perseverance, and something Angela Duckworth calls "**grit**."

Making money on the markets is not art. It is a skill. In the early 80s, Richard Dennis and William Eckhardt assembled a team, including a poker player, a drug dealer, and other people from all walks of life. They were given a system, starting capital, and sent off to trade futures. Decades later, some of these people still trade. Were they talented? Maybe some of them had some predisposition, but it did not matter. They worked on and at a system, the result of which might have looked like art.

Scientists like to explain the world with definitive formulas. This approach works well for simple and even complicated systems (which can usually be broken down into several simple systems) but not for complex systems:

- Simple system: how much fuel do you need to send a rocket to Mars?
- Complicated system: how do you send someone to Mars? (This can be broken down into simple systems, such as fuel consumption.)
- Complex system: how do you sustain life on Mars?

Markets are complex systems. Unlike complicated systems, complex ones cannot be broken down into a series of simple systems. The moment you think you have a definitive formula that explains stock prices, *ceteris paribus*, the markets will adapt and morph into something else.

The point I'm trying to make is that we do not see things as they are. We see things as we think they are. Context filters our perception. If we think something is going to be hard, it is probably not going to be easy.

If we think the stock market is an art, we will marvel at the masterpiece but fail to appreciate the craft. If we think of it as a science, we will look for a definitive formula, only to be fooled by randomness time and again. If we see it as a game, then the child in us will play.

How do you win this complex, infinite, random game?

"There are known knowns, things we know that we know; and there are known unknowns, things that we know we don't know. But there are also unknown unknowns, things we do not know we don't know."

– Donald Rumsfeld

Share prices may reflect fundamentals over time, but the journey is likely to be a random walk. The random walk theory was popularized by Burton Malkiel in *A Random Walk Down Wall Street*. It essentially postulates that every financial asset has an intrinsic value, yet market prices are hard to accurately predict. Randomness routinely throws market participants off. When even the best of the best in the business succeed roughly 50% of the time, the only conclusion is that randomness cannot be eradicated.

There are two types of games: finite and infinite. A finite game has a clear set of rules, participants, a beginning, a middle, and an end. An infinite game has no set of rules, no beginning, and no end. The objective of a finite game is to win the game. The objective of an infinite game is to stay in the game.

Let's illustrate this with an example. A professional poker player meets a professional trader. The trader plays risky hands throughout the night and wins the game. The next day, the poker player buys a stock the trader recommended. The trader stops out the trade two weeks later, while the gambler forgets about it and doubles his money over the next 3 years. For the trader, poker is a hobby, and he won the poker night because he knew he could afford more risk. Meanwhile, the poker player took calculated risks. He accepted the short-term loss as part of winning the long-term game. When the poker player followed the investment tip, he rode it through the ups and downs, as he was merely using a disposable asset. On the other hand, when the trader closed the same stock and missed the ensuing rally, he was executing risk management.

For the trader, the poker night was a finite game. On the other hand, the stock tip was a finite game for the poker player. They both could afford a higher risk tolerance in each other's games because they knew the game was finite. However, when a game turns from a hobby to a livelihood, we become more risk-averse.

Jack Schwager, best-selling author of the *Market Wizards* series, often says that no sane person would buy a book on surgery, read it over the weekend, and believe they would be ready to operate on someone's head by Monday. Yet, people buy books on investment, subscribe to a couple of newsletters, and think it is perfectly reasonable to start trading by Monday. It may work for amateurs with a very small sample. After all, there is a 50-50 chance of winning. The same randomness that favors the amateurs hurts the pros who have a much larger sample. The game becomes infinite the moment a hobby turns into work. The gambler may have budgeted for a few bad poker nights a year. Similarly, the trader follows a tight risk management policy. Poker players and star traders have one thing in common: they go to work; it is not supposed to be fun.

This leads us to the central question of this book: how do you beat an infinite complex random game?

How do you win an infinite game?

If you are in an infinite game, you don't win by winning one game or all the games. You win by staying in the game. You win some, you lose some, but you get to stay in the game as long as your average wins multiplied by your win rate exceeds your average loss multiplied by your loss rate. You win as long as your **gain expectancy** stays positive. Your job as a stock picker, trader, investor, speculator, or whatever you choose to call yourself, is to maximize that gain expectancy. That is the part where, out of all the stocks you picked, the ones you keep need to look good, the result of which may eventually look like art. This is what we are going to work on in *Part II, The Outer Game: Developing a Robust Trading Edge*, so keep reading, Michelangelo.

How do you beat complexity?

When faced with a complex problem, we intuitively believe the solution must be complicated. Not always. The trajectory of a fast projectile is rocket science, quite literally. Now, when was the last time you saw Serena Williams solving stochastic equations by the side of the court? This is called the gaze heuristic: see, run, intercept, repeat. Complex problems have simple solutions.

Many quantitative traders, affectionately referred to as quants, believe they have to justify their PhDs with convoluted equations. Proof by mathematical intimidation undoubtedly strokes the ego, and yet a high IQ does not rhyme with high performance. The stock market is the place where Nobel prize winners go to get humbled.

On the other hand, it appears there is a simple heuristic hiding in plain sight that beats the complexity of the market. This simple mantra is: "cut your losers, run your winners." *Part II, The Outer Game: Developing a Robust Trading Edge*, will give practical techniques to reduce the drag of losers.

How do you beat randomness?

As a species, our survival has depended on how we deal with randomness. The same survival mechanism we instinctively apply in daily life does not transfer to the markets. Understanding randomness is critical to the development of a healthy short selling practice. First, let us look at how we approach randomness in the markets. Second, let us look at how we deal with randomness in real life. Third, we will see how we can apply this skill to the markets.

Let us say we design a system to pick stocks. When we build a strategy, we start with some assumptions. If stocks meet certain expectations [insert laundry list of criteria here…], we go long or short. In theory, rich valuations, far above reasonable market expectations, revert to "fair," fair valuation being the price some market participants are willing to pay for the value they perceive. In theory, bad businesses are expected to go bust. In theory, overbought stocks are expected to revert to the mean and vice versa for oversold issues. *In theory*, this should work. Now, it is time to take the idea for a spin. Randomness can be summarized in the outcome matrix below:

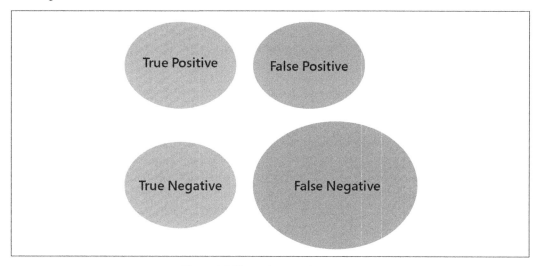

Figure 1.1: Figurative matrix outcome

True positives are when outcomes match expectations. **True negatives** occur when stocks did not pass our test and went on to exhibit poor performance as predicted. This is when theory has its first encounter with reality. In theory, markets are efficient: all publicly available information should be reflected in the price immediately. In practice, this is not always the case.

Back to the drawing board, the presence of **false positives**, when outcomes do not match expectations (for example, stocks passed our tests but flopped in practice), suggests we have missed something. In practice, valuations can get and remain rich longer than clients will stay invested. In practice, overbought and oversold technical indicators are signs of sustained strength and weakness, respectively. They indicate the continuation of a trend rather than a reversion to the mean. We are confused and frustrated. Our natural inclination is to refine our thesis, adding layers of complexity to reduce false positives. This approach generates fewer signals, yet false positives do not disappear entirely.

A side effect and classic pitfall for intermediate short sellers of over-filtering are **false negatives**. This is when stocks exhibit desired behavior but go completely undetected as a result of our more stringent tests. A real-life analogy is dating by checklist. Sometimes people show up with a long laundry list of unattainable standards and unrealistic expectations. In the same way, market participants reject good enough ideas because of their own self-limiting belief systems all the time. They essentially seek reassurance that their pick will perform as expected by applying superfluous filters, but they fail to see that some of those conditions are mutually exclusive or unrealistic. As a result, they systematically price themselves out of the market and miss all the perfectly fine opportunities passing them by. This explains the bloated size of the false negative circle in *Figure 1.1*.

Structural/crowded shorts are classic examples of over-filtering. They tick all the bad boxes, except obvious trades are rarely profitable. Conversely, high dividend yield value traps are classic examples of false negatives or blind spots. Those stocks have cheap valuations and dividend support. They do not participate in bull markets. They do not provide adequate support in prolonged bear phases either. They are slow-burning underperformers, relegated to the purgatory of forgotten issues. The bottom line is, despite all best efforts, some stocks still fail to be profitable, on the short and long sides. This is a lot more complex than we originally thought. More confusion. Back to the drawing board again.

Continuing with the dating by checklist scenario, one way to beat randomness is as follows. On paper, a person ticks all the boxes. In practice, big red flags pop up: that person does not laugh at your jokes, hates broccoli, stubbornly refuses to debate Kant's "critique of pure reason" with your goldfish—all the classic important stuff.

In real life, you deal with this seemingly random response by aborting the mission. You don't wait until you are married with a couple of kids in tow, a dead goldfish in a bowl, and a mountain of green vegetables rotting in the fridge to break up. It's the same with the markets. A stock might tick all the boxes, but something unforeseen or overlooked pops up and you bail. When we focus all our energy on stock picking, we try to solve randomness with certainty. Trying harder next time to pick the right stock does not solve randomness. Perfectionism is a form of procrastination. The only way to deal with randomness is to accept our fallibility. The faster we fail, the faster we move on.

Let's illustrate this concept with a practical example. We can all agree that stocks underperforming their benchmark have peaked out relative to the index. Within the population that has hit a ceiling, there are 100% of the future underperformers (which would be our key target for short selling) plus some stocks that will meander sideways and go nowhere until they trend again. There is simply no easy way to discriminate the former from the latter *a priori*. There are, however, simple techniques to deal with freeloaders *a posteriori*. The way to beat randomness is not to try and be a better stock picker. The way to beat randomness is to accept that at one point or another, you will pick losers and learn how to deal with them. People see all those great market wizards for the few picks that worked well. They do not look at all the ones that were discarded along the way. We have it backward. We want the medal before the race. Great stock pickers should be judged on what they choose to keep, rather than the less profitable picks they discard along the way.

Playing the short selling game

"*Follow me if you want to live.*"

– *Arnold Schwarzenegger, Terminator*

The mechanics of short selling are deceptively simple. For example, you sell a stock at 100, buy it back at 90, and pocket the 10. It works in **absolute** or **relative** to a benchmark. There is only one additional step that needs to take place before the short sale. Short sellers deliver shares they do not own. So, they borrow those shares from a stock lending desk with their brokerage house first. Once they buy the shares back and close the trade, they return those shares.

Do not let that simplicity fool you. Due to the infinite, complex, random nature of the game that we have considered in this chapter, 90% of market participants fail. Of the remaining 10%, fewer than half will ever engage in short selling. That is the unapologetic reality of the markets.

Our objective is to navigate these challenges and succeed on both sides of the portfolio, despite the complexity. If we travel down the same road as everybody else, we will end up with the same results, minus one standard deviation for good measure.

If virtually everyone fails on the forgiving abundance of the long side, then for you to survive on the merciless aridity of the short side, this book must be intentionally different. This book will take you on a road far less traveled. You might disagree with parts of it, but you will come out transformed. For example, like 100% of the people before you, you will conclude that stock picking is bankrupt. You will also get to see for yourself exactly where the money is generated within the investment process.

Summary

In this chapter, we set the context for the rest of the book. The stock market is neither an art form nor a science. Market wizards are not born, nor do they need to be supremely intelligent. They are forged in the crucible of adversity. The stock market is an infinite, complex, random game. The only way to win this game is to stay in it, by adapting your strategy to the market's infinite, complex, random nature, and to pick stocks and cut losses accordingly. In the coming chapters, we will consider how to incorporate short selling into your trading strategy, and implement techniques to improve your success rate and gain expectancy.

Market participants are generally less comfortable selling short than buying long. This is down to a number of technical factors, but also because of a general fear of the practice, propagated by the number of myths related to short selling. We will discuss and disprove these in the next chapter.

2

10 Classic Myths About Short Selling

Since the 1975 movie *Jaws*, whenever we get in the water, we all have this instinctive apprehension about what swims beneath. Sharks are unparalleled killing machines. They have a better detection system than the most technologically advanced sonar. They swim faster than speed boats. They have three rows of razor-sharp teeth that continuously regrow. Yet, did you know that deep in the comfort of your home, somewhere in the dark, there is something a thousand times deadlier than any great white? There are, on average, 80 shark attacks every year, mostly exploratory bites and mistaken identity. Meanwhile, falling out of bed carries a far greater probability. Sharks are majestic creatures. If they wanted us dead, we would be. Apparently, they don't like junk food.

Short sellers are like sharks, a little less majestic, but still vastly misunderstood and not as deadly as you might think. You know you have a bit of a reputational issue when your brethren, in allegedly the most reviled industry, would still gladly sharpen pitchforks at the single mention of your profession. In this chapter, we will debunk 10 of the most enduring myths surrounding short selling:

- Myth #1: Short sellers destroy pensions
- Myth #2: Short sellers destroy companies
- Myth #3: Short sellers destroy value
- Myth #4: Short sellers are evil speculators
- Myth #5: Short selling has unlimited loss potential but limited profit potential

- Myth #6: Short selling increases risk
- Myth #7: Short selling increases market volatility
- Myth #8: Short selling collapses share prices
- Myth #9: Short selling is unnecessary during bull markets
- Myth #10: The myth of the "structural short"

Myth #1: Short sellers destroy pensions

"Do you believe in God, Monsieur Le Chiffre?"

"I believe in a reasonable rate of return."

– *James Bond, Casino Royale*

During the **Great Financial Crisis (GFC)** of 2008, many influential figures encouraged market participants to buy stocks to "shore up the market." They claimed it was "the patriotic thing to do." I grew up in an era when patriots were altruistic individuals who put their lives at risk so that others may have a better future. Somewhere along Wall Street, a patriot became someone who put other people's money at risk in order to guarantee an end-of-year bonus and ego massage.

In the GFC, short sellers did not decimate anyone's pension for a simple reason: pension funds did not allocate to short sellers. Neither did they cause the GFC. Short sellers did not securitize toxic debt or cause the real estate market bubble, nor were they responsible for its collapse. Their crime was to do their homework, take the other side, and profit from the debacle.

Traders make one of two things. Either they make money, or they make excuses. When they make money, performance does the talking. When they don't, they scramble for excuses. Short sellers are the perfect scapegoats. The most vitriolic critics of short sellers are not exactly fund management nobility.

Besides, it might be counter-productive in the long term to blame short sellers for one's misfortunes. There are only two ways you can live your life: as a hero or as a victim. A hero takes responsibility, lives up to the challenges, and triumphs over adversity. A victim will blame others for their failures. The "patriots" who blame short sellers choose the path of the victim. Next time asset allocators decide on their allocation, who do you think they would rather allocate to: heroes or victims?

Now, do short sellers really decimate pensions? The single most important question about your own pension is: "do I want to retire on stories, or do I want to retire on numbers?" The day after your retirement, what will matter to you: all those buzz investment themes or the balance in your bank account?

If you think they are one and the same, then keep churning, and wait for either the handshake and the gold watch, or the tap on the shoulder from the line manager for a life-altering conversation. If you choose to retire on numbers, however, then let's have a look at them.

Nothing illustrates the "story versus numbers" dichotomy better than the active versus passive investing debate. Active management refers to fund managers taking bets away from the benchmark, a practice referred to as active money. Passive investing refers to minimizing the tracking error by mimicking the index. Active managers claim their stock-picking ability and portfolio management skills deliver superior returns. However, the numbers tell a different story. According to S&P's *Index versus Active* reports, the vast majority of active managers underperform the S&P 500 benchmark on 1, 3, and 5 year-horizons. This means that their cumulative compounded returns are lower than the benchmark. **Exchange-Traded Funds**, or **ETFs**, fared better than active managers every year on record, even during the most severe market downturns.

 A more detailed report regarding active manager performance compared to the benchmarks can be accessed via S&P's SPIVA reports: `https://www.spglobal.com/spdji/en/spiva/#/reports/regions`.

The proof is in the pudding. The burden of proof is no longer on ETFs but on active managers to prove that they can deliver more than the index. The debate has gradually shifted from "which manager should we allocate to?" to "remind me again why we should be going with an expensive underperforming benchmark hugger when there is a liquid, better, cheaper alternative?"

Unfortunately, there is more. The penalty for deviating from the benchmark is severe. If managers deviate and outperform, they are knighted as "stock pickers." Yet, when they stray and underperform, they are dubbed as having "high tracking errors." This often leads to redemptions, the kiss of death for fund managers. When the choice is between becoming a hero or keeping your job, self-preservation compels active managers to mirror the benchmark, a practice referred to as **closet indexing**. This is the famous "*no-one ever got fired for holding [insert big safe blue-chip stock here...]*" line. If active managers end up mirroring their benchmark, then the "active versus passive" debate is a misnomer. It really comes down to a choice between low-cost indexing via an index fund versus expensive closet indexing via a self-preserving active manager. Either way, you get the same index, but with the latter, you also have to pay a middle-man, called an active manager. As John Boggle, founder of Vanguard, used to say: "*in investing, you get what you don't pay for.*"

That does not mean active management should die an unceremonious death. There are exceptional active managers worth every penny of their management fees. It simply means that the average active mutual fund manager gives active management a bad name. Investors who go down the active management route not only take an equity risk premium. They also take an active management risk premium. The current crisis of active management is nothing but the time-honored routine of the middle man in every industry who realizes that they can no longer delay efficiency.

Next, let's look at what happens during bear markets. Markets have returned between 6.3% and 8% on average. Compounded returns over a century are astronomical. So, in theory, you should stay invested for the long run. Explain that again to the cohorts who retired in 2001 and 2009. Markets have gone down 50% twice in a decade. When the response to "too big to fail" and "too much leverage" was to make them bigger, hyper-leverage, and put the same people responsible for the GFC back in the driver's seat, rest assured that markets are bound to hit "soft patches" again. Long-only active managers may display heroic grace under fire during bear markets but, when your net worth has gone down by 50%, a 1 or 2% outperformance is a rounding error. Two double diamond black slopes in a decade and everyone wants bear market insurance: "What should I buy during a bear market?"

Let us reframe the question. Imagine someone walking up to you and asking: "There is a bull market going on. What should I be short selling?" Pause for a second and then consider your reaction. If selling a bull market does not make any sense, then why would you buy anything during a bear market? There is no safe harbor asset class that will magically rise. The only thing that goes up in a bear market is correlation. There will be ample time to buy at bargain-basement prices once the rain of falling knives stops.

During a bear market, the only market participants who can guarantee a reasonable rate of return are those whose mandate is inversely correlated with the index. These people are short sellers. You do not have to like them. You do not even have to stay invested with them during bull markets. More than any other market participants, they understand the cyclicality of inflows and redemptions. If you choose to retire on numbers, then you owe your pension to consider allocating to short sellers.

This brings us to a counter-intuitive conclusion. If you choose to retire on numbers instead of stories, then passive investing is the way to go on the long side. For capital protection and alpha generation during downturns, investors need to allocate to short sellers. In the active management space, the only market participants who will deliver a reasonable rate of return on your pension are short sellers.

Another counter-intuitive conclusion for practitioners is evolution. Active fund managers face an unprecedented existential crisis. If they want to survive, they need to evolve, adapt, and acquire new skills. Short selling might very well be a rare skill uniquely suited to market participants who are determined to stay relevant.

Myth #2: Short sellers destroy companies

"Round up the usual suspects."

– Capitaine Renaud, Casablanca

When the real estate bubble burst in 2007, what were the short sellers in the risk committee and boards of directors at Lehman Brothers doing? Nothing. They did strictly nothing to prevent or remedy the situation because none of them ever sat on any of those committees. In the history of capitalism, no short seller has ever sat on the board of directors of a company whose stock they were selling short.

We can agree that fundamentals drive share prices in the long run. The driving force is the quality of management. Mark Zuckerberg is the genius behind Facebook. Warren Buffett turned an ailing textile company named Berkshire Hathaway into an industrial conglomerate. Jeff Bezos built Amazon. Steve Jobs 2.0 was the architect of Apple's renaissance. If top management is so eager to take credit for success, then it should equally be held responsible for failure. Steve Jobs 1.0 ran Apple into the ground. Kay Whitmore buried Kodak. The responsibility for Bears Stearns, Lehman Brothers, Merrill Lynch, and AIG falls squarely on the shoulders of those at the helm. Short sellers did not make any of the bad decisions that destroyed those companies. Bad management makes bad decisions that lead to bad outcomes, the same way that good management makes good decisions that lead to good results.

No one captured what happens at the highest echelon of companies better than Steve Jobs in his 1995 Lost Interview. He mentioned that "groupthink" amidst the rarefied atmosphere of top management in venerable institutions sometimes leads to a cognitive bias called the Dunning-Kruger effect. As an example, Kodak was once an iconic brand. Management believed they were so ahead of the game they could indefinitely delay innovation. They took a step backward to their old core technology when the world was moving forward. As tragic as it was back then, there is no flower on Kodak's grave today. The world, and even the 50,000 Kodak employees laid off, have moved on. Today, Kodak is a case study in the failure of management to embrace innovation.

Top management love to surround themselves with bozocrats, non-threatening obedient "yes-men," whose sole purpose is to reassure the upper crust of their brilliance, reinforcing a fatal belief in infallibility. Dissent is squashed. Innovation, branded as cannibalization, is swiftly buried in the Kodak sarcophagus of innovation.

Top management becomes so infatuated with their brilliance that they do not even realize they are detached from reality. Given sufficient time, their obsolete products destroy them from the inside. Short sellers simply ride arrogance to its dusty end.

The history of capitalism is the story of evolution. During World War I, the dominant mode of transportation was the horse. On the first day of World War II, the world woke up in horror to a German panzer division mowing down the Polish cavalry. The cruel lesson is that evolution does not take prisoners. Out of the hundreds of car manufacturers between the two world wars emerged a few winners. The rest of the industry went out of business. For every winner, there are countless losers. Today, everyone is perfectly happy with horse-carts running around Central Park, but no one sheds tears over the defunct horse-cart industry. Everyone has forgotten the names of all those small car manufacturers. The world has moved on.

We often see the S&P 500 as this monolithic hall of corporate fame and power, but we forget that since the index was formed in 1957, only 86 of the original 500 constituents are still in the index. The other 414 have either gone bankrupt or been merged into larger companies. Radio Shack did not go out of business because of short sellers. It went out of business because it could not evolve to face the competition of Amazon and the likes of Best Buy. Short sellers do not destroy companies. They escort obsolescence out of the inexorable march of evolution.

Myth #3: Short sellers destroy value

"Price is what you pay, value is what you get."

– Warren Buffett

Market commentators love to put a dollar sign on the destruction of value every time share prices tank. The net worth of Mr Zuckerberg shrank by $12 billion on July 26, 2018. Since short sellers stand to profit from the drop, they are guilty of value destruction by association. For example, George Soros is often associated with the fall of the British pound in 1995. How could one man single-handedly bring down the currency of one of the wealthiest nations on earth? He bet big on the Bank of England's unsustainable stance.

At the heart of this is a confusion between intrinsic and market values. One is value, the other is valuation. Intrinsic value is the net wealth companies create through the sale of products and services. Market value is the price market participants are willing to pay. Market and intrinsic value live in parallel universes that rarely intersect. One is hard work. The other is the fabled Keynesian beauty contest. The bottom line is that shareholders do not create any more value than short sellers destroy any.

Myth #4: Short sellers are evil speculators

"I am soft, I am lovable. But what I really want to do is reach in, rip out their heart, and eat it before they die."

– Richard Fuld, fallen angel, on short sellers

People often forget that when Steve Jobs returned to the helm, the iconic logo once again made the cover of magazines in a casket. Amazon was not always the darling of Wall Street. What is now considered visionary management was, for a long time, branded as stubborn disrespect for shareholders.

When executives whine about vicious rumors spread by short sellers and their agents, they forget that Steve Jobs and Jeff Bezos had to stomach the same vitriol for years. They came up with the best antidote against short sellers. Make products that sell, manage your company properly, and short sellers will go away. Today, no short seller would ever take a stab at Apple. Note to all CEOs, the vaccine against short sellers is: put the interests of the company, its employees, its customers, the environment, its shareholders, and its management in that order and things will be fine.

If your approach is instead to hollow out resources from R&D, customer service, randomly "restructure" personnel, and flatten the organization chart, to engage in aggressive accounting practices, and vote for ridiculous stock option plans for the board, to gobble up sterile acquisitions and, above all, finance share buy-back plans, then, one day, there will be a pot of gold on the other side of the rainbow to be shared among short sellers.

In 2007, Mathew Rothman, global head of quantitative research, published a note about the demise of quants that went on to become the most circulated piece of research in the history of Lehman Brothers. As the battle between short sellers and Lehman escalated, he showed top management a white paper from Owen Lamont entitled *Go Down Fighting: Short Sellers vs. Firms*. Richard Fuld was not amused. He blamed short sellers for spreading vicious rumors that drove Lehman's share price down. A decade later, the dust settled. Every other article about the GFC and banker's hubris is illustrated with a picture of Richard Fuld's testimony before the House committee. Being the poster child of the GFC is a rough way to go down in history, even by cold calculating investment bankers' standards. My heart goes out to Mr Fuld…

 Owen A. Lamont's *Go Down Fighting* paper can be accessed in full at *Oxford Academic* here: `https://academic.oup.com/raps/article/2/1/1/1563177`.

However, if all it took to bring down companies, markets, and currencies were bad breath, colorful language, and small positions relative to the overall float, then faith in capitalism should join the great white shark and polar bear in the list of endangered species. The national sport of short sellers is to unveil paradoxes in the fabric of the corporate space-time continuum. Ignorance and competence cannot exist in the same place at the same time. Basically, you cannot pretend to know what you are doing if you don't know what is going on. Strangely enough, this is a lie embattled CEOs would like us to believe. Whenever they are questioned about the illicit activities of their subordinates, their first line of defense is to feign indignation and throw them under the Bentley, pretending that they were unaware of the illicit actions perpetrated by a few isolated rogue individuals. That's commendable, except every single person on this planet knows that money does not grow on trees. Money leaves a trail. Bonuses are not charitable contributions.

Besides, company size is not a valid excuse either. For example, war is a dirty business. Generals are often far removed from the theater of operations. Yet, it does not mean their lowest-ranked soldiers can run around pillaging and looting with impunity. So, when CEOs claim they are not aware of fraud perpetrated by their underlings, either they are willfully blind and therefore complicit in the cover-up, or they really do not know what is going on and therefore incompetent. Either way, they are unfit for duty and undeserving of their compensation packages. That explains why, whenever short sellers uncover malfeasance, top management goes on the offensive and portrays short sellers as evil speculators who spread vicious unfounded rumors. Companies who have nothing to fear may not be happy, but they rarely waste time on legal action against short sellers.

Short sellers are the cicadas of the markets. No one has ever blamed cicadas for heralding the end of summer. When short sellers show up, this may herald the end of good times. They do not just talk trash. They put their money where their mouth is. If someone is willing to put capital at risk, the least long holders should do is revisit their bullish stance. Short sellers are often blamed for spreading vicious rumors and profiting from the decline. Companies will take analysts with Buy ratings for dinner and short sellers to court. Short sellers must therefore be careful about their facts and wording. Secondly, regulators do not take kindly to short sellers shorting across pension funds' large holdings. They are audited on a regular basis. Compliance is a survival mechanism. If your business model is to manipulate share price by spreading rumors and trade on it, then drop this book and go buy coffee mugs because "los federales" are about to establish a base camp in your meeting room.

"If we are victorious in one more battle with the Romans, we shall be utterly ruined."

– Plutarch on Pyrrhus

A word of caution for fellow short sellers. Short selling is an immature and fragile segment of the industry. On the one hand, short sellers want recognition for the value they bring to the markets. In the words of James Surowiecki, they balance out "Wall Street's inherent bullish bias," and play "a vital role in uncovering malfeasance." Short sellers also want to be treated fairly, just like any other market participant.

The preceding quotes are extracted from a 2015 New Yorker article by James Surowiecki, accessible here: `https://www.newyorker.com/magazine/2015/03/23/in-praise-of-short-sellers`.

Yet, on the other hand, short sellers come across as the enemy for a good reason. Airing commercials or sponsoring documentaries to expose companies as frauds and their management as crooks is a double-edged sword. Every successful campaign builds up resentment amidst corporations, regulators, and the public. Every short-term pyrrhic skirmish won makes the long-term victory ever more elusive. Many jurisdictions still ban short selling. Those that allow short selling have cumbersome administrative rules such as the uptick rule, an obligation to secure "borrow" before trading. The uptick rule stipulates that a short sale can only take place following an uptick in traded price.

Respect is never due but consistently earned. As long as short sellers fight dirty, they deserve to be treated with equal disdain. The most powerful incentive is probably the attitude of investors. Short sellers have such a sulfurous reputation that many investors will simply refuse to allocate to short sellers.

The premise of this book is that short selling does not have to be conflictual. Please be kind to top management. Do not remind them of their obsolescence. Time and markets are cruel enough already. The middle ground is simply to say you are shorting underperformers relative to the benchmark. Looking for relative shorts does not infuriate corporations, quite the opposite in fact. Every start up entrepreneur in Silicon Valley knows that markets have only two seasons, bull and bear. A bull market is series A and IPO season. A bear market is "go back working for the man" season. Executives in defensive sectors, such as food or utilities, do not expect their stocks to be assets of choice during bull markets. In fact, they would probably rescind their pension mandate to a manager who would gulp up their stock in a bull market, unless of course you are Warren Buffett and you talk to Coca-Cola.

Myth #5: Short selling has unlimited loss potential but limited profit potential

"Not all is lost until the lesson is lost."

– Mother Teresa

Share prices may go up multiple times but can only go down 100%. Short sellers therefore open themselves up for infinite losses and limited profits. The not-so-secret dream of every fund manager is to pass their name down to posterity. "Managers" who just sit back watching their shorts going up multiple times against them deserve to have this dream come true. They have earned the right to have their name on a plaque… at the bottom of a public urinal. There is simply no excuse for bad risk management.

On a different note, meet Joe Campbell, a young dynamic entrepreneur, and investor in his spare time. On November 18, 2015, he sold short Kalobios (KBIO) at an average cost of $2 for a total market value of $33,000. Enter Pharma Bro, Martin Shkreli, who disclosed 50% ownership of Kalobios after the close. The share price roofed at 800% in the after-hours market. Borrow vanished overnight. Unable to meet his margin call, the unfortunate short seller appealed to the sympathy of fellow traders by launching a crowdfunding campaign on GoFundMe, only to face the humiliating double whammy of market participants "revenge trading" vitriolic comments. My sympathy goes to Mr Campbell and may at least his story serve as a lesson to aspiring short sellers:

- Penny stocks are tourist traps. Tourists do not care about the quality of borrow. They salivate over the story. When a recall happens, they scramble to locate. When no borrow is available, they are forced to cover, which eventually snowballs into short squeezes.

- Penny stocks are binary events. Either they go to zero, or there is a corporate action, and the share price goes ballistic. Penny stocks are high-risk, low reward trades. Get a few dan on your black belt before taking on Bruce Lee. 90% of market participants are unprofitable. The majority of the remaining 10% still refrain from short selling.

If it is any solace to Mr Campbell, Pharma Bro has since become a convicted felon.

Myth #6: Short selling increases risk

"Facts do not cease to exist because they are ignored."

– Aldous Huxley

Short selling is risky. Not knowing how to sell short is, however, a lot riskier. Market participants are not risk-averse when they choose not to learn the craft. They are conservative to the point of being risk-seeking. Think of it as emergency drills. A refusal to practice the drills does not make the risks of fire, tsunami, or earthquake go away. People choose to go about their business unprepared for rare but life-threatening events. Being a market participant is not just about buy-and-hope, fair-weather sailing. Things can, and will, get rough.

At a subconscious level, every single market participant has this nagging subconscious fear of a bear market around the corner. They know they will give back some of the gains. Their best-case scenario is to sell before the bear and wait it out. This sometimes drives them to sell too early and miss out on big moves. As Peter Lynch said: "Far more money has been lost by investors preparing for corrections, or trying to anticipate corrections, than has been lost in corrections themselves."

Since no amount of academic research is ever going to drive the point across, let's look inside and play a game. Pick two pieces of paper, draw two columns. On the first one, write down your fears about bear markets. What is going to happen to your gains, portfolio, net worth, and job? How do you prepare for it? Be specific about when and how it manifests in your daily work. For example, do you check the markets more often than you think you should? Do you scan news for potentially bearish catalysts? Are you overly conservative or do you take risky bets while you think you can?

Next, imagine you were so serene about your ability to make money in down markets as to casually say: "Bull markets. Bear markets. They all taste like chicken." What would you do differently? Would you hold your positions longer? Would you size them differently? Would you be checking the news all the time? Write all the feelings on the second piece of paper. Once this is done, pick the first piece of paper and address all the fears one by one in the right-hand column. About half of your fears are emotional vampires that rob you of energy. They dissipate under the light of logical scrutiny.

Deep down, we all know that not being able to sell short is a lot riskier than not shorting at all because it gives you the ability to profit from both bull and bear markets.

Myth #7: Short selling increases market volatility

In 2008, banking top executives were contemplating the abyss from the parapet of their corner offices. The banking lobby promptly marched up to Washington to demand a moratorium on short selling. In response, the U.S. **Securities and Exchange Commission** (**SEC**) put a temporary ban on short selling in the country in an effort to "restore equilibrium to the markets." This was lifted a short time later. Once the dust had settled, some analysis was done on the effect of the short selling ban, and the Federal Reserve published a report in which they concluded that short selling actually reduces volatility.

In the boxing ring called the stock market, it is not every day that the U.S. Federal Reserve is in the corner of short sellers. Without further ado, see the opening paragraph of their report:

> *"In response to the sharp decline in prices of financial stocks in the fall of 2008, regulators in a number of countries banned short selling of particular stocks and industries. Evidence suggests that these bans did little to stop the slide in stock prices, but significantly increased costs of liquidity. In August 2011, the U.S. market experienced a large decline when Standard and Poor's announced a downgrade of U.S. debt. Our cross-sectional tests suggest that the decline in stock prices was not significantly driven or amplified by short selling. Short selling does not appear to be the root cause of recent stock market declines. Furthermore, banning short selling does not appear to prevent stock prices from falling when firm-specific or economy-wide economic fundamentals are weak, and may impose high costs on market participants."*

 The title of the report is as follows: The New York Federal Reserve, *Market Declines: What Is Accomplished by Banning Short-Selling?*, Robert Battalio, Hamid Mehran, and Paul Schultz, Volume 18, Number 5, 2012.

Market participants sell short for various reasons. Options traders, convertible managers, and indexers need to delta-hedge their positions. The inability to sell short reduces liquidity and the offering of financial products. Restrictions on short selling are therefore a sign of market immaturity.

Myth #8: Short selling collapses share prices

Short sellers simply do not have the firepower to torpedo share prices. Short sellers need to borrow shares in order to sell short. This comes from shareholders who lend a fraction of their holdings to stock loan desks. Borrow availability usually averages less than 10% of the free float, in other words, the portion of shares available to public investors. This means that short sellers represent a fraction of the overall sell volume.

The BB guns of short sellers may have a punctual market impact, but the real damage is inflicted by the heavy artillery of institutional investors selling. This leads us to an interesting point about short selling. Making money on the short side is not about spotting stocks that could potentially go down. It is about riding the tail of institutional investors liquidating their positions.

Myth #9: Short selling is unnecessary during bull markets

> *"The best time to fix the roof is when the sun is shining."*
>
> *– John F. Kennedy*

Some market participants do not want to sell short during bull markets. They lament the scarcity of "good short ideas." Besides, they do not want to trail their competitors by wasting precious alpha shorting stocks. They procrastinate about sharpening the saw until it is rusty.

No bull market has ever boosted anyone's IQ. Market participants do not get smarter in bull markets; they become complacent. Just as waiting for a first heart attack to get in shape is not healthy, waiting for a bear market to learn short selling is an unprofessional way to manage other people's money. Short selling is a muscle that atrophies when not flexed.

The reason why investors keep their money in long/short funds is downside protection. Investors will forgive mediocre performance and stomach high fees through a bull market as long as they know there is downside protection in a bear market.

Beta jockeys believe there will be ample time to pick up short selling when the broader market turns bearish. After all, the outer game of short selling, tools, and techniques may be a little more sophisticated than the long side, but it is not rocket science. Short selling is, first and foremost, an inner game. Do not underestimate the time it takes to internalize the mental discipline of short selling.

The wrong time to start is when the long side is hemorrhaging money, and investors are breathing down your neck.

Myth #10: The myth of the "structural short"

"With great power comes great responsibility."

– Uncle Ben, Spider-Man

Structural shorts are stocks perceived as irreversibly doomed; horse carriages in the 1930s, print papers in the digital age, and coal mines in the renewable energy era. They are supposedly compelling shorts because the dynamics of their business models or industries are structurally flawed.

Structural shorts are as cheap as market gurus flapping their mouths in the media, a dime a dozen. Profitable structural shorts are the unicorns of the financial services industry, as rare and elusive as market wizards.

In *Chapter 3, Take a Walk on the Wild Short Side*, we dispel the myth of structural shorts. For now, let us focus on what it means to look for structural shorts when managing other people's money. Market participants have held the comfortable belief that somewhere out there, there is a stock that they just can sell short and throw away the key. Since it will see itself to bankruptcy, it does not need any further maintenance.

Now, they do not hold reciprocal beliefs about their longs. Of course, they believe they require continuous maintenance. They believe in meeting with management, updating earnings models, calls with analysts, and so on. So, they believe in rigorous work ethics on the long side and passivity on the short side. In the real world, everyone knows that the short side is considerably harder than the long. So, how come complacent laziness would work on the difficult side when hard work barely pays off on the easy one?

When people publicly hold this kind of asymmetrical unquestioned beliefs, the inconvenient truth is that they have not given much thought to the short side. They do not know how to sell short. They have obviously not tried very hard either. If they had, reality would quickly have slapped them into submission. Yet, they still hope things will magically take care of themselves. They confidently market a skill they do not possess, happy to take on other people's money and milk generous fees. Yet they have no intention of taking responsibility for the inevitable discomfiture. In the Queen's English, this is called dereliction of duty. In execution trader English, those individuals are called clowns. For the rest of the book, let's embellish their status to *chrematocoulrophones* (*chremato*: money, *coulro*: clowns, *phones*: voice).

Summary

Short selling has long been this terra incognita on our doorstep. There are more books and whitepapers published in relation to modern techniques such as artificial intelligence or machine learning than short selling, which has been around for centuries. Dispelling myths is particularly important if we want to give the technique a letter of nobility, rehabilitate the discipline, and attract talented minds.

In the next chapter, we will discuss the market dynamics of the short side and explain how a deep understanding of them is critical to success.

3

Take a Walk on the Wild Short Side

"In theory, theory and practice are the same. In practice, they are different."

– Yogi Berra, Yankees philosopher

Short selling is a secret fantasy for many long-only participants. They have all come across some stock they have analyzed, concluded it was doomed to fail, and wished they could short it. Then, they watched it crater. They feel confident their analytical superpowers would work wonders on the short side as well. It all works well in theory until it has to work in practice. When market participants come to the world of short selling, they assume they should simply do the opposite of what they do on the long side.

In this chapter, we will map the journey from the long side to the short side. We consider why most traders think they can sell short yet fail in practice. First, we will look at why shorting on valuations fails. Then, we will eviscerate the structural short tourist trap for good. We will meander in the purgatory of learned helplessness, before waking to the reality of short selling. In the second part of this chapter, we will start to dive into the world of short selling and its unique idiosyncrasies.

Along the way, we will cover the following topics:

- The long side world according to GARP
- Structural shorts: the unicorns of the financial services industry
- Overcoming learned helplessness

- Money "is" made between events that "should" happen
- The unique challenges of the short side

The long side world according to GARP

"He wished he could arrange a maiming as a kind of moral lesson."

– John Irving, *The World According to Garp*

On the long side, market participants often look for stocks with solid long-term prospects that are temporarily mispriced. They want to buy something that grows at a discount, the famous "margin of safety." This approach is known as **Growth At a Reasonable Price** (**GARP**). If that seems to work fine on the long side, then do the opposite on the short side and voila, right? It could even sound something like **Dive at a Record Price** (**DARP**).

The first logical step is the easiest one: find stocks with surreal pricing. There is always a stock, sometimes an entire industry, that seems to defy the conventional laws of gravity. With monetary authorities around the world asleep on the "print" button, there is no shortage of absurdly priced stocks. The second step is to do some analysis on esoteric business models, sustainability of growth rate, cash flow burn rate, and so on. Once the stars align and you spot levitating valuations coupled with a sinking business model, it is time to teach manners to those insolent stocks with some carefully crafted short positions. Past a certain point, no matter how good business models might be, valuations stop making sense and things should revert to fair anyway.

Despite the apparent logic of this approach, let's consider why this might not be the case. The concept of GARP implicitly relies on fairness. Cheap valuations revert to fair. The objective is to catch stocks when they are cheap and ride the correction up. For technically versed market participants, buy deeply oversold stocks and wait for the rebound. It is fair and makes logical sense. It would therefore be fair and logical to assume that unsustainable pricing would revert down to fair valuation. The problem is that carrying this subconscious belief in fairness into the short world proves to be a fatal virtue.

Stocks that have reached stratospheric valuations often have enough momentum to push to the ionosphere, before gravity reels them back in. Stocks with a **Price/ Earnings** (**PE**) ratio (a valuation metric calculated as share price divided by earnings per share) of 100 have escaped the gravity of reason. They might as well go to 150, 200, or 3000.

Champagne stocks in bubbly territory still have fizz, which is when the Wall Street cheerleaders conveniently roll out the same old routine: "permanently high plateau," "this time it's different," "paradigm change," "new economy." Market participants may see themselves as the lonely voice of reason amid a delusional crowd. Yet, as Seneca, patron saint of investment bankers by day and stoic philosopher by night, would attest, a single sane mind against an insane mob is still an unfair fight.

After a geometric ascent comes the parabolic "grand finale" rise in share price. This is when fundamental short sellers suffer the curse of reason: they leave early, because positions are unsustainable. We have all been there. We buy back our short positions, close the final top, and walk away in disgust, only to find out that Newtonian physics does not discriminate between fruits, thermonuclear intercontinental ballistic missiles, and Icarus stocks.

Moral of the story: Short selling a stock that does not make sense does not make sense either. As Keynes used to say, "*markets can stay irrational longer than we can stay solvent.*"

Structural shorts: the unicorns of the financial services industry

"If you want a guarantee, buy a toaster."

– Clint Eastwood

Once market participants have been burned a few times trying to melt the wings of Icarus stocks, they change approach. They crave certainty. They look for stocks that already tick all the "bad" boxes: Bad company in bad industry with bad products, bad management, bad valuations, bad news flow, bad ratings, and so on. They go on a hunt for **structural shorts**. Fortunately, there are a lot more companies traveling down the boulevard of failure than up the narrow path of success.

The problem is timing. Every bit of information has a price tag attached to it. This gets discounted in the share price. By the time short sellers accumulate enough evidence to conclude beyond the shadow of a doubt that they have encountered a structural short, institutional long holders have already left the building. The only shareholders left are stable long-term investors, such as founders and strategic partners. Short selling "structural shorts" becomes a binary event. Either they go out of business, or a major corporate event such as a company merger or acquisition happens. In simple terms, share price either drops to zero or stays up.

Besides, short selling is a bit more complicated than long buying. Short sellers need to sell stock they do not own in the first place. So, they conveniently borrow them from stock lending desks, who charge a lending fee. Lending fees are a direct function of supply and demand. They go from general collateral 0.25%-0.5% to double-digits for hard-to-locate issues. Structural shorts happen to be also referred to as crowded shorts, the lending fee for which would make Shakespeare's Shylock blush with envy. Share price may go down but borrowing is prohibitively expensive, and any bit of buying pressure triggers a vicious short squeeze, where you might find that you've made 1-2% over 2 months, only for stock price to rally 15% in 3 days.

Structural shorts are cheap, just like market gurus: a dime a dozen. Profitable structural shorts are like market wizards: the unicorns of financial services, the exceptions that prove there is no rule.

Overcoming learned helplessness

> *"Remember no man is really defeated unless he is discouraged."*
>
> *– Bruce Lee, Chinese American philosopher*

After a few unsuccessful attempts at ball trapping shooting stars and chewing dry bones, market participants find themselves at a loss, financially and emotionally. No battle plan, however well drafted, ever survived its first encounter with the enemy. The short side turns into an endless source of frustration, its logic defying logic.

Dogs are a man's best friend and unfortunately one of his favorite lab test subjects too. In a famous experiment, Martin Seligman, pioneer of the positive psychology movement, deprived dogs of the chance of reward. Randomness in the attribution of reward further deprived test dogs of hope. They gradually became apathetic. They stopped trying even when they had a clear chance of success. They just passed up "free-money" trades. Those dogs had learned helplessness.

Symptoms of learned helplessness among the financial wolves manifest as a few token shorts, large short index futures, and structurally high net exposure. In execution trader English, they give up trying to short specific stocks. They only keep sporadic token short ideas. They hedge, or balance the long and short sides, by selling futures. What seemed easy when watching the game from the long side bench feels insurmountably difficult now that they have been bruised a few times on the field.

Frustrated market participants then retreat to their comfort zone: the long side. This even transpires in their marketing material. They still talk about downside protection, but the savvy stock picks they advertise to investors are almost all on the long side.

At this point, they unknowingly betray their sole "raison d'etre" as long/short players: their ability to generate alpha regardless of the market's moody gyrations. A quick way to tell if market participants are serious short sellers is to look at the ratio of short to long ideas they publish in their marketing materials.

Fortunately, learned helplessness is a reversible condition. It can be unlearned. This is part of what this book is about.

Money "is" made between events that "should" happen

"Most decisions should probably be made with somewhere around 70% of the information you wish you had."

– Jeff Bezos

The reality of short selling is that money is made in the time between events that "should" happen. Let me explain what I mean. When stocks reach unsustainable levels, they "should" go down. When companies are in complete disarray, they "should" go under. Between the fatal moment of implosion in orbit like an old satellite and the languishing purgatory of zombie stocks, they were not magically beamed down by some market Scottie. Between the time when they "should" go down and the time when they "should" go bust, the reality is that they actually "did" come down a long way, over a long time, unnoticed, unappreciated, but still in a very profitable way to a few savvy short sellers.

They faded from the conversation. They did not have extravagant valuations all the way down, quite the opposite in fact. They were on par with or marginally cheaper than their peers and the broader market, but they stayed cheap for a reason. They disappointed. Institutions gradually sold their holdings. Retailers were busy chasing the new next buzz stocks. Market participants had no reason to hold them anymore. They committed the ultimate crime in the market beauty contest: they were boring.

Think about it for one second: on the long side, you would not own a boring stock. Other less talented market participants might eventually come to the same conclusion. They would either sell or stay away. Unattractive stocks do not outperform. Over time, small underperformance compounds into big disappointment. In a nutshell, the stocks you do not want to own on the long side are potential candidates for the short book.

The key to finding good shorts is to accept a counterintuitive truth about short selling: It isn't sexy. Good shorts are boring. They don't stand out as either too expensive or too flawed, and their valuations tend to be similar to their peers'. They are just boring underperformers.

The unique challenges of the short side

"When things go wrong, don't go with them."

– Elvis Presley, the King

People fail at short selling because they overlook three critical factors working against them: market dynamics, scarcity mentality, and asymmetry of information.

Market dynamics: short selling is not a stock-picking contest, but a position-sizing exercise

"This is space, the environment does not cooperate."

– The Martian

Successful longs expand. Successful shorts contract. On the long side, the market does the heavy lifting. On the short side, the market does not cooperate. Unsuccessful shorts balloon, while the successful ones shrink.

To illustrate this point, let's take a look at the table below. Imagine we have four stocks: two on the long side (A and B) and two on the short (C and D). The objective here is to illustrate how the long and short sides behave differently. To keep things simple, let us start with 4 stocks priced at $100 on day 1. The open long market value is +$200 and short market value is -$200. The gross exposure (absolute value of the long and short books) is $400, and total net exposure (the difference between the long and short books) is $0. In financial creole, a net exposure below 10% is usually classified as market neutral. It may sounds more intelligent and safer, but it is definitely not risk-free.

100 days later, A, B, C, and D are worth 110, 95, 90, and 105 respectively.

Ticker	Day 1	Day 100	Profit & Loss
A	100	110	10
B	100	95	-5
Market Value Long	200	205	5
C	-100	-90	10
D	-100	-105	-5
Market Value Short	-200	-195	5
Gross Exposure	400	400	10
Net Exposure	0	10	10

The gross exposure is still $400, but the net exposure is now +$10. On the long side, there is more of something that works and less of something that doesn't. On the short side, however, there is less of something that works and more of something that doesn't. Even though the absolute movement on each of the shorted stocks (C and D) equals the absolute movement of the long positions (A and B), the net exposure naturally moves up. Successful longs expand and shorts contract. This results in a natural healthy upward drift of the net exposure. This means that long and short exposures are not matched.

Stocks are usually classified in sectors, industries, and sub-industries. Market participants tend to shop in similar sectors to hedge their bets. That could be Toyota versus General Motors, for instance. Sector exposure also experiences dislocation. On the long side, sectors that contribute increase in size. Meanwhile, on the short side, sectors that hurt increase in size.

Beta is sensitivity to the market. In high school soporific math class, this is a covariance matrix of discrete returns of a stock versus its benchmark. In execution trader English, this is how much a stock fluctuates when the index moves. Things are even worse when factoring Beta. The long side benefits from the expansion, but the short side experiences a net drag from the contraction. The bottom line is that on the short side, the market does not cooperate.

Any clean-shaven academic would logically argue that the solution is to increase the hit ratio and oversize short positions. It would be fine if market participants were right 100% of the time. Short positions could be oversized. In the real world, any battered and bruised short selling practitioner would cry insanity. Increasing the hit ratio means becoming a better stock picker. This is what everyone strives to accomplish every day. The problem is that even investment legends still have win rates of between 30 to 50% on the long side and somewhere between 20 to 40% on the short side. So, the solution would be to do more of the same and expect different results. Welcome to the world of insane marginal contribution.

Well, since the odds are lower, short selling armchair strategists would proceed to argue that the solution is obviously to size positions smaller to contain losses. The problem again is market dynamics. Successful shorts shrink. For example, taking a -0.50% bet means that a -10% decline would yield +0.05% profit, hardly the kind of return that gets investors to write big tickets.

The naked truth is that short selling is not a stock-picking contest. It is a position-sizing exercise. The difficulty is to size positions so that they contribute when they work but do not kill performance when they don't.

Since longs and shorts have opposite dynamics, there are only two ways to balance net exposure:

- Top up winners: this is the short side version of "ride winners, cut losers." Successful shorts need to be periodically replenished.

- Keep more short positions than longs: idea generation on the short side is a big stumbling block for most market participants.

This leads us to the next problem.

Scarcity mentality

"It is not down on any map; true places never are."

– Herman Melville, Moby-Dick

The need to come up with a steady supply of ideas leads us to the second factor working against short sellers: scarcity mentality. Market participants who approach the short side with a fundamental long-only perspective tend to carefully research and pick stocks. This means that their good picks tend to be few and far between. Long market participants tend to be whale hunters. It works on the long side because successful longs expand over time. However, bring this whale-hunting mindset to the short side and it turns into a wild narwhal chase.

The short side requires a different mindset. It requires an abundance mentality in which quantity prevails over quality. If long investors are whale hunters, short sellers need to be sardine fishers. Sardine fishing may not be the most inspirational material for classic novels, but at least it puts food on the table—good luck bringing back one of those elusive unicorn whales from the Arctic Circle. Short sellers need to avoid over-filtering. They need to make it easy to get into the portfolio but hard to stay. The key is to expect every short position to fail.

This leads us to the third challenge. There is not much information about short candidates.

Asymmetry of information

"It is difficult to get a man to understand something, when his salary depends on his not understanding it."

– Upton Sinclair

In addition to skewed market dynamics that drive the need for a steady supply of new ideas, short sellers also face the challenge of limited information. Neither corporates nor the street have an incentive to volunteer information that may adversely impact share price. Short sellers are on their own.

Stock options and transparency

"Profit is sweet, even if it comes from deception."

– Sophocles

Stock options are a popular way to attract, incentivize, and retain talented employees. When the remuneration of company officers is directly tied to share price performance, there is no incentive to volunteer information that could rock the boat. Short sellers encounter three types of difficulties:

- Companies have the privilege to turn down requests for corporate access to declared short sellers. They are under no obligation to answer thorny questions from investors. This *omertà* is a perfectly understandable human behavior, particularly when short sellers are adversarial.

- Secondly, top management sometimes takes a hostile stance toward short sellers. The good news is that when managements are thin-skinned enough to take short sellers to court, they are often aggressive in their business practices and accounting policies too.

- Thirdly, transparency is a one-way street. Companies are extroverts about their achievements but introverts about their failures. There is no budget freeze on public relations when it comes to success, but permafrost tundra when it comes to failures. Public self-flagellation is for martyrs, not corporate warriors.

In practice, it means it takes twice as much effort to gather half as much information to make an investment decision twice as risky.

Sell-side analysts are the guardians of the financial galaxy

"I am Groot."

– Groot, Guardians of the Galaxy

Finance is the only competitive sport where cheerleaders wear pinstripe suits. The sell-side industry is ill equipped to meet the needs of short sellers. In analysts' defense, it is difficult to champion a "sell" recommendation when the bonus pool of the entire food chain of any investment bank depends on rationalizing a "buy" recommendation by whatever means necessary.

There is no incentive for sell-side analysts to encourage selling or short selling. Corporations refinance on capital markets via the issuance of instruments such as stocks, commercial paper, and debt. They might feel marginally disinclined to award the mandate to a shop whose resident Einstein clamors that the next chapter in their corporate history will be either 11 or 13.

Analysts devote their lives to getting close to top management. The buy-side community rewards them with their ability to facilitate corporate access to top management. As James Montier used to put it, they are glorified secretaries. There is therefore no incentive to alienate management with a sell rating. When everyone proudly harbors a "buy" rating, sending a request for a company via an analyst with a sell rating rarely puts management in a friendly predisposition. It is an unnecessary shot across the bow.

Finally, analysts alienate existing investors. Who said that institutional investors never return calls from the sell side? Try and put a "sell" recommendation on one of their big long positions and they will remember your phone number.

As a result, sell-side analysts are the guardians of the financial galaxy. More precisely, they are Groot, the walking tree with a unique one-liner: "I am Groot," which in this context equates to "it's a buy." When share price performance disagrees, rationalizations can be quite supercalifragilisticexpialidocious, as the great expert on all things financial, Mary Poppins, would say. So, here is a way to decipher the enigma of the street creole:

- "This is a one-off, it's a buy": *Share price tanked unexpectedly. I am Groot.*
- "Negative earnings growth due to cyclical inventory adjustment, it's a buy": *Earnings have hit a "soft patch" and share price underperforms. I am Groot.*
- "The market is wrong, it's a buy": *Stock fails to rally along with the broader market. I am Groot.*
- "Buy on weakness, buy the dips": *Underperformance continues. I am Groot.*
- "We have lowered our estimates, adjusted our target price, stretched our investment horizon to 2057, but kept our rating, because the long-term story is still intact, it's a buy": *Underperformance sets in. I am Groot.*
- "Buy for the long-term investor, it's a buy": *Nothing works, it is cheap and getting cheaper. I am Groot.*

- "News flow is so bad, it is good news, it's a buy": *Share price falls through the floor – at that price, something will happen. I am Groot.*

- "Bad news is already baked in the valuations, it's a buy": *Nothing happened, share price languishes. I am Groot.*

- "This is a structural short, sell": *The investment banking department does not expect any deal in the near future. It is therefore OK to burn that bridge. If a stock does not bulge after a salvo of sell-side rating downgrades, then it is time to melt the family silver and BUY BUY BUY.*

Apparently, there is a "sell" recommendation still available at most shops. Yet it is like the "close doors" button in elevators: generally disconnected and here purely for placebic purposes.

Bottom line: this makes the rating grid a bit difficult to understand. Financial creole can be hard to decipher. Here is a simple guide to analyst ratings, what they mean, and how you should react:

Recommendation	Translation	Action
Strong buy	Momentum stock or investment banking deal in the pipeline	Buy
Buy	Default rating	What's for dinner? Movies on Friday?
Neutral	Negative opinion	Sell or sell short
Sell	Capitulation, not afraid to burn the bridge with the company	Cover short and look for long set up
Strong sell	Revenge rating	If recent long set up, melt the family silver and BUY, BUY, BUY, else buy to cover at market
Drop coverage	Underperformer	Check borrow utilization before selling short

Ratings are sticky. In all honesty, integrity is not the kind of currency that puts Ferraris in the garage. While analysts have a natural incentive to maintain a favorable rating, they enjoy more freedom with their numbers. They will slash their estimates, stretch their investment horizon, and bargain with their upside potential. This is the bargaining stage.

This is an admission that things may not be working as well as expected. Declining earnings momentum is a popular signal among short sellers. They may not be able to change their ratings, but they will be more honest with their numbers.

If market participants base their investment decisions on analyst estimates, they should probably be aware of their forecast accuracy. Forecasting does not seem to be analysts' strong suit either. Marco Dion, then head of quantitative research at JP Morgan, compiled a sell-side forecast accuracy report back in 2007 before the GFC. The object of the paper was to calculate how accurate analysts were in their forecasts one year out on a rolling basis.

The conclusion from this research paper largely explained why strategies focus on earnings momentum, also referred to as direction over time, as opposed to accuracy. What was really fascinating was the in-sample forecast accuracy. Analysts had a 2% chance of being spot-on for their earnings forecasts one year out. They had a 25% chance of being 10% away. At 2%, being spot-on is called a statistical error. At a 25% chance of being 10% away, even if accuracy miraculously doubled, it would still have the long-term probability of a coin toss.

Pulling back the curtain on financial analysts may have revealed fallible magicians. If you are not happy, blame the game, not the players. Analysts are brilliant, passionate, hard-working people, with encyclopaedic knowledge of their sectors and companies. However, they operate in a game rigged to make people trade, not necessarily to make them money.

Summary

Market participants tend to follow a predictable arc from the moment they proudly first set foot on the short selling terra incognita to the time they subconsciously abdicate sovereignty. The most important thing to remember is that the short side is *not* the inverse of the long. You cannot rely on mispriced stocks to revert to their fair valuations, and "structural shorts" are only profitable in the minds of short selling tourists. The short side obeys its own laws.

Among the challenges short sellers face that long-only market participants don't are overcoming a scarcity of information and bringing an abundance mindset to successfully counteract distorted exposures.

Now that we have dispelled a few myths about short selling and analyzed the idiosyncratic dynamics of the short side, the next parts of this book will be about building a short selling practice from the ground up. In *Part II, The Outer Game: Developing a Robust Trading Edge*, we will look at the outer game, or how to develop an advantageous trading edge.

In *Part III, The Long/Short Game: Building a Long/Short Product*, we will put everything together and consider how to build a long/short portfolio that investors will be interested in.

Beginning in the next chapter, we will take up the discussion of how to choose an effective trading methodology and begin to develop your short side trading edge.

4

Long/Short Methodologies: Absolute and Relative

In this chapter, we will be comparing methodologies, with a particular focus on absolute versus relative series. Absolute series are the **Open High Low Close (OHLC)** prices you can see on any website or platform. They often come either adjusted for dividends, stock splits, and other corporate actions. Relative series are the above absolute series divided by the closing price of the benchmark, adjusted for currency.

We hope to demonstrate the weaknesses of the absolute method, and strengths of the relative weakness method, which will define our methodology for the rest of the book. We will cover the following topics on the way:

- Importing libraries
- Long/Short 1.0: The absolute method
- Long/Short 2.0: The relative weakness method

 You can access color versions of all images in this chapter via the following link: `https://static.packt-cdn.com/downloads/9781801815192_ColorImages.pdf`. You can also access source code for this chapter via the book's GitHub repository: `https://github.com/PacktPublishing/Algorithmic-Short-Selling-with-Python-Published-by-Packt`.

Importing libraries

The following code, and indeed most of the code in the book, first requires the installation of the yfinance package:

```
pip install yfinance
```

yfinance can then be imported:

```
import yfinance as yf
```

For this chapter and the rest of the book, we will also be working with pandas, numpy, and matplotlib. So, please remember to import them first:

```
# Import Libraries
import pandas as pd
import numpy as np
%matplotlib inline
import matplotlib.pyplot as plt
```

Long/Short 1.0: the absolute method

> "'But the Emperor has nothing at all on!', said a little child.
>
> 'Listen to the voice of innocence!', exclaimed his father."
>
> – *Arthur Andersen*

The absolute method makes intuitive sense: buy stocks that go up, short stocks that go down. There is a one-to-one relationship between data coming from various providers, price charts on the screen, and what goes into the portfolio. Everybody speaks the same language. Investors, market commentators, and various other market participants talk about the same price and generally valuation levels. Shorting stocks that go down in absolute value generates cash that can be used to buy additional stocks on the long side and increase leverage.

There is only one small problem: the product does not always do what it says on the tin. Let's keep it civil: the absolute method has been a crass utter failure from the get-go and the following sections will consider why.

Ineffective at decreasing correlation with the benchmark

Investors explicitly pay premium fees for uncorrelated returns. In execution trader English, investors want their money to grow, regardless of Mr. Market's mood swings. Let's look at why the absolute method fails to deliver on this promise.

In bull markets, the tide lifts all boats. Few stocks go down, but when they do, they attract a lot of attention. Long holders exit the stock while short sellers pile on. These stocks become crowded shorts. Popular shorts are notoriously difficult to trade — they are illiquid and notoriously volatile. Getting in and out of these stocks has some adverse market impact, borrow fees are expensive, and they are also prone to short squeezes, those violent rallies at the end of a bearish descent. Since no one wants to be too cornered through a short squeeze, this puts a natural cap on bet sizes, leading to atrophied short books.

On the other hand, long books are overdeveloped in bull markets. This results in high structural positive net exposures, which is an explicit bet on upwards market direction. In financial creole, those are known as "directional hedge funds." These fund managers talk a good game about ambidextrous and agile management, but as soon as the market turns bearish, they seek refuge under the comfort of their desks. Conversely, in bear markets, few stocks tend to go up. Short ideas are plentiful, but in practice, exposures rarely cross into negative territory. This means that investors cushion the blow but still lose money.

The following chart shows the S&P 500 index and a count of all the constituents in either the bull or bear regime using the absolute price series.

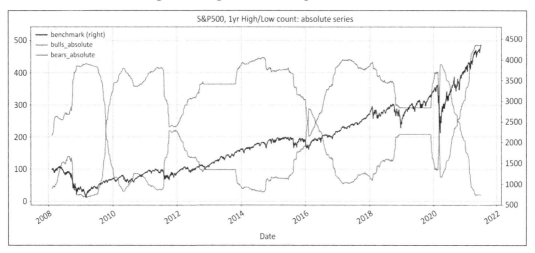

Figure 4.1: The number of stocks in bullish or bearish territory greatly fluctuates with market gyrations

The preceding chart, and another chart comparing this method with the relative weakness method (which we will come back to in the *Consistent supply of fresh ideas on both sides* section), can be produced by executing the following source code:

```
# S&P500 dataframe: list of tickers
sp_df = pd.read_html('https://en.wikipedia.org/wiki/List_of_S%26P_500_
companies')[0]
sp_df['Symbol'] = sp_df['Symbol'].str.replace('.', '-')
bm_ticker = '^GSPC'
tickers_list = [bm_ticker] + list(sp_df['Symbol'])[:]

# Variables instantiation
window = 252
df_abs = pd.DataFrame()
batch_size = 20
loop_size = int(len(tickers_list) // batch_size) + 2

for t in range(1,loop_size): # Batch download
    m = (t - 1) * batch_size
    n = t * batch_size
    batch_list = tickers_list[m:n]
    print(batch_list,m,n)
    batch_download = yf.download(tickers= batch_list,
                                 start= '2007-01-01', end = None,
                                 interval = "1d",group_by = 'column',
                                 auto_adjust = True,
                                 prepost = True, treads = True,
                                 proxy = None)['Close']
    df_abs = df_abs.join(batch_download, how='outer')

### removed for brevity: check GitHub repo for full code ###

bullbear['bulls_absolute'] = df_abs[df_abs > 0].count(axis=1)
bullbear['bears_absolute'] = df_abs[df_abs < 0].count(axis=1)
bullbear['bulls_relative'] = df_rel[df_rel > 0].count(axis=1)
bullbear['bears_relative'] = df_rel[df_rel < 0].count(axis=1)

bullbear[280:][['benchmark','bulls_absolute', 'bears_absolute',
            ]].plot(figsize=(20,8),
              style=['k', 'g', 'r'],grid=True,secondary_
y=['benchmark'],
```

```
                 title = 'S&P500, 1yr High/Low count: absolute series' )

bullbear[280:][['benchmark','bulls_absolute', 'bears_absolute', 'bulls_
relative', 'bears_relative']].plot(figsize=(20,8),
               style=['k', 'g', 'r','g:', 'r:'],grid=True,secondary_
y=['benchmark'],
               title = 'S&P500, 1yr High/Low count: absolute &
relative series')
```

The structure of the preceding code is fairly compact and straightforward:

1. Import the yfinance module to enable downloading from Yahoo Finance.
2. Download the latest S&P 500 constituents using the pandas.read_html method. Extract the ticker list and replace . with - to ensure compatibility with Yahoo Finance.
3. Instantiate dataframes and variables to process data and aggregate results. Calculate the batch size using the modulo // function.
4. Add a loop to the batch download close prices. Add to df_abs using the join method.
5. Create df_rel by dividing df_abs by the bm_ticker column (specified with axis=0) then rebasing it by the first value of the index:
    1. Use the np.where method to define bullish/bearish regimes: If close is the highest of 252 periods assign 1, if close is the lowest of 252 periods assign –1; otherwise, assign np.nan.
    2. Propagate 1 and -1 across np.nan missing values.
6. Aggregate results on the bullbear dataframe, adding the horizontal count (axis=1) across absolute and relative dataframes.
7. Plot benchmark, bullish, and bearish counts.

When the market goes up, the number of bullish stocks rises. When the market turns sideways or bearish, the number of stocks in bearish territory rises. This demonstrates that the absolute method is by definition correlated to the markets. It should suffice to look at the track record of long/short funds to conclude that the absolute method has failed to deliver uncorrelated attractive returns.

The next few sections will consider a number of weaknesses of the absolute method.

Ineffective at reducing volatility

Since the short side has fewer ideas than the other, the way to balance exposures is to supersize the more concentrated book. This translates into a diluted, relatively low volatility long portfolio and a few concentrated "structural short" bets. As we saw in *Chapter 3, Take a Walk on the Wild Short Side*, crowded shorts are illiquid and therefore more prone to volatility spikes. There is no shortage of sellers, but courageous buyers are scarce.

Volatility on the short side drives the entire portfolio. Underwhelming performance divided by high residual volatility only yields unattractive volatility adjusted returns.

Little, if any, historical downside protection

The absolute method might post positive returns during bull markets. But every time the market tanks, performance hits a "soft patch."

During the **Great Financial Crisis (GFC)**, one would have expected net exposures to drop below zero. After all, everyone was talking of financial Armageddon. If long/short players were as comfortable shorting as they claimed to be, net exposures should have dropped below 0. The numbers told a different story. With net beta at +0.5, market participants were residually bullish.

The way absolute method practitioners reduced their net exposure was to reduce their long exposure, and hoard cash. When it came down to pulling the trigger on the short side, they fertilized their pants. Years of trading in a bull market had atrophied their short selling muscle. If you want to beat Mike Tyson, you need to show up at the gym and get your smile rectified a few times.

Lesser investment vehicle

The absolute method has earned its existential crisis. Long/Short 1.0 is neither a sophisticated, nor a safe investment vehicle. It is a lesser vehicle in every single respect. It makes less money than mutual funds and index funds in bull markets. It only loses less money than the index in bear markets. After fees, investors compound less money with the absolute method than they would with low-tech plain-vanilla index funds. There is less transparency and less liquidity than in classical mutual funds. It is therefore little surprise that those funds have failed to attract and retain pension money looking for stable, uncorrelated returns. Absolute long/shorts funds are in the business of making money for themselves and occasionally for their investors.

Laggard indicator

"La gravité est le bouclier des sots [Gravity is the shield of fools]."

– Montesquieu, French philosopher

Stocks are not intercontinental ballistic missiles. They do not simply fall out of the sky because they could not score enough marine-grade diesel to fill up a whole fuel tank:

1. First, they lag behind their immediate competitors.
2. Second, they trail behind other stocks in their industry.
3. Third, they fall behind within their sector.
4. Fourth, they underperform the broader index.
5. Fifth, they finally go down in absolute value.

The bottom line is, by the time those stocks pop up on people's radar screens, they have already shed a lot of value. In an industry where creative colorful insults are an occupational pastime, few zingers sting as much as being called a laggard indicator. Yet it seems to be the dominant business model in the long/short business.

Long/short market participants are most certainly not imbeciles. They are highly educated, dedicated, hard-working people. Going 'long on strength' and 'short on weakness' is the right idea—the absolute data series is just the wrong data set. As an alternative, the next section will discuss the benefits of using the relative series over absolute prices.

Long/Short 2.0: the relative weakness method

"Truth is by nature self-evident. As soon as you remove the cobwebs of ignorance that surround it, it shines clear."

– Mahatma Gandhi

Indices such as S&P 500, Nasdaq 100, FTSE 100, and Topix are the market capitalization weighted average of their constituents. Roughly half the stocks will do better and the rest worse than the index over any timeframe. There are many more stocks to pick from the large contingent of relative underperformers than the few and far between stocks that drop in absolute value.

Below is the source code to calculate relative series:

```python
def relative(df,_o,_h,_l,_c, bm_df, bm_col, ccy_df, ccy_col, dgt,
start, end,rebase=True):
    '''
    df: df
    bm_df, bm_col: df benchmark dataframe & column name
    ccy_df,ccy_col: currency dataframe & column name
    dgt: rounding decimal
    start/end: string or offset
    rebase: boolean rebase to beginning or continuous series
    '''
    # Slice df dataframe from start to end period: either offset or
datetime
    df = df[start:end]

    # inner join of benchmark & currency: only common values are
preserved
    df = df.join(bm_df[[bm_col]],how='inner')
    df = df.join(ccy_df[[ccy_col]],how='inner')

    # rename benchmark name as bm and currency as ccy
    df.rename(columns={bm_col:'bm', ccy_col:'ccy'},inplace=True)

    # Adjustment factor: calculate the scalar product of benchmark and
currency
    df['bmfx'] = round(df['bm'].mul(df['ccy']),dgt).
fillna(method='ffill')
    if rebase == True:
        df['bmfx'] = df['bmfx'].div(df['bmfx'][0])

    # Divide absolute price by fxcy adjustment factor and rebase to
first value
    df['r' + str(_o)] = round(df[_o].div(df['bmfx']),dgt)
    df['r' + str(_h)] = round(df[_h].div(df['bmfx']),dgt)
    df['r'+ str(_l)] = round(df[_l].div(df['bmfx']),dgt)
    df['r'+ str(_c)] = round(df[_c].div(df['bmfx']),dgt)
    df = df.drop(['bm','ccy','bmfx'],axis=1)

    return (df)
```

Next, we will take this function for a spin. Softbank (9984.T) is a company listed on the **Tokyo Stock Exchange (TSE)**. It trades in Japanese yen. The company has been a major player in the US tech industry for almost three decades. Softbank will therefore be benchmarked against Nasdaq in USD:

```
ticker = '9984.T' # Softbank
ohlc = ['Open','High','Low','Close']
_o,_h,_l,_c = [ohlc[h] for h in range(len(ohlc))]
start= '2018-12-30'
end = None
df =  round(yf.download(tickers= ticker,start= start, end = end,
                        interval = "1d",group_by = 'column',
                        auto_adjust= True, prepost= True,
                        treads = True, proxy = None),2)
bm_df = pd.DataFrame()
bm_ticker = '^IXIC' #Nasdaq
bm_col = 'nasdaq'
ccy_df = pd.DataFrame()
ccy_ticker = 'USDJPY=X'
ccy_col = 'JPY'
dgt = 5

bm_df[bm_col] =  yf.download(tickers= bm_ticker,start= start, end = end,
                             interval = "1d",group_by = 'column',
                             auto_adjust = True, prepost = True,
                             treads = True, proxy = None)['Close']
ccy_df[ccy_col] =  yf.download(tickers= ccy_ticker,start= start,
                               end = end, interval= "1d",
                               group_by = 'column',auto_adjust = True,
                               prepost = True, treads = True,
                               proxy = None)['Close']

df = relative(df,_o,_h,_l,_c, bm_df, bm_col, ccy_df, ccy_col, dgt,
start, end,rebase=True)

df[['Close','rClose']].plot(figsize=(20,8),grid=True,
           title= 'Softbank Absolute in JPY vs relative to Nasdaq in
USD rebased' )
```

This code calculates the relative series rebased to the beginning of the dataframe compared to the absolute series, using Softbank as an example. First, we download Softbank in OHLC local currency. Then we download the close prices of the benchmark Nasdaq and the currency, US dollar.

We run the relative series function rebased to the beginning of the dataframe by keeping the boolean flag `rebase=True`.

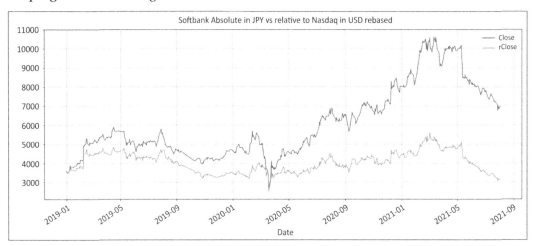

Figure 4.2: Softbank in absolute JPY versus relative to Nasdaq in USD rebased

When telephones lost their cord, people carried them everywhere and gradually enchained themselves. Softbank has been a powerhouse on the TSE since telephones have enchained mankind. Yet, Softbank has been a lackluster performer when benchmarked against the Nasdaq index and labelled in USD. For the rest of the book, we will be using Softbank series in absolute value and Japanese Yen simply for demonstration purposes. The concept is simple: buy the outperformers, sell short the underperformers, make money on the spread. The idea of focusing on the excess returns over the index is nothing new. Mutual funds managers are assessed on their outperformance over the benchmark. When focusing on only the long side, the mission is to overweigh outperformers and underweigh underperformers. The difference in weight over the benchmark is called "**active money**."

The relative weakness method takes a similar approach. A long/short portfolio is the net sum of two relative books. The long side is a classic mutual fund-type long book. The short side is composed of underperformers benchmarked to the inverse of the index. The only difference with a mutual fund is instead of staying away from underperformers, managers take active bets on the short side. Performance comes from the spread between outperformance on the long side and underperformance on the short. Below is a simple example. General Electric, General Motors, and Goldman Sachs are in three different industries. Yet, they have two things in common. Firstly, they are constituents of the same S&P 500 index. Secondly, when combined together, their tickers have this lovely acronym: GEMS.

The code below shows price series in absolute value and then returns relative to the benchmark.

```
tickers_list = ['GE','GM','GS']

# Dataframes instantiation
gems = pd.DataFrame()
start = '2020-03-31'
benchmark = yf.download(tickers= '^GSPC',start= start, end = None,
                        interval = "1d",group_by = 'column',
                        auto_adjust = True, prepost = True,
                        treads = True, proxy = None)['Close']
failed = []
rel_ticker_list = []
for n,ticker in enumerate(tickers_list):
    try: #7 Download & process data
        gems[ticker] = yf.download(tickers= ticker,start= start,
                                   end = None, interval = "1d",
                                   group_by = 'column',
                                   auto_adjust = True, prepost = True,
                                   treads = True, proxy = None)['Close']
        gems['rel_'+ticker] = gems[ticker].div(benchmark * gems[ticker]
[0]) * benchmark[0]
        rel_ticker_list.append('rel_'+ticker)
    except:
        failed.append(ticker)
gems = gems[tickers_list+rel_ticker_list]
gems.plot(figsize= (20,8),secondary_y= rel_ticker_list,style=['r','b','
g','r:','b:','g:'],
          title= 'GEMS Absolute Prices vs Relative Series' )
```

The code takes the following steps:

1. The gems dataframe is instantiated. start could be either a date—2019-12-31, for instance, or an offset period such as –254. Lists are instantiated.

2. Run a loop to download price information from Yahoo Finance. Add absolute series to the gems dataframe.

3. For the relative series, divide by the benchmark and rebase at the beginning of the series.

4. Append rel_list_ticker to obtain a list of tickers with the prefix el. This will be used to sort columns later.

5. Re-order the columns and print.

The result shows the absolute prices along with the relative series on dotted lines of **General Electric (GE)**, **General Motors (GM)**, and **Goldman Sachs (GS)**:

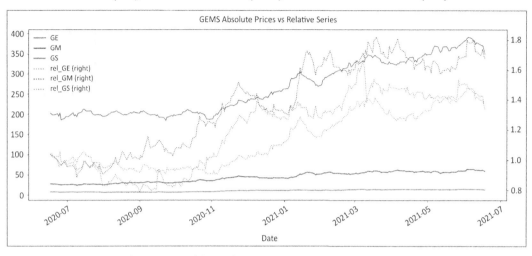

Figure 4.3: Absolute vs Relative prices of General Electric (GE), General Motors (GM), and Goldman Sachs (GS)

The chart illustrates that relative series are a bit more indicative of a stock's relative strength compared to the market. Prices are restarted versus the benchmark at the beginning of the period, but they provide uniform series across sectors. At first, it may seem unnatural to enter a short position on a rising stock. Losing money does not come naturally to absolute return players. To understand the concept, let's reframe it by picturing what happens in a bear market. When the big bear pounds the market, nothing goes up. This means that you'll be looking to buy long defensive stocks that hold their ground or fall slower than the broader index. You will be losing less than the market on the long side. Typically you would be buying non-cyclical utilities, railways, or food stocks.

Conversely, you will be looking to short stocks that drop faster than the benchmark. Those tend to be cyclical stocks for which performance ebbs and flows with the economic cycle, such as airline companies. By the way, you can keep the darlings of the previous bull markets in your portfolio, but remember to switch sides. Leaders of bull markets tend to attract late-cycle momentum players. Those are the weakest market participants, late to the game, with no real game plan. They bail as soon as the going gets tough, which leads to sudden performance disgorgement. The relative series open a whole new world of possibilities compared with the classic absolute method. Below are 10 reasons that assert the superiority of the relative weakness method.

Consistent supply of fresh ideas on both sides

Indices are generally the market cap weighted average of all its constituents. This means that roughly half the issues will outperform while the other half trail the market. At first, this plethora of ideas appears disconcerting to market participants who have consistently focused on absolute performance. Market participants can be tempted to continue to trade the long side using the absolute method and the short one using the relative method. This awful idea often leads to buying and shorting underperformers. The long side must be a mirror image of the type of strategy and series deployed on the short side.

Let's revisit the script we wrote in the *Ineffective at decreasing correlation with the benchmark* section about the number of stocks in bullish and bearish territory. As we mentioned there, the code produces two charts. We originally published a lateral count using the absolute series, which is also shown here:

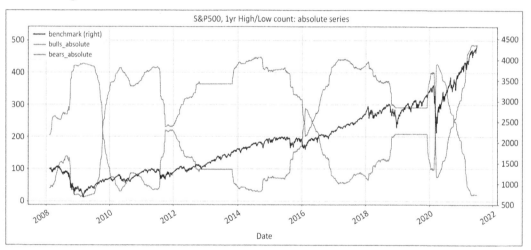

Figure 4.4: Stocks in the S&P 500 in bullish or bearish territory using the absolute series

It illustrates that the S&P 500 has been in bullish territory for over 12 years, with a few hiccups along the way. Overall, there are many more stocks in bullish than bearish territory. Short candidates are few and far between. As the adage goes, the tide lifts all boats.

However, let's compare this with the relative series. This is a simple lateral count on daily bars. In comparison, the chart below shows the number of stocks in bullish and bearish territory using both absolute and relative series side by side, the price divided by the close of the index:

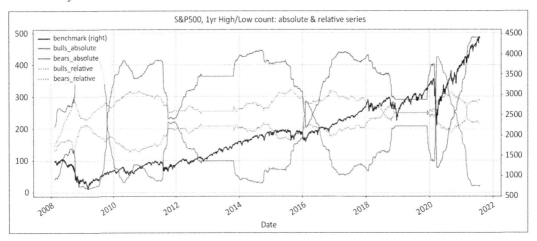

Figure 4.5: Number of stocks in the S&P 500 in bullish or bearish territory
using the absolute series compared to relative to the index

The dotted lines represent the number of stocks in either bullish or bearish territory relative to the index. Unsurprisingly, there are roughly half the stocks in the bull camp and the others in bearish mode at any point in time. This provides a plethora of ideas to choose from on both sides.

The list of constituents does not feature historical inclusions/ deletions. Stocks that perform poorly, go bankrupt, or are absorbed are deleted from the index. This creates an artificial upward drift referred to as survivorship bias. Survivorship bias does not affect short selling strategies as their validity is measured only against the strongest stocks.

There is a consistent supply of fresh ideas, regardless of the index. The absolute series has massive fluctuations depending on the market's ever-changing mood. Meanwhile, the number of stocks in bullish or bearish territory remains fairly constant using the relative series. This implies there are always plenty of ideas on both sides of the book at any given time.

As the breadth narrows, the number of underperformers may even exceed that of outperformers. That directly contradicts the widely held belief that short ideas are few and far between. In reality, it is not rare to have more underperformers than outperformers.

The index is the market capitalization weighted average of its constituents. It is dominated by the largest 100 capitalizations. In sideways or turbulent times, smaller capitalizations tend to be reminded of Newtonian physics. Gravity hits hard on illiquid stocks.

Focus on sector rotation

In the absolute method, the objective is to time the top and the bottom of the market. Every seasoned market participant will tell you that only two types of people consistently manage to time tops and bottoms. They are either amnesiac or charlatans, more often a combination of both. When restating everything in relative series, the objective is to focus on sector rotation. As we saw in the above chart, the number of stocks in either territory does not fluctuate much over time. This does not mean the same stocks underperform for eternity. The market may go up for years, but it will reward different industries, sectors, and even market caps over time. Using the relative weakness method, this means buying nascent outperformers and shorting early underperformers. Imagine the impact on clients when you tell them after a successful bear campaign it is now time to switch sides and go for long early cyclicals and small caps amidst the ambient doomsday gloom.

Provides a low-correlation product

Dividing everything by the benchmark strips the effect of the underlying index. This mechanically removes correlation to the index. The focus is now on excess returns over the benchmark. It may come across as repetitive, but it drives the point home. The absolute series has large fluctuations in the number of names in either regime depending on the state of the market.

Conversely, the relative series has a fairly consistent number of names on either side. Market gyrations do not greatly affect the size of the pool of candidates, as demonstrated in the *Consistent supply of fresh ideas on both sides* section. This is also basic arithmetic. Dividing the absolute series by the index strips the effect of the benchmark across the entire population. The only two factors remaining are currency impact and stock-specific performance.

Provides a low-volatility product

This is a direct consequence of the abundance of underperformers. When there are a plethora of short candidates to choose from, market participants enjoy greater diversification in their portfolios. They also have lower concentration. This reduces volatility.

Reduces the cost of borrow fees

Crowded shorts are notoriously expensive to borrow. Institutional shareholders rarely abide by an old maritime code of honor. They do not sink with the ship. They tend to liquidate their positions when underperformance persists. This makes borrowing even harder to locate over time.

On the other hand, underperformers still benefit from some inertia. Borrowing is close to general collateral, in other words, cheap and plentiful. When bad news sinks in and absolute players lurk around, relative short sellers can pass the baton to their less sophisticated counterparts. The former can move to cheap easy-to-borrow shorts, while the latter are left to chew on expensive, dry, hard-to-borrow names.

Provides scalability

One of the problems with the absolute method is its lack of scalability. Stocks that go down in absolute value are usually popular. Crowded shorts are volatile and illiquid. It is difficult to build large profitable positions.

In 2007, quantitative funds, often referred to as quants, learned the hard way that there was a limit to short selling crowded issues. When there is an ample supply of ideas on both sides, concentration can be kept low as **Assets Under Management (AUM)** continue to grow.

Non-confrontational

The relative method is non-confrontational. Relative short sellers do not need to make things personal. Management of defensive companies understand that their stocks are bound to underperform in bull markets. They do not take offense when their stocks are either sold short or bought long on this premise. Conversely, high-flying tech entrepreneurs know that bear markets are not exactly IPO season.

Currency adjustment becomes an advantage

Managers with regional or global mandates juggle multiple currencies and indices. Converting everything into fund currency relative to a global or regional benchmark puts all stocks on the same playfield.

There is no need for an additional layer of macro-view, currency hedging, risk management. Everything is rebased in the same currency and benchmark adjusted unit. For example, the Japanese market soared as its currency was devalued by 40%. Managers operating in Japanese yen (JPY) did well in local currency; their counterparts denominated in USD fared poorly despite having the exact same stocks in their portfolios. The depreciation of the Japanese yen ate all gains away.

But managing a currency-adjusted relative portfolio is not intuitive. Everything from stock selection to portfolio management must be adjusted for the benchmark and fund currency. Decisions such as entry, exit, and position-sizing need to be made in currency-adjusted relative prices. Charts in absolute and local currency provided by most data vendors answer questions that relative market participants should never be asking themselves. Comparing stocks' absolute value with currencies is like comparing apples and oranges. Converting the entire investment universe into relative series is a bit more involved up front, but a lot easier to manipulate thereafter.

Other market participants cannot guess your levels

Market participants often complain that "they" are triggering their stop loss, or "they" work their orders. Market participants tend to place stop losses at support/resistance levels, round numbers. Some algorithms are specifically designed to game resting orders. When all the price levels are calculated relative to the index and adjusted for currency, those sniper algorithms are ineffective. The series that relative participants react to are different from the absolute levels.

The flipside is that stop losses have to be actively managed. In execution trader English, orders that do not match prices coming from the exchange cannot be filled.

You will look like an investment genius

As we saw earlier, stocks do not drop in absolute value out of nowhere. Underperformance starts with their competitors and extends to the industry, sector, and broader market before tumbling down in absolute value. Entering a short on a relative basis may be mildly painful for a while. It will, however, appear prescient to those fixated on absolute prices.

A picture is worth a thousand words. The following chart plots both the relative and absolute performance of **Wells Fargo (WFC)**:

```
ticker = 'WFC'
benchmark = '^GSPC'
tickers_list = [benchmark] + [ticker]

data = round(yf.download(tickers= tickers_list,start= '2015-09-07', end
= None,
             interval = "1d",group_by = 'column',auto_adjust = True,
             prepost = True, treads = True, proxy = None)['Close'],2)

data['r'+str(ticker)] = round(data[ticker].div(data[benchmark])*data[be
nchmark][0] ,2)
data[[ticker,'r'+str(ticker)]].plot(figsize=(20,8),grid=True,
title= str.upper(ticker)+ ' Absolute vs Relative series')
```

This produces the following chart:

Figure 4.6: Wells Fargo in absolute and relative series one year before the scandal (to date)

The chart starts one year and one day before the scandal erupted. Underperformance began long before the absolute share price factored in what was about to come. Relative performance discounts the absolute performance months in advance.

Now, imagine you had started to short Wells Fargo even 6 months before the scandal. Is there a better selling point to all those investors who are so desperate to find one good short seller? There is no better marketing pitch than a chart in absolute value plotting the trades you took according to changes relative to the index. Imagine anchoring short positions in all the Enrons, Lehmans, GMs, and Kodaks of this world long before they even made the news.

Getting in ahead of everyone gives a margin of safety. Positions are less vulnerable to bear market rallies. This is, however, only half of the equation. Getting out on the short side can be messy. Volume thins out as shorts gain in popularity. This is where the relative method offers a decisive advantage. At some point, selling pressure will be done. Relative short sellers have ample time to cover their shorts, while their absolute counterparts double down on their vitriolic crusade. Stocks begin to outperform, imperceptibly at first, stubbornly then, before rising defiantly. This invariably catches absolute fundamental short sellers who bank on a double-dip that never comes.

Summary

In this chapter, we outlined the benefits of switching from absolute OHLC prices to the relative series. Absolute participants are laggard indicators while relative players lead the pack. Market participants who adopt the methodology outlined in this chapter will have a distinct edge. They will be able to build and liquidate positions ahead of the crowd. They will look like prescient investment geniuses. They will have more ideas to choose from. Their portfolios will have lower correlation to the markets, and lower volatility as well. These are traits investors are looking for.

Once all stocks are rebased relative to the benchmark in fund currency, the next step is to reclassify the investment universe according to their regime: bullish, bearish, sideways. We take this up in the next chapter.

5
Regime Definition

During the Napoleonic wars, field surgeons with limited resources had to make quick decisions as to whom would need surgery, who could survive without, and the unfortunate ones for whom nothing could be done. Triage was born out of necessity to allocate limited time and resources in the most efficient and humane way possible. In the stock market, regime is another word for triage. Some are bullish, some are bearish, and some are inconclusive.

Markets tend to "stay wrong" a lot longer than investors tend to stick with you. Segregating stocks into different regime buckets—triaging them—before performing in-depth analysis is an efficient allocation of resources. The objective of this initial triage is not to predict where stocks could, would, or should be headed, but to practice the long-lost art of actively listening to what the market has to say.

Some market participants like to spend time and resources on building bear theses for stocks that stubbornly defy the gravity of reason. This is not efficient for two reasons. First, they expect reversion to the mean. On the long side, they trade trends and ride outperformers, expecting them to continue to do well. Meanwhile, on the short side, they trade mean reversion and expect expensive stocks to choke on humble pie and come back down to cheap prices again.

As we will analyze in the coming chapters, trend following and mean reversion have opposite pay-offs and risk profiles. Long trend-following and short mean-reversion does not reduce risk. It compounds it. For now, it suffices to say that market participants must make a choice. Either they trade trends expecting them to develop, or inefficiencies expecting them to correct. When they choose to trade both trends and inefficiencies, their investment style is incongruent. They invite the worst outcome of each style, which unsurprisingly tends to happen simultaneously at the worst time.

Secondly, expecting stocks to revert is essentially like trying to time the top. It is like standing in the middle of the tracks expecting freight train after freight train to stop. Bull regimes tend to outlast investors' patience for gallantry. It is more prudent to wait for more information to surface and the tide to turn bearish before placing a short.

As a different approach, establishing a market regime is something that could really help fundamental short-sellers. They often show up too early. They place their bets long before the broader market starts to factor in the information. The difference between a short selling guru and the dreaded tap on the shoulder is 6 months. Short internet stocks in 1999, and you'll be teaching math to bored university students in 2000. Short the same stocks as early as late January 2000, and a new short selling star is born.

In the following sections, we will look at various regime definition methods, before comparing them:

- Importing libraries
- Creating a charting function
- Breakout/breakdown
- Moving averages
- Higher highs/higher lows
- Floor/ceiling
- Methodology comparison
- Let the market regime dictate the best strategy

 You can access color versions of all images in this chapter via the following link: `https://static.packt-cdn.com/downloads/9781801815192_ColorImages.pdf`. You can also access source code for this chapter via the book's GitHub repository: `https://github.com/PacktPublishing/Algorithmic-Short-Selling-with-Python-Published-by-Packt`

Importing libraries

For this chapter and the rest of the book, we will be working with the `pandas`, `numpy`, `yfinance`, and `matplotlib` libraries. We will also be working with `find_peaks` from the ScientificPython library.

So, please remember to import them first:

```
# Import Libraries
import pandas as pd
import numpy as np
import yfinance as yf
%matplotlib inline
import matplotlib.pyplot as plt
from scipy.signal import find_peaks
```

Creating a charting function

Before we visually compare various regime methods, let's publish the source code for a colorful charting function called graph_regime_combo. The parameters will gradually make sense as we unveil each method.

The code is as digestible as Japanese mochi rice, a common cause of death by asphyxiation for toddlers, elderly people, and foreigners, like the author, in Japan. The structure is however simple, like the author as well. Everything depends on whether the floor/ceiling method is instantiated in the rg variable, or not. If floor/ceiling is present, then it supersedes everything else. If not, the other two methods (breakout and moving average crossover) are printed. The ax1.fill_between method identifies the boundaries. Read all of them to understand the conditions. The rest is uneventful:

```
#### Graph Regimes ####
def graph_regime_combo(ticker,df,_c,rg,lo,hi,slo,shi,clg,flr,rg_ch,
                       ma_st,ma_mt,ma_lt,lt_lo,lt_hi,st_lo,st_hi):

    '''

    https://www.color-hex.com/color-names.html
    ticker,df,_c: _c is closing price
    rg: regime -1/0/1 using floor/ceiling method
    lo,hi: small, noisy highs/lows
    slo,shi: swing lows/highs
    clg,flr: ceiling/floor
    rg_ch: regime change base
    ma_st,ma_mt,ma_lt: moving averages ST/MT/LT
    lt_lo,lt_hi: range breakout High/Low LT
    st_lo,st_hi: range breakout High/Low ST
    '''

    fig = plt.figure(figsize=(20,8))
```

```
    ax1 = plt.subplot2grid((1,1), (0,0))
    date = df.index
    close = df[_c]
    ax1.plot_date(df.index, close,'-', color='k',  label=ticker.
upper())
    try:
        if pd.notnull(rg):
            base = df[rg_ch]
            regime = df[rg]

#### removed for brevity: check GitHub repo for full code ####

    for label in ax1.xaxis.get_ticklabels():
        label.set_rotation(45)
    ax1.grid(True)
    ax1.xaxis.label.set_color('k')
    ax1.yaxis.label.set_color('k')
    plt.xlabel('Date')
    plt.ylabel(str.upper(ticker) + ' Price')
    plt.title(str.upper(ticker))
    plt.legend()
#### Graph Regimes Combo ####
```

Now that this deadly code is out of the way, survivors may proceed to the next stage: range breakout.

Breakout/breakdown

"Kites rise highest against the wind – not with it."

– Winston Churchill

This is the oldest and simplest trend-following method. It works for both bull and bear markets. If the price makes a new high over *x* number of periods, the regime is bullish. If the price makes a fresh low over *x* number of periods, the regime is bearish. This method is computationally easy to implement.

Popular durations are 252 trading days (which works out as 52 weeks), and 100 and 50 trading days. Below, here is a simple rendition of this regime methodology:

```
def regime_breakout(df,_h,_l,window):
    hl =  np.where(df[_h] == df[_h].rolling(window).max(),1,
                        np.where(df[_l] == df[_l].
                            rolling(window).min(), -1,np.nan))
    roll_hl = pd.Series(index= df.index, data= hl).fillna(method=
'ffill')
    return roll_hl


ticker = '9984.T' # Softbank ticker
start= '2016-12-31'
end = None
df = yf.download(tickers= ticker,start= start, end = end,
                interval = "1d",group_by = 'column',
                auto_adjust = True, prepost = True,
                treads = True, proxy = None)


window = 252
df['hi_'+str(window)] = df['High'].rolling(window).max()
df['lo_'+str(window)] = df['Low'].rolling(window).min()
df['bo_'+ str(window)]= regime_breakout(df= df,_h= 'High',_l=
'Low',window= window)
df[['Close','hi_'+str(window),'lo_'+str(window),
    'bo_'+ str(window)]].plot(secondary_y= ['bo_'+ str(window)],
        figsize=(20,5), style=['k','g:','r:','b-.'],
        title = str.upper(ticker)+' '+str(window)+' days high/low')
```

The way this code functions is simple:

1. If the high is the highest of x periods, then hl is 1.
2. Otherwise, if the low is the lowest of x periods, then hl is -1.
3. If neither of these conditions is true, hl is N/A.
4. We want to propagate the latest values forward along the missing values using the fillna method. First, we convert the numpy array to a pandas series.
5. Then, we fill missing values using the fillna forward fill method.

6. Download the data, run the function, and plot the chart:

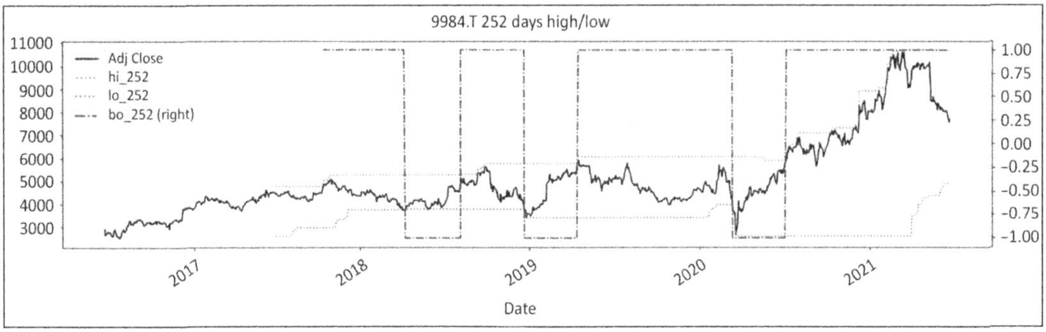

Figure 5.1: Softbank one year high/low regime breakout definition

This range breakout strategy works wonders when the price breaks out after consolidation or a sideways market. Sideways markets are the interim periods between up or downward trends, when the old regime is dead and the new is not obvious yet. In a sideways undulating market, price oscillates in a range.

Bulls fight bears in a Gilgamesh epic battle. When prices break out from the upper or lower bound, this signals one side has thrown in the towel. Pent-up energy is released. The price moves effortlessly along the line of least resistance. This breakout method is therefore the weapon for choice for range breakouts/breakdowns.

The main drawback of this method is its built-in lag, which comes as a result of the duration. In financial revisionist jargon, the waiting period is called **confirmation**. Market participants rarely have the patience to wait 50 days, 100 days, or even a year to finally find some resolution. Time is money. Stocks late on their rent should either be reduced or kicked out. Market participants that use this method with a long duration may want to re-introduce a time exit into their strategy.

The main advantages of this method are computational simplicity and stability. The major drawbacks are its inherent lag and the discomfort of giving back large amounts of profits. This leads us to the next iteration: the asymmetrical range breakout strategy.

Further refinements to the breakout regime definition method include dissociated periods for entries and exits. For example, the legendary Chicago Turtle Traders entered on 50-day highs and closed on 20-day lows:

```
# CHAPTER 5 Turtle for dummies

def turtle_trader(df, _h, _l, slow, fast):
    '''
    "    _slow: Long/Short direction\n",
    "    _fast: trailing stop loss\n",
    '''
```

```
    _slow = regime_breakout(df,_h,_l,window = slow)
    _fast = regime_breakout(df,_h,_l,window = fast)
    turtle = pd. Series(index= df.index,
                        data = np.where(_slow == 1,np.where(_fast ==
1,1,0),
                                        np.where(_slow == -1, np.where(_fast
==-1,-1,0),0)))
    return turtle


slow = 50
fast = 20
ohlc = ['Open','High','Low','Close']
_o,_h,_l,_c = [ohlc[h] for h in range(len(ohlc))]

df['bo_'+ str(slow)] = regime_breakout(df,_h,_l,window = slow)
df['bo_'+ str(fast)] = regime_breakout(df,_h,_l,window = fast)
df['turtle_'+ str(slow)+str(fast)] = turtle_trader(df, _h, _l, slow,
fast)
rg_cols = ['bo_'+str(slow),'bo_'+ str(fast),'turtle_'+
str(slow)+str(fast)]
df[['Close','bo_'+str(slow),'bo_'+ str(fast),'turtle_'+
str(slow)+str(fast)] ].plot(
    secondary_y= rg_cols,figsize=(20,5), style=
['k','orange','g:','b-.'],
                              title = str.upper(ticker)+' '+str(rg_
cols))
```

This asymmetrical duration enables traders to capture small profits in nimble markets:

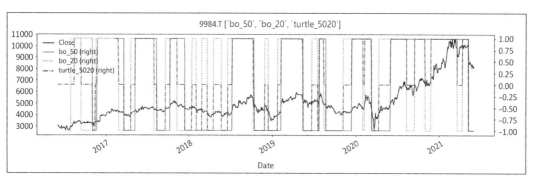

Figure 5.2: Softbank with asymmetrical regime breakout duration (turtle traders for dummies)

The preceding graph shows the closing price of Softbank, the slow regime breakout (orange solid line), the fast regime breakout (green dotted line), and the blue dashed-dotted line as the combination of both. The blue dashed-dotted line gives entries and exits. It is a bit difficult to read, so we will use a visually friendlier chart below.

The turtle strategy outlined above is a rudimentary script inspired by the legendary Turtle Traders. It is composed of two range breakout regimes. The slower duration is used for entries. The faster duration is used for exits. This asymmetrical duration for entry and exit relies on a time-honored principle: be prudent and deliberate to confirm trends, but quick and decisive to cut losses and protect profits. This last regime will be renamed *Turtle for dummies* from now on.

We will be recycling this basic strategy throughout this book to illustrate examples, purely for educational purposes. However, do not do this at home— it is realistic enough for educational purposes, but too simplistic to be deployed in real-money production.

A more visual representation of the turtle for dummies strategies using graph_regime_combo is as follows:

```
ma_st = ma_mt = ma_lt = 0
rg=lo=hi=slo=shi=clg=flr=rg_ch = None

ohlc = ['Open','High','Low','Close']
_o,_h,_l,_c = [ohlc[h] for h in range(len(ohlc))]


bo_lt = 200
bo_st = 50

lt_lo = df[_l].rolling(window= bo_lt).min()
lt_hi = df[_h].rolling(window= bo_lt).max()
st_lo = df[_l].rolling(window= bo_st).min()
st_hi = df[_h].rolling(window= bo_st).max()


graph_regime_combo(ticker,df,_c,rg,lo,hi,slo,shi,clg,flr,rg_ch,ma_
st,ma_mt,ma_lt,lt_lo,lt_hi,st_lo,st_hi)
```

This gives the chart below:

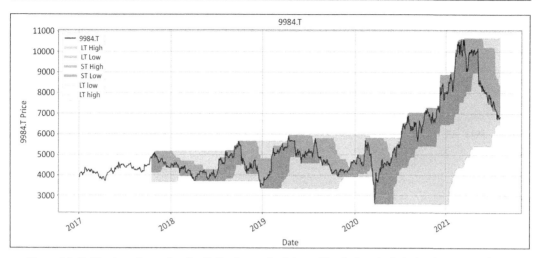

Figure 5.3: Softbank regime using Turtle Trader methodology. The darker shade is the shorter timeframe

The longer duration gives the direction; long or short. This is the blue line, based on the 50-day high/low. The shorter duration is the stop loss. We will discuss stop losses in detail in *Chapter 7, Improve Your Trading Edge*. Shorter duration protects profits by narrowing the range. The flipside of this is an elevated trading frequency. This set of parameters for the Turtle strategy does not work well in choppy markets as we can see throughout 2018. It also struggles in sideways markets as in 2019.

Moving average crossover

Moving averages are another popular regime definition method. This method is so simple and prevalent that even the most hardcore fundamental analysts who claim never to look at charts still like to have a 200-day simple moving average. This method is also computationally easy. There may be further refinements as to the type of moving averages from simple to exponential, triangular, adaptive. Yet, the principle is the same. When the faster moving average is above the slower one, the regime is bullish. When it is below the slower one, the regime is bearish. The code below shows how to calculate the regime with two moving averages using simple and exponential moving averages (SMA and EMA respectively):

```
#### Regime SMA EMA ####
def regime_sma(df,_c,st,lt):
    '''
    bull +1: sma_st >= sma_lt , bear -1: sma_st <= sma_lt
    '''
    sma_lt = df[_c].rolling(lt).mean()
    sma_st = df[_c].rolling(st).mean()
    rg_sma = np.sign(sma_st - sma_lt)
```

```
        return rg_sma

def regime_ema(df,_c,st,lt):
    '''
    bull +1: ema_st >= ema_lt , bear -1: ema_st <= ema_lt
    '''
    ema_st = df[_c].ewm(span=st,min_periods = st).mean()
    ema_lt = df[_c].ewm(span=lt,min_periods = lt).mean()
    rg_ema = np.sign(ema_st - ema_lt)
    return rg_ema


st = 50
lt = 200
df['sma_' + str(st) + str(lt)] = regime_sma(df, _c='Close', st= st,
lt= lt)
df['ema_' + str(st) + str(lt)] = regime_ema(df, _c='Close', st= st,
lt= lt)


ohlc = ['Open','High','Low','Close']
_o,_h,_l,_c = [ohlc[h] for h in range(len(ohlc))]
rgme_cols = ['sma_' + str(st) + str(lt), 'ema_' + str(st) +
str(lt),'turtle_'+ str(slow)+str(fast) ]
df[['Close','sma_' + str(st) + str(lt), 'ema_' + str(st) +
str(lt),'turtle_'+ str(slow)+str(fast)] ].plot(
    secondary_y= rgme_cols,figsize=(20,8), style=['k','orange','m--
','b-.'],
                                    title = str.upper(ticker)+'
'+str(rgme_cols))
```

This produces the chart below:

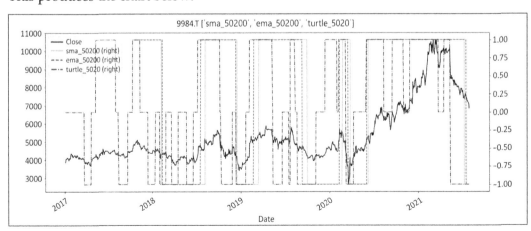

Figure 5.4: Softbank regimes using turtle breakout, SMA, and EMA

Here, we compare three regime methods. We have our new freshly minted, best-friend-forever *Turtle for dummies* in the dashed-dotted blue line. We have the SMA in orange, and the EMA in the purple dashed line. The results are predictably close for the moving average series. The exponential moving average is more reactive than the simple one. We can now visualize the results using the `graph_regime_combo` chart function:

```
rg=lo=hi=slo=shi=clg=flr=rg_ch = None
lt_lo = lt_hi = st_lo = st_hi = 0

ma_st = df[_c].rolling(window=50).mean()
ma_mt = df[_c].rolling(window=200).mean()
ma_lt = df[_c].rolling(window=200).mean()

ohlc = ['Open','High','Low','Close']
_o,_h,_l,_c = [ohlc[h] for h in range(len(ohlc))]

graph_regime_combo(ticker,df,_c,rg,lo,hi,slo,shi,clg,flr,rg_ch,
ma_st,ma_mt,ma_lt,lt_lo,lt_hi,st_lo,st_hi)
```

The function accommodates up to three moving averages. To obtain a chart with only two moving averages, like has been done here, set the mid-term and long-term to the same values (in this instance, med-term and long-term have been set to 200). Below is the resulting visual rendition of a moving average crossover regime. Areas in light green and light red are where the regime is either bullish or bearish and profitable. Areas in dark green and dark red are where the regime is either bullish or bearish and unprofitable:

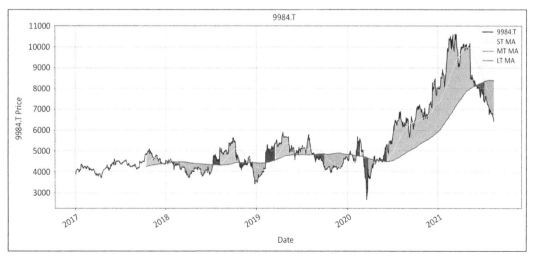

Figure 5.5: Crossover on Softbank darker zones are loss-making areas

This strategy has a rough time in sideways and volatile markets. Fast- and slow-moving averages converge to a flat line with low amplitude sinusoidal oscillations. Trading frequency and loss rate increase while win rate collapses.

A more succinct way to instantiate the three moving averages is via a list comprehension. First, we create a list of moving average variables. Second, we instantiate variables through a comprehension list. Let's write the above with a few list comprehensions:

```
mav = [50, 200, 200]
ma_st,ma_mt,ma_lt = [df[_c].rolling(mav[t]).mean() for t in
range(len(mav))]

bo = [50, 252]
st_lo,lt_lo = [df[_l].rolling(bo[t]).min() for t in range(len(bo))]
st_hi,lt_hi = [df[_h].rolling(bo[t]).max() for t in range(len(bo))]

ohlc = ['Open','High','Low','Close']
_o,_h,_l,_c = [ohlc[h] for h in range(len(ohlc))]

graph_regime_combo(ticker,df,_c,rg,lo,hi,slo,shi,clg,flr,rg_ch,
ma_st,ma_mt,ma_lt,lt_lo,lt_hi,st_lo,st_hi)
```

This would be something like this:

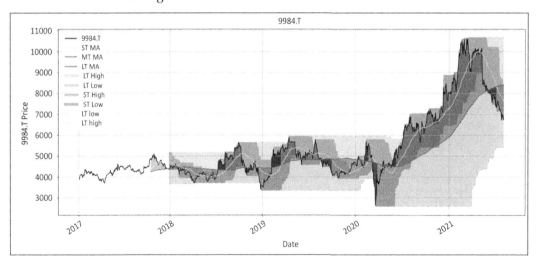

Figure 5.6: Softbank crossover imposed on the Turtle for dummies

This increasingly colorful chart shows the combination of two regime methods. It unfortunately adds more confusion than problems it solves. Market participants are sometimes tempted to add multiple conditions hoping to weed out false positives. But unfortunately it's easier to accept randomness than to try and eradicate it.

The two-line crossover is the most popular version of the moving crossover method. The slower line defines the regime while the shorter duration line times entries and exits. The most popular duration is 50/200, known as **golden/death cross**. In theory, this combination makes sense. 200 days is a robust long-term measure, while 50 days is a good momentum indicator. In practice, this combination has an awful hit rate. It only works for big long-term trends. Unfortunately, they come few and far between, hence the win rate hovering around 20%. The rest of the time the faster moving-average flip-flops back and forth around the slower one like a career politician.

These weaknesses lead moving-average aficionados to the next iteration of three moving averages. In the following example, we improve on the previous golden cross 50/200 moving average crossover by adding another shorter-duration moving average. For the sake of simplicity, we use 20, 50, and 200 days. The 200 days gives the regime, while the 20/50 permutation gives entries and exits.

All we have to do is change one variable in the following code:

```
rg=lo=hi=slo=shi=clg=flr=rg_ch = None
lt_lo = lt_hi = st_lo = st_hi = 0

mav = [20, 50, 200]
ma_st,ma_mt,ma_lt = [df[_c].rolling(mav[t]).mean() for t in
range(len(mav))]

ohlc = ['Open','High','Low','Close']
_o,_h,_l,_c = [ohlc[h] for h in range(len(ohlc))]

graph_regime_combo(ticker,df,_c,rg,lo,hi,slo,shi,clg,flr,rg_ch,
ma_st,ma_mt,ma_lt,lt_lo,lt_hi,st_lo,st_hi)
```

We can see the resulting chart below:

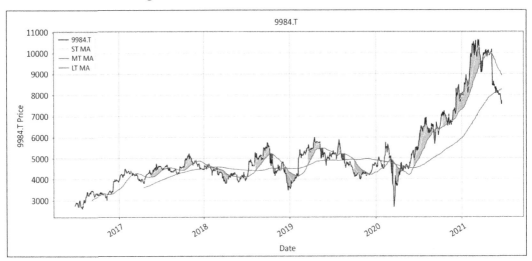

Figure 5.7: Softbank triple moving average crossover

The longest duration determines the regime. The two medium- and short-term durations time entries and exits respectively. Rather than a long paragraph, the logic can best be summarized as follows:

1. **Long**: Enter and stay long as the short-term moving average is the highest, followed by the mid- and long-term moving averages

2. **Short**: Enter and stay short as long as the short-term moving average is below the mid-term, which in turn needs to be below long-term moving average.

3. **Else**: Neutral, no position.

This method is probably the most practical compromise between following long-term established trends and maintaining decent risk management.

Unlike the double-moving average graph we saw earlier, the triple-moving average does not persist in the wrong direction for long. It does a much better job at cutting positions early. Those are the colorless and shorter darker areas. The flip side is the increase in trading frequency. Another drawback is the inherent lag of this method. As evidenced in the middle portion of the chart, in sideways markets, price will move a fair bit in either direction before a signal is generated.

The main reason why market participants abandon the moving average method is sideways markets. When markets undulate sideways, moving averages oscillate around one another. This generates many false-positive signals, which tend to erode both the financial and the emotional capital bases. After a few costly false starts, market participants tend to look for less noisy methods.

Rather than tweaking moving-average durations or abandoning the method altogether, a better solution might be to play with bet size instead. Size smaller at the first sign of sideways markets and then increase weight as trends gain momentum.

Higher highs/higher lows

This is another popular method. Stocks that trend up make higher highs and higher lows. Conversely, stocks trending down make lower lows and lower highs in that order, and therefore suggest sustained weakness. This method makes intuitive sense. Unfortunately, it is not statistically as robust as it looks. Markets sometimes print lower/higher lows/highs that throw calculations off, before resuming their journey. Secondly, this method requires three conditions to be simultaneously met:

1. A lower low.
2. A lower high.
3. Both lower low and lower high conditions must be met sequentially, which only works in orderly markets.

Those three conditions have to be met consecutively in that precise order for the regime to turn bearish. Markets are random and noisier than people generally assume.

The main advantage of this method are entries and exits. On the long side, buy long on a low and exit on a high. On the short side, sell short on a high and exit on a low. Those counter-trend entries and exits enable market participants to capture profits. Furthermore, stop losses are objectively defined at the higher low on the long side and at the lower high on the short side.

Overall, the premise of this method makes logical sense. Stocks that print higher highs and higher lows are pulled upward, and vice versa on the way down. Unfortunately, this method struggles in noisy markets where there is no neat succession of highs and lows—I have therefore omitted the code from this chapter.

The following method uses the same swing highs and swing lows to define the regime in a much more powerful way. It is simple and statistically robust.

The floor/ceiling method

That method is originally a variation on the higher high/higher low method. Everyone has intuitively used it and yet it is so obvious that no-one has apparently bothered to formalise it. Unlike the higher high/higher low method, only one of the two following conditions has to be fulfilled for the regime to change:

1. **Bearish**: A swing high has to be materially lower than the peak.
2. **Bullish**: A swing low has to be materially higher than the bottom.

The swings do not even have to be consecutive for the regime to change. For example, markets sometimes shoot up, then retreat and print sideways swings for a while. Those periods are known as **consolidation**. The regime does not turn bearish until one swing high is markedly below the peak.

The classic definition is always valid regardless of the time frame and the asset class. Lows will be materially higher than the bottom in a bull market. Conversely, highs will be materially lower than the peak in bear markets.

Randomness triggers exceptions that are handled in a simple elegant way. There are two methods:

1. **Conservative**:
    *   If the regime is bearish and the price crosses over the ceiling, the regime turns bullish.
    *   If the regime is bullish and the price crosses under the floor, the regime turns bearish.

2. **Aggressive**:
    *   If the regime is bearish and the price crosses over the discovery swing high, the regime turns bullish.
    *   If the regime is bullish and the price crosses under the discovery swing low, the regime turns bearish.

This floor/ceiling method has only two regimes: bull or bear. A sideways regime is a pause within a broader bull or bear context. This method brings stability to regime definition. In practice, nothing is more frustrating than flip-flopping around a moving average. Stability enables market participants to better manage their positions.

The floor/ceiling methodology is conceptually simple. It is however not easy to calculate. It is a two-step process:

1. Swing detection
2. Regime definition

The market does not go up in a straight line. It goes up and down along a dominant trend. It marks local highs and lows along the way. Those are called **swing highs** and **swing lows**.

Swing detection is 80% of the work in the floor/ceiling method. Not all swing highs and lows are born equal. The main difficulty is in separating noise from the signal. Since regime definition is based upon swings, faulty swing detection inevitably leads to faulty regime definition.

The logic of the code is simple. It relies on two tests: retest and distance. We will go through the entire sequence from swing high to swing low, which is illustrated in *Figure 5.8*:

1. The price makes a new high from a previous swing low.
2. The price drops from that all-time high.
3. The price retests that all-time high, but it fails and drops below that post-high low.
4. Once the price closes below the highest low, sellers may be in charge. The algorithm is designed to continuously reset to the highest low after the all-time high.

The following are the equivalent steps for a swing low:

1. The price prints a lowest low: the first low.
2. It rebounds to a first high.
3. The price retreats to its latest low, but fails to take the lowest low.
4. The price subsequently starts traveling upward. Either it takes out the first high (always the highest high following the lowest low) or prints a lower high, called the latest high. When the price closes above the first or latest high, this suggests that buyers may be in charge now.

    This sequence repeats itself until the price closes above or below the latest high or low. In isolation, retests are not statistically significant. They occur quite frequently. When coupled with a distance test, retests tend to be more meaningful.

5. **Distance test**: This is the distance from the swing high to the lowest low. This test is either in units of volatility or percentage points. The further away from a swing, the more likely it indicates an exhaustion of the trend:

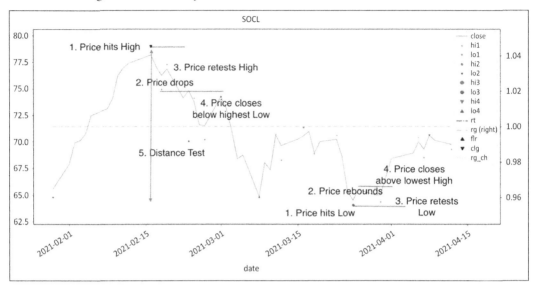

Figure 5.8: Swing detection visual explanation: distance and retest

Now, let's zoom out and look at the big picture. The swing high in the above figure is the peak in the chart below:

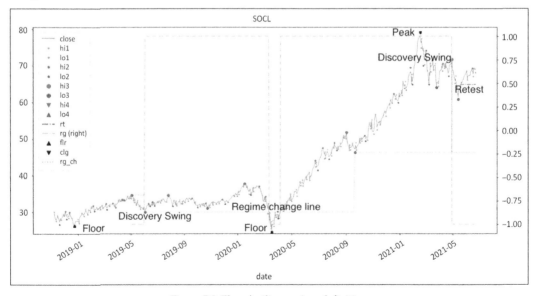

Figure 5.9: Floor/ceiling regime definition

The line on the secondary axis is the regime. The regime turns bullish after finding a swing low substantially higher than the bottom. This swing low is now the regime change line. Should the price cross below that level, the regime will turn bearish. This happens in the first quarter of 2020, at which time the regime turns bearish. The price crosses above that level again and the regime reverts to bullish. The price prints an all-time high at the beginning of 2021, tanks, then rebounds, but rolls over before the high. The regime turns bearish. It is now time to switch side from the long to the short. Yet, the borrow on that issue was prohibitively expensive, so that juicy trade did not graduate to a round trip.

In the following sections, we will go through the source code required to calculate this. The conceptual framework was inspired by the seminal work of Belgian mathematician Benoit Mandelbrot on fractals. We start with a noisy series of small highs and lows and zoom out using the previous reduced series. This method is a bit more computationally intense than other methods. The result is however surprisingly intuitive. It broadly falls in two phases: **swing detection** and **regime definition**. Swing detection is a succession of small functions.

Swing detection

Swing detection splits in two parts: historical swings and last swing adjustment. The first two functions, `historical_swings` and `hilo_alternation`, accomplish 90% of the work. The rest is a succession of small functions that ensure the last swing is relevant. This might look a little verbose at first sight, so we will slowly walk through all the functions and explain their relevance.

Historical swings and high/low alternation

Let's start with downloading historical prices. We are using using SPY, a proxy **Exchange-Traded Fund** (**ETF**) for the S&P 500, but you can experiment by using a different ticker if you like:

```
# CHAPTER 5 Swing detection
ticker = 'SPY'

start= '2016-12-31'
end = None
raw_data = round(yf.download(tickers= ticker,start= start,
end = end,interval = "1d",
                group_by = 'column',auto_adjust = True,
prepost = True,
                treads = True, proxy = None),2)
ohlc = ['Open','High','Low','Close']
_o,_h,_l,_c = [ohlc[h] for h in range(len(ohlc))]
```

Next, we will present each function sequentially and illustrate the progression with charts or attributes. We pick up where the previous function left off and march on. Finally, we will publish a full recap with all the functions at once and put out a chart:

```python
#### hilo_alternation(hilo, dist= None, hurdle= None) ####
def hilo_alternation(hilo, dist= None, hurdle= None):
    i=0
    while (np.sign(hilo .shift(1)) == np.sign(hilo)).any(): # runs
until duplicates are eliminated
        # removes swing lows > swing highs
        hilo.loc[(np.sign(hilo.shift(1)) != np.sign(hilo)) & # hilo
alternation test
                (hilo.shift(1)<0) &  # previous datapoint: high
                (np.abs(hilo.shift(1)) < np.abs(hilo) )] = np.nan #
high[-1] < low, eliminate low


        hilo.loc[(np.sign(hilo.shift(1)) != np.sign(hilo)) &  # hilo
alternation
                (hilo.shift(1)>0) &  # previous swing: low
                (np.abs(hilo ) < hilo.shift(1))] = np.nan # swing high
< swing low[-1]


#### removed for brevity: check GitHub repo for full code ####
#### hilo_alternation(hilo, dist= None, hurdle= None) ####



#### historical_swings(df,_o,_h,_l,_c, dist= None, hurdle= None) ####
def historical_swings(df,_o,_h,_l,_c, dist= None, hurdle= None):

    reduction = df[[_o,_h,_l,_c]].copy()
    reduction['avg_px'] = round(reduction[[_h,_l,_c]].mean(axis=1),2)
    highs = reduction['avg_px'].values
    lows = - reduction['avg_px'].values
    reduction_target =  len(reduction) // 100

    n = 0
    while len(reduction) >= reduction_target:
        highs_list = find_peaks(highs, distance = 1, width = 0)
        lows_list = find_peaks(lows, distance = 1, width = 0)
        hilo = reduction.iloc[lows_list[0]][_l].sub(reduction.
iloc[highs_list[0]][_h],fill_value=0)


#### removed for brevity: check GitHub repo for full code ####
```

```
#### historical_swings(df,_o,_h,_l,_c, dist= None, hurdle= None) ####

df = raw_data.copy()
ohlc = ['Open','High','Low','Close']
_o,_h,_l,_c = [ohlc[h] for h in range(len(ohlc))]
rhs = ['Hi1', 'Lo1','Hi2', 'Lo2', 'Hi3', 'Lo3']
rt_hi,rt_lo,_hi,_lo,shi,slo = [rhs[h] for h in range(len(rhs))]

df= historical_swings(df,_o,_h,_l,_c,dist= None, hurdle= None)

df[[_c,rt_hi,rt_lo,_hi,_lo,shi,slo ]].plot(
    style=['grey','y.', 'c.','r.', 'g.', 'rv', 'g^'],
    figsize=(20,5),grid=True, title = str.upper(ticker))
df[[_c,shi,slo]].plot(style=['grey','rv', 'g^'],
        figsize=(20,5),grid=True, title = str.upper(ticker))
```

The `hilo_alternation` function loops through the reduction dataframe until the series is neatly constituted of alternating highs and lows. It eliminates:

1. Same side consecutive highs and lows: highs are assigned a minus sign. lows have a positive sign. When there are two consecutive highs or lows, the lowest value marks the extreme point.

2. Lows higher than surrounding highs. Randomness cannot be eliminated: in theory, this should not exist, but in practice, anomalies persist.

3. Noisy short-distance highs and lows. The distance test is not entirely relevant as the alternation loop is contained within a larger multi-level loop. This is the fractal part of the algorithm where we look for the same pattern while zooming out. The feature is however an elegant option to shorten the number of loops.

4. At the end of every iteration the `hilo df` is reduced using the `dropna` method.

The `historical_swings` function takes the following steps:

1. Reduction dataframe: Copy the main dataframe and instantiate a new series from high, low, and average values.

2. Loop to reduce the dataframe.

3. Calculate two series of highs and lows (by assigning a minus sign to the average series). The only requirement for a high is that the preceding and succeeding bars must be lower and vice versa for troughs.

4. Run the `hilo_alternation` function to reduce the dataframe.

5. Populate the reduced dataframe and reduce further via the dropna method.

6. Populate the main dataframe for each level. Stop when the length of the reduction is <1% of the main dataframe, or no more reduction is possible, or 10 iterations have been passed.

The above code returns this splendidly noisy chart:

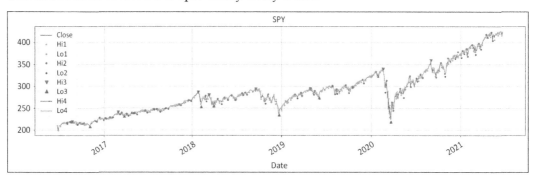

Figure 5.10: SPY fractal highs/lows level 1 to 3

The first level is the small dots labeled Hi1 and Lo1 above and below the closing price. Level 2 is the red and green dots labeled Hi2 and Lo2. It is less frequent, but still relatively noisy. Next, we really need to identify meaningful inflexions to base our analysis on. So, we go up one level. Triangles are level 3. Prices have been filtered twice. The original dataframe has been reduced by 99%.

The following chart simply shows price and level 3 data:

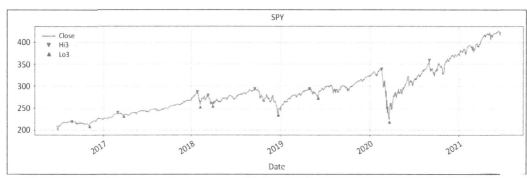

Figure 5.11: SPY historical swings

The last triangle is below the highest close. This is clearly a false positive. The swing high is clearly neither the highest point, nor followed by a swing low. The rest of the functions will adjust for the last swing. So, let's make this false positive disappear:

1. **Swing high**: The price continues to move higher than the latest swing high.

2. **Swing low**: The price continues to move lower than the latest swing low.

The `cleanup_latest_swing()` function removes false positives from the latest swing high and low:

```
#### cleanup_latest_swing(df, shi, slo, rt_hi, rt_lo) ####
def cleanup_latest_swing(df, shi, slo, rt_hi, rt_lo):
    '''
    removes false positives
    '''
    # Latest swing
    shi_dt = df.loc[pd.notnull(df[shi]), shi].index[-1]
    s_hi = df.loc[pd.notnull(df[shi]), shi][-1]
    slo_dt = df.loc[pd.notnull(df[slo]), slo].index[-1]
    s_lo = df.loc[pd.notnull(df[slo]), slo][-1]
    len_shi_dt = len(df[:shi_dt])
    len_slo_dt = len(df[:slo_dt])


    # Reset false positives to np.nan
    for i in range(2):

        if (len_shi_dt > len_slo_dt) & ((df.loc[shi_dt:,rt_hi].max()>
s_hi) | (s_hi<s_lo)):
            df.loc[shi_dt, shi] = np.nan
            len_shi_dt = 0
        elif (len_slo_dt > len_shi_dt) &
((df.loc[slo_dt:,rt_lo].min()< s_lo)| (s_hi<s_lo)):
            df.loc[slo_dt, slo] = np.nan
            len_slo_dt = 0
        else:
            pass

    return df
#### cleanup_latest_swing(df, shi, slo, rt_hi, rt_lo) ####

df[[_c,shi,slo]].plot(style=['grey','rv', 'g^'],
        figsize=(20,5),grid=True, title = str.upper(ticker) + ' pre-
adjustment')

df = cleanup_latest_swing(df, shi,slo,rt_hi,rt_lo)

df[[_c,shi,slo]].plot(style=['grey', 'rv', 'g^'],
        figsize=(20,5),grid=True, title = str.upper(ticker) + ' post-
adjustment')
```

The code takes the following steps:

1. The code identifies the latest swing low and high.
2. Identify the most recent swing.
3. If a false positive, assign N/A.

The following charts, before and after adjustment, demonstrate that the function has removed false positives from the data:

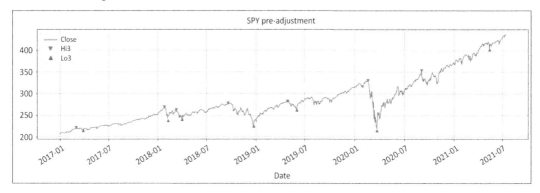

Figure 5.12: SPY before: last swing high and low are false positives

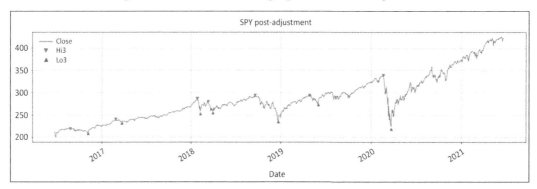

Figure 5.13: SPY after: both swings are deleted

The two charts are self-explanatory. The last two triangles have to be removed. The last swing low symbolized by a green triangle is higher than the preceding swing high. Besides, this swing high is invalid as there is no lower swing low. So, both are removed when we loop once over the last two swings. The chart now goes all the way back to the March 2020 low. Next, we will instantiate all the variables necessary for the rest of the process using the latest_swing_variables() function. This function calculates the variables that will be used in the next few functions. They are respectively:

- ud: Direction, up +1 , down -1.

- bs: Base, either swing low or high.

- bs_dt: The swing date.

- _rt: The series name that will be used to detect swing. Either retest low, rt_
  lo, for a swing high, or retest high, rt_hi, for a swing low.

- _swg: The series to assign the value; shi for swing high and slo for swing
  low.

- hh_ll: Either the lowest low or highest high.

- hh_ll_dt: The date of the highest high or lowest low.

We will make use of list comprehension to declare variables:

```
#### latest_swings(df, shi, slo, rt_hi, rt_lo, _h, _l, _c, _vol) ####
def latest_swing_variables(df, shi, slo, rt_hi, rt_lo, _h, _l, _c):
    '''
    Latest swings dates & values
    '''
    shi_dt = df.loc[pd.notnull(df[shi]), shi].index[-1]
    slo_dt = df.loc[pd.notnull(df[slo]), slo].index[-1]
    s_hi = df.loc[pd.notnull(df[shi]), shi][-1]
    s_lo = df.loc[pd.notnull(df[slo]), slo][-1]

    if slo_dt > shi_dt:
        swg_var = [1,s_lo,slo_dt,rt_lo,shi, df.loc[slo_dt:,_h].max(),
df.loc[slo_dt:, _h].idxmax()]
    elif shi_dt > slo_dt:
        swg_var = [-1,s_hi,shi_dt,rt_hi,slo, df.loc[shi_dt:, _l].
min(),df.loc[shi_dt:, _l].idxmin()]
    else:
        ud = 0
    ud, bs, bs_dt, _rt, _swg, hh_ll, hh_ll_dt = [swg_var[h] for h in
range(len(swg_var))]

    return ud, bs, bs_dt, _rt, _swg, hh_ll, hh_ll_dt
#### latest_swings(df, shi, slo, rt_hi, rt_lo, _h, _l, _c, _vol) ####

ud,bs,bs_dt,_rt,_swg,hh_ll,hh_ll_dt = latest_swing_
variables(df,shi,slo,rt_hi,rt_lo,_h,_l,_c)

ud, bs, bs_dt, _rt, _swg, hh_ll, hh_ll_dt
```

This will produce output like the following:

```
(1,
 213.43,
 Timestamp('2020-03-23 00:00:00'),
 'Lo1',
 'Hi3',
 452.6,
 Timestamp('2021-09-02 00:00:00'))
```

The variables declared above will be used in the subsections to come.

Establishing trend exhaustion

Everything we have done up to this point is two-fold. We have detected historical swings and cleaned them up. Then, we have declared variables that we will be using to find the latest swing in real time. The method we use to detect the final swing is called a **retest**. In the context of the SPY chart, the market prints a highest high from the swing low. The price comes down a little then goes back up but fails to take the highest high. The price then penetrates the post-high low. Retests are essentially hesitations. They are quite frequent. Markets can and do remain indecisive more often than not. However, when retests happen at the end of a sustained move, this may signal an exhaustion of the trend and a possible reversal in the market direction.

This distance test acts as a filter. This function has two built-in tests:

1. Distance expressed as a multiple of volatility. We use a measure of volatility **Average True Range** (**ATR**) or standard deviations.

2. Distance as a fixed percentage.

The default setting of the function is no distance test, which will return a de facto pass. A successful test is either -1 for a swing low or +1 for a swing high, and 0 for a failed test. We will also define a function that calculates the ATR. This is classic volatility measure originally built by legendary Welles Wilder:

```
#### test_distance(ud, bs, hh_ll, vlty, dist_vol, dist_pct) ####
def test_distance(ud,bs, hh_ll, dist_vol, dist_pct):

    # priority: 1. Vol 2. pct 3. dflt
    if (dist_vol > 0):
        distance_test = np.sign(abs(hh_ll - bs) - dist_vol)
    elif (dist_pct > 0):
        distance_test = np.sign(abs(hh_ll / bs - 1) - dist_pct)
    else:
        distance_test = np.sign(dist_pct)
```

```
    return int(max(distance_test,0) * ud)
#### test_distance(ud, bs, hh_ll, vlty, dist_vol, dist_pct) ####
#### ATR ####
def average_true_range(df, _h, _l, _c, n):
    '''

    http://stockcharts.com/school/doku.php?id=chart_school:technical_
indicators:average_true_range_atr
    '''

    atr =  (df[_h].combine(df[_c].shift(), max) - df[_l].
combine(df[_c].shift(), min)).rolling(window=n).mean()
    return atr


#### ATR ####

dist_vol = round(average_true_range(df,_h,_l,_c,n=63)[hh_ll_dt] * 2,2)
dist_pct = 0.05
_sign = test_distance(ud,bs, hh_ll, dist_vol, dist_pct)
_sign
```

This will produce the following output:

This distance test verifies that between the latest swing to the most extreme price expressed either in units of volatility or in percentage points is big enough to suggest a potential trend exhaustion. This filter reduces the occurrence of false positives.

Retest swing

All the functions led us to this moment: swing detection. This little function packs a surprisingly good punch. The logic is symmetrical for a swing high or low. We will therefore concentrate on a swing high:

1. Detect the highest high from swing low.
2. From the highest high, identify the highest retest low.
3. When the price closes below the highest retest low: swing high = highest high.

It works just as well to identify swing lows. This is how the sequence would unfold:

1. Detect the lowest low from the swing high.
2. From the lowest low, identify the lowest retest high.
3. When the price closes above the lowest retest high: swing low = lowest low.

Note that the function will always reset to the highest retest low. Sometimes, price drops precipitously and then tries to regain some composure only to falter later. When resetting to the highest retest low, the function will waste no time identifying the earliest moment a trend has potentially reversed.

The function will also create series rt in absolute or rrt in relative to show which retest is used to detect swings. This optional feature may come useful if you want to visualize which retest was used to detect swings.

In *Figure 5.14*, this is the black dot:

```
#### retest_swing(df, _sign, _rt, hh_ll_dt, hh_ll, _c, _swg) ####
def retest_swing(df, _sign, _rt, hh_ll_dt, hh_ll, _c, _swg):
    rt_sgmt = df.loc[hh_ll_dt:, _rt]

    if (rt_sgmt.count() > 0) & (_sign != 0): # Retests exist and
distance test met
        if _sign == 1: #
            rt_list =
[rt_sgmt.idxmax(),rt_sgmt.max(),df.loc[rt_sgmt.idxmax():, _c].cummin()]

        elif _sign == -1:
            rt_list = [rt_sgmt.idxmin(), rt_sgmt.min(),
df.loc[rt_sgmt.idxmin():, _c].cummax()]
        rt_dt,rt_hurdle, rt_px = [rt_list[h] for h in
range(len(rt_list))]

        if str(_c)[0] == 'r':
            df.loc[rt_dt,'rrt'] = rt_hurdle
        elif str(_c)[0] != 'r':
            df.loc[rt_dt,'rt'] = rt_hurdle

        if (np.sign(rt_px - rt_hurdle) == - np.sign(_sign)).any():
            df.at[hh_ll_dt, _swg] = hh_ll
    return df
#### retest_swing(df, _sign, _rt, hh_ll_dt, hh_ll, _c, _swg) ####

df = retest_swing(df, _sign, _rt, hh_ll_dt, hh_ll, _c, _swg)

try:
    df['rt '] = df['rt'].fillna(method='ffill')
```

```
    df[bs_dt:][[_c, rt_hi, rt_lo,
        shi, slo,'rt']].plot(style=['grey', 'c.','y.',
        'rv', 'g^', 'ko'],figsize=(20,5),grid=True, title =
str.upper(ticker))
except:
    df[bs_dt:][[_c, rt_hi, rt_lo,
        shi, slo]].plot(style=['grey', 'c.','y.',
        'rv', 'g^', 'ko'],figsize=(20,5),grid=True, title =
str.upper(ticker))
```

The black dot at the very end of the resulting chart is the highest retest low. Note that this will periodically disappear as the function resets when it meets either a new high or new low, so don't worry if it isn't visible when you run the function:

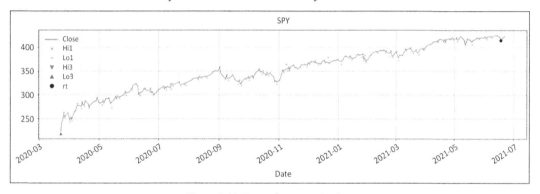

Figure 5.14: Retest from a swing low

As long as the price keeps making new highs, the retest resets along the way. There will be false positives along the way, but this is part of the journey.

Some readers may not agree with the retest method, whatever the reasons might be. So, we introduce an alternative method of swing detection.

Retracement swing

This function is an alternative to the retest method. It relies solely on a retracement from the extreme value. The main benefit of this method is its conceptual simplicity. Once the price has moved far enough in the opposite direction, then it is usually safe to conclude that a swing has been printed. This instrument is blunt, however. It usually works but fails in sideways or highly volatile markets:

1. Calculate the retracement from the extreme value, either the minimum from the top or the maximum from the bottom.
2. Distance test in units of volatility or in percentage points.

This function acts as a failsafe in case a retest does not materialize quickly enough:

```
#### retracement_swing(df, _sign, _swg, _c, hh_ll_dt, hh_ll, vlty,
retrace_vol, retrace_pct)
def retracement_swing(df, _sign, _swg, _c, hh_ll_dt, hh_ll, vlty,
retrace_pct):
    if _sign == 1: #
        retracement = df.loc[hh_ll_dt:, _c].min() - hh_ll

#### removed for brevity: check GitHub repo for full code ####
#### retracement_swing(df, _sign, _swg, _c, hh_ll_dt, hh_ll, vlty,
retrace_vol, retrace_pct) ####

vlty = round(average_true_range(df=df, _h= _h, _l= _l, _c= _c , n=63)
[hh_ll_dt],2)
dist_vol = 5 * vlty
dist_pct = 0.05
_sign = test_distance(ud,bs, hh_ll, dist_vol, dist_pct)
df = retest_swing(df, _sign, _rt, hh_ll_dt, hh_ll, _c, _swg)
retrace_vol = 2.5 * vlty
retrace_pct = 0.05
df = retracement_swing(df,_sign,_swg,_c,hh_ll_dt,hh_ll, vlty,retrace_
vol, retrace_pct)

df[[_c,_hi,_lo,shi,slo]].plot(
    style=['grey','r.', 'g.', 'rv', 'g^'],
    figsize=(20,5),grid=True, title = str.upper(ticker))

df[[_c,shi,slo]].plot(style=['grey','rv', 'g^'],
            figsize=(20,5),grid=True, title = str.upper(ticker))
```

This creates the following graphs:

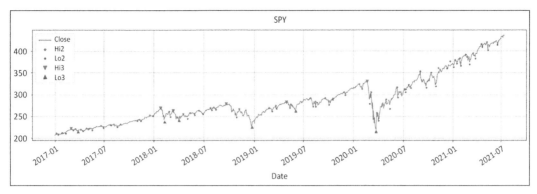

Figure 5.15: Retracement swing function levels 2 and 3

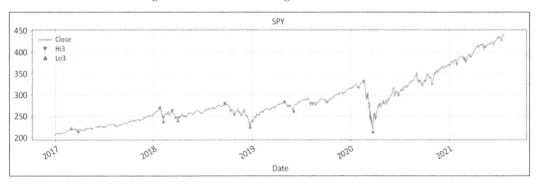

Figure 5.16: Retracement swing function swing highs and lows

This final function acts as a failsafe when markets move brutally one way or another. Both functions (retest and retracement) can be used concurrently.

So, we went through all this verbose code to come up with a few meaningful datapoints called **swing highs** and **lows**. Next, we will use those swings as a basis for regime detection.

Putting it all together: regime detection

Let's do a quick recap using all the functions. To demonstrate the versatility of the functions, we will spice things a little. First, we publish the code for the relative function again. Then we will run SPY in absolute, then benchmark it against ONEQ (a proxy ETF for Nasdaq).

We will plot three charts to show where your money is best allocated:

```
### RELATIVE
def relative(df,_o,_h,_l,_c, bm_df, bm_col, ccy_df, ccy_col, dgt,
start, end,rebase=True):
    '''
    df: df
    bm_df, bm_col: df benchmark dataframe & column name
    ccy_df,ccy_col: currency dataframe & column name
    dgt: rounding decimal
    start/end: string or offset
    rebase: boolean rebase to beginning or continuous series
    '''
#### removed for brevity: check GitHub repo for full code ####
### RELATIVE ###

bm_df = pd.DataFrame()
bm_col = 'ONEQ'
ccy_col = 'USD'
dgt= 3
bm_df[bm_col] = round(yf.download(tickers= bm_col,start= start, end =
end,interval = "1d",
                 group_by = 'column',auto_adjust = True, prepost =
True,
                 treads = True, proxy = None)['Close'],2)
bm_df[ccy_col] = 1

df = raw_data.copy()
ohlc = ['Open','High','Low','Close']
_o,_h,_l,_c = [ohlc[h] for h in range(len(ohlc))]
rhs = ['Hi1', 'Lo1','Hi2', 'Lo2', 'Hi3', 'Lo3']
rt_hi,rt_lo,_hi,_lo,shi,slo = [rhs[h] for h in range(len(rhs))]
df= relative(df,_o,_h,_l,_c, bm_df, bm_col, ccy_df=bm_df,
          ccy_col=ccy_col, dgt= dgt, start=start, end=
end,rebase=True)

for a in np.arange(0,2):
    df = historical_swings(df,_o,_h,_l,_c, dist= None, hurdle= None)
    df = cleanup_latest_swing(df, shi, slo, rt_hi, rt_lo)
    ud, bs, bs_dt, _rt, _swg, hh_ll, hh_ll_dt = latest_swing_
variables(df, shi, slo,rt_hi,rt_lo,_h, _l,_c)
    vlty = round(average_true_range(df=df, _h= _h, _l= _l, _c= _c ,
n=63)[hh_ll_dt],2)
    dist_vol = 5 * vlty
    dist_pct = 0.05
    _sign = test_distance(ud,bs, hh_ll, dist_vol, dist_pct)
```

```
    df = retest_swing(df, _sign, _rt, hh_ll_dt, hh_ll, _c, _swg)
    retrace_vol = 2.5 * vlty
    retrace_pct = 0.05
    df = retracement_swing(df,_sign,_swg,_c,hh_ll_dt,hh_ll,
vlty,retrace_vol, retrace_pct)
    rohlc = ['rOpen','rHigh','rLow','rClose']
    _o,_h,_l,_c = [rohlc[h] for h in range(len(rohlc)) ]
    rrhs = ['rH1', 'rL1','rH2', 'rL2', 'rH3', 'rL3']
    rt_hi,rt_lo,_hi,_lo,shi,slo = [rrhs[h] for h in range(len(rrhs))]
```

Let's run through the key steps covered by this code:

1. We instantiate the benchmark ONEQ. The currency is USD.

2. We instantiate df by copying the raw data. We run two list comprehensions to declare the variables.

3. We run the relative function to get the relative prices.

4. The for loop will run once over the absolute series. At the end of the first run, we run two list comprehensions to declare the relative variables.

5. In the second loop, the absolute variables are replaced with relative ones. Everything is symmetrical. The parameters remain the same. The only things that have changed are the input series.

Finally, we print four charts:

```
df[['Close','Hi1','Lo1','Hi2','Lo2','Hi3','Lo3']].
plot(style=['grey','y.', 'c.','r.', 'g.', 'rv', 'g^'],
     figsize=(20,5),grid=True, title = str.upper(ticker))
df[['Close','Hi3','Lo3']].plot(
     style=['grey', 'rv', 'g^'],
     figsize=(20,5),grid=True, title = str.upper(ticker))


df[['Close','Hi3','Lo3',_c,shi,slo]].plot(
     style=['grey','rv', 'g^','k:','mv','b^'],
            figsize=(20,5),grid=True, title = str.upper(ticker)+' vs
'+str.upper(bm_col))


rohlc = ['rOpen','rHigh','rLow','rClose']
_o,_h,_l,_c = [rohlc[h] for h in range(len(rohlc)) ]


df[[_c,shi,slo]].plot(
     style=['k:','mv','b^'],
            figsize=(20,5),grid=True, title = str.upper(ticker)+' vs
'+str.upper(bm_col))
```

The first one is the Christmas tree-looking chart with all the small dots:

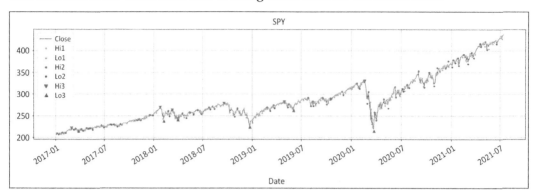

Figure 5.17: SPY with highs/lows level 1 to 3

All the information is present. The chart is noisy. The second one is a clean **SPY** chart:

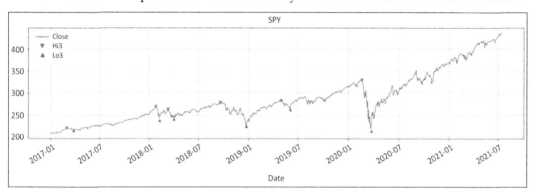

Figure 5.18: SPY with swing highs and lows

This is a clean chart of **SPY**. The false positives have been removed. And now for the grand finale; **SPY** versus **ONEQ**:

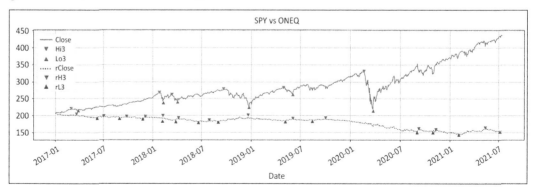

Figure 5.19: SPY in absolute and relative to ONEQ

SPY has clearly underperformed **ONEQ**, meaning the S&P 500 has underperformed the Nasdaq for a few years straight. Swings in relative value tend to mirror the absolute ones. Interestingly enough, looking at the fourth and final chart, it seems like the relative value may have bottomed out, meaning the last swing low seems to be substantially higher than the lowest low:

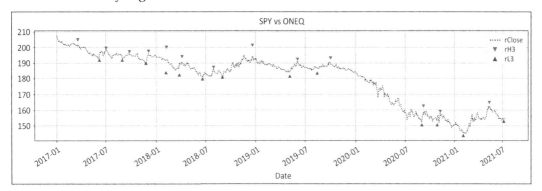

Figure 5.20: Has SPY finally bottomed out versus ONEQ?

When we print the relative chart, it seems like the last swing low may be substantially higher than the lowest low. This means the relative chart may have bottomed out. This could be an early indication that the S&P 500 might start to outperform the Nasdaq. This neatly leads us into the next section on floor/ceiling regime definition.

Regime definition

A bear market ends when new lows are materially higher than the lowest low. At some point, the market will print a bottom. Every subsequent low will settle higher. Measure all lows versus the bottom. Once the distance expressed in volatility-adjusted units or even percentage points is wide enough, the market has found a floor. In execution trader English, if all the pessimism of the sellers fails to penetrate the low, then the market is no longer bearish.

A bull market ends when all advances retreat below the top. At some point, the market will print a top. If every subsequent rally settles below the top, the market has found a ceiling. In execution trader English, if all the bullishness cannot take the high, then this bull is over. When a ceiling is found, the market can turn either sideways or bearish. Conversely, when a floor is found, the market can turn either sideways or bullish.

The formula is a **z-score** of the distance from peak/trough to subsequent swing highs/lows. The z-score is a delta expressed in units of volatility (ATR, standard deviations, realized or implied). The code below may look a bit verbose. The principle is however conceptually simple.

A classic bull regime is defined as follows:

1. Look for a ceiling: The search window starts from the floor.

2. Measure the current swing versus the ceiling: `ceiling_test = (swing_high[i]-top)/stdev[i]`.

3. If the distance to the ceiling is fewer than *x* standard deviations, the regime has turned bearish.

A classic bear regime is defined as follows:

1. Look for a floor: The search window starts from the ceiling.

2. Measure the current swing versus the floor: `floor_test = (swing_low[i]-bottom)/stdev[i]`.

3. If the distance to the floor is greater than *x* standard deviations, the regime has turned bullish.

The code for the floor/ceiling function is this chapter's *pièce de résistance*. The function is as follows:

```
#### regime_floor_ceiling(df, hi,lo,cl, slo, shi,flr,clg,rg,rg_
ch,stdev,threshold) ####
def regime_floor_ceiling(df, _h,_l,_c,slo, shi,flr,clg,rg,rg_
ch,stdev,threshold):
    # Lists instantiation
    threshold_test,rg_ch_ix_list,rg_ch_list = [],[], []
    floor_ix_list, floor_list, ceiling_ix_list, ceiling_list =
[],[],[],[]

    ### Range initialisation to 1st swing
    floor_ix_list.append(df.index[0])
    ceiling_ix_list.append(df.index[0])

    ### Boolean variables
    ceiling_found = floor_found = breakdown = breakout = False

    ### Swings lists
    swing_highs = list(df[pd.notnull(df[shi])][shi])
    swing_highs_ix = list(df[pd.notnull(df[shi])].index)
    swing_lows = list(df[pd.notnull(df[slo])][slo])
    swing_lows_ix = list(df[pd.notnull(df[slo])].index)
    loop_size = np.maximum(len(swing_highs),len(swing_lows))

    ### Loop through swings
    for i in range(loop_size):
```

```
        ### asymetric swing list: default to last swing if shorter list
#### removed for brevity: check GitHub repo for full code ####


        ### CLASSIC CEILING DISCOVERY
#### removed for brevity: check GitHub repo for full code ####


        ### EXCEPTION HANDLING: price penetrates discovery swing
#### removed for brevity: check GitHub repo for full code ####


        ### CLASSIC FLOOR DISCOVERY
#### removed for brevity: check GitHub repo for full code ####


        ### EXCEPTION HANDLING: price penetrates discovery swing
#### removed for brevity: check GitHub repo for full code ####


    ### POPULATE FLOOR,CEILING, RG CHANGE COLUMNS
#### removed for brevity: check GitHub repo for full code ####


#### regime_floor_ceiling(df, hi,lo,cl, slo, shi,flr,clg,rg,rg_
ch,stdev,threshold) ####

ohlc = ['Open','High','Low','Close']
_o,_h,_l,_c = [ohlc[h] for h in range(len(ohlc))]

rg_val = ['Hi3','Lo3','flr','clg','rg','rg_ch',1.5]
slo, shi,flr,clg,rg,rg_ch,threshold = [rg_val[s] for s in range(len(rg_
val))]
stdev = df[_c].rolling(63).std(ddof=0)

df = regime_floor_ceiling(df,_h,_l,_c,slo, shi,flr,clg,rg,rg_
ch,stdev,threshold)

df[[_c,'Hi3', 'Lo3','clg','flr','rg_ch','rg']].plot(
    style=['grey', 'ro', 'go', 'kv', 'k^','c:','y-.'],
    secondary_y= ['rg'],figsize=(20,5),
    grid=True, title = str.upper(ticker))
```

Behind this intimidatingly verbose code is simple logic. Let's go through its main articulations. There are broadly two logics:

1. **Classic floor and ceiling discovery**: We loop through the swings to identify peaks and subsequent falling swing highs as well as bottoms and rising swing lows. This type of setup is referred to as classic floor and ceiling discovery inside the code.

2. **Exception handling**: This happens when price penetrates discovery swings:

   • Initial penetration: For a floor, we look for the lowest low since the discovery swing low. For a ceiling, we look for the highest high since the discovery swing high. The regime is reset to the previously dominant one.

   • Reversion: Sometimes prices bounce around. This roundtrip exception handling ensures the regime responds well to randomness.

3. Once the loop is over, columns are populated.

After those clarifications, voila! The floor/ceiling regime is the dashed horizontal line on the secondary *y* axis. This regime methodology is the definition of stability:

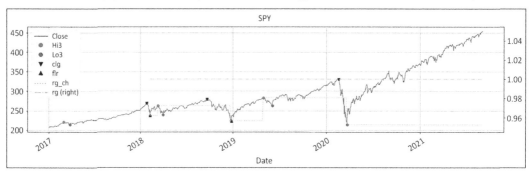

Figure 5.21: SPY close and floor/ceiling bullish regime

The regime has remained bullish throughout the entire period. The market "hit a soft patch," financial creole for puking its guts out, in early 2020. The regime did not even blink. This does not mean this regime definition is not responsive. It does not mean that market participants should "buy and hope." It simply means the regime did not change. This stability allows market participants to articulate strategies and manage risk in a calm, composed manner.

Methodology comparison

"Learning to choose is hard. Learning to choose well is harder. And learning to choose well in a world of unlimited possibilities is harder still."

– Barry Schwartz on the paradox of choice

In 2004, Barry Schwartz rocked the world with something we have always intuitively felt. The more choices we have, the more stress we experience. We have outlined a few methods. Let's compare them graphically and hope the winner will visually stand out.

Firstly, let's print the floor/ceiling alone. The small dots are level 1. The big dots are level 2. The black triangle is the floor. The shade is the length of the regime. It starts from the first swing low and goes all the way to the right. Even the pandemic "soft patch" did not put a dent in it. This is as stable as it possibly can be:

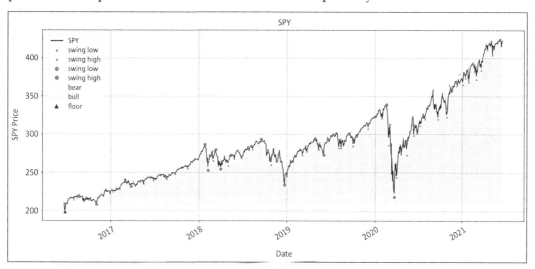

Figure 5.22: SPY floor/ceiling bullish regime forever

This could come across as unresponsive to market gyrations and to a certain extent it is. In Q1 of 2020, the world seemed to bound for AC/DC's proverbial "highway to hell" in a hand basket. And yet, the regime was not swayed. It probably flashed bearishly on the ascent in late May 2020, but promptly reverted back to a Robert de Niro "raging bull" market. It is neither good nor bad. It is simply how this regime method works. The vast majority of market participants are long-term trend followers. They want to buy stuff to pass on to future generations along with their Philippe Patek watch collection.

It does not mean that they will do nothing for the next decade. Market participants often add to their positions as markets tank, something known as **buy on weakness**. This is the perfect regime definition method to accomplish this. The unparalleled stability of this regime detection methodology sets the long-term background context. The regime is either bullish or bearish. Then, market participants can superimpose all kinds of strategies to either "buy on weakness" or "sell on strength" depending on the dominant regime.

More importantly, Warren Buffett said that we should buy when there is blood on the streets. Easier said than done when the market has dropped like a stone and our limbic brain feels trapped. This is where this regime method brings the reassurance needed to pull the trigger.

Secondly, we print out the moving average and range breakout regime methodologies:

```
ohlc = ['Open','High','Low','Close']
_o,_h,_l,_c = [ohlc[h] for h in range(len(ohlc))]


mav = [20, 50, 200]
ma_st,ma_mt,ma_lt = [df[_c].rolling(mav[t]).mean() for t in
range(len(mav))]


bo = [50, 252]
st_lo,lt_lo = [df[_l].rolling(bo[t]).min() for t in range(len(bo))]
st_hi,lt_hi = [df[_h].rolling(bo[t]).max() for t in range(len(bo))]


rg=lo=hi=slo=shi=clg=flr=rg_ch = None
graph_regime_combo(ticker,df,_c,rg,lo,hi,slo,shi,clg,flr,rg_ch,ma_
st,ma_mt,ma_lt,lt_lo,lt_hi,st_lo,st_hi)


rg_combo = ['Close','rg','Lo3','Hi3','Lo3','Hi3','clg','flr','rg_ch']
_c,rg,lo,hi,slo,shi,clg,flr,rg_ch =[rg_combo[r] for r in range(len(rg_
combo)) ]


graph_regime_combo(ticker,df,_c,rg,lo,hi,slo,shi,clg,flr,rg_ch,ma_
st,ma_mt,ma_lt,lt_lo,lt_hi,st_lo,st_hi)
```

This will produce the following two charts:

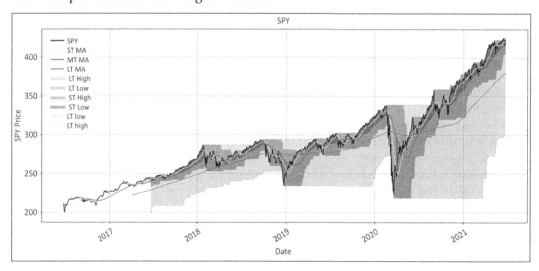

Figure 5.23: SPY regime breakout and moving average crossover

Variables are deliberately much longer than the patience of the average market participant. The range breakout is set at 252 days breakout and 50 days stop loss. The triple moving average has the famous golden cross and 20 days as entry/exit. Those variables deliberately calibrate for long-term trends. They are not supposed to flip-flop like a senator. And yet, there are still a few changes along the way.

The second chart overlays the floor/ceiling method. This is the lightest shade of blue that stretches from the first swing to the end of the chart:

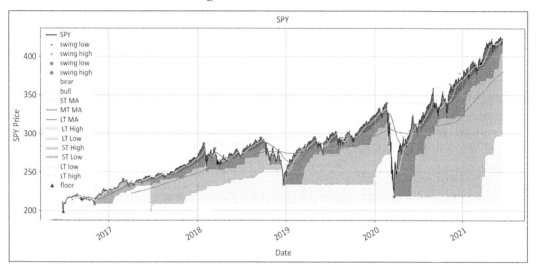

Figure 5.24: SPY floor/ceiling, breakout, and moving average crossover regimes

The above chart combines all three methods in one crisp visualization. The floor/ceiling is the lightest shade of blue. Note that the floor/ceiling regime supersedes all other methodologies. Bearish phases using the breakout or moving average crossover methodologies are not reflected unless the floor/ceiling regime changes.

The big takeaway is that the floor/ceiling method provides stability upon which to build strategies. There is tremendous value in knowing that the market is still bullish and dips should be bought. No other method out there provides this level of stability. Institutional investors move big tickets. Getting in and out erodes profitability. This is why they will privilege from stability over accuracy. When conditions change, they change their mind. Until then, this is usual drama. Market participants can then articulate strategies however they see fit. It could be swing detection, moving averages, range breakout, or risk reversal. The only thing that matters is the knowledge that the market is still in bullish territory.

For market participants who favor action over patience, there are two ways to overclock the floor/ceiling methodology. It relies on swings. Increase the number of swings and the regime will mechanically be more nervous.

- **Method 1**: Use level 2 instead of level 3 swings. Level 3 filters out a lot of noise. This also makes it less responsive. If you do not mind the noise, go ahead

- **Method 2**: Faster periodicity. This data was processed on daily bar timeframe. Keep the same level 3 but accelerate the periodicity to a 4 hour interval. This second method gives some fascinating results. Try downloading data at a 1-5 minute interval. Process the swing detection sequence and watch the fractals paint a near perfect picture up to daily frame. Warning: this method works well for historical data, but generates numerous false positives. As such, we did not generate the data to promote the method.

The above ticker is a example on the long side. It looks a bit incongruous in a book on short selling. Yet, the message is easier to convey to market participants coming from the long side. This methodology is rigorously symmetrical on the short side. It is therefore time to revisit our beloved scandalous Wells Fargo example. We will run the sequence in both absolute and relative to the S&P500 and publish the respective charts:

```
params = ['2014-12-31', None, 63, 0.05, 0.05, 1.5, 2]
start, end, vlty_n,dist_pct,retrace_pct,threshold,dgt= [params[h] for h
in range(len(params))]


rel_var = ['^GSPC','SP500', 'USD']
bm_ticker, bm_col, ccy_col = [rel_var[h] for h in range(len(rel_var))]
bm_df = pd.DataFrame()
bm_df[bm_col] = round(yf.download(tickers= bm_ticker,start= start, end
= end,interval = "1d",
                group_by = 'column',auto_adjust = True, prepost =
True,
                treads = True, proxy = None)['Close'],dgt)
bm_df[ccy_col] = 1


ticker = 'WFC'
df = round(yf.download(tickers= ticker,start= start, end =
end,interval = "1d",
                group_by = 'column',auto_adjust = True, prepost =
True,
                treads = True, proxy = None),2)
ohlc = ['Open','High','Low','Close']
_o,_h,_l,_c = [ohlc[h] for h in range(len(ohlc))]
df= relative(df=df,_o=_o,_h=_h,_l=_l,_c=_c, bm_df=bm_df, bm_col= bm_
col, ccy_df=bm_df,
```

```
            ccy_col=ccy_col, dgt= dgt, start=start, end=
end,rebase=True)

df[['Close','rClose']].plot(figsize=(20,5),style=['k','grey'],
                        title = str.upper(ticker)+ ' Relative &
Absolute')
```

This will generate a graph like the following:

Figure 5.25: Wells Fargo in absolute and relative to the S&P 500

The above code is a repeat of something we already saw in a previous chapter. Next, we will run the sequence. One thing worth noting is that the calculation regarding the benchmark and currency precedes the single stock calculation. Should you want to run the same calculation across an entire investment universe, all you have to do is insert a loop to iterate tickers.

Next, we run the swing detection and regime definition twice. First, we run it on the absolute series. At the end of the loop, we re-initialize the variables to the relative series. And then we run the sequence on the relative series:

```
swing_val = ['rg','Lo1','Hi1','Lo3','Hi3','clg','flr','rg_ch']
rg,rt_lo,rt_hi,slo,shi,clg,flr,rg_ch = [swing_val[s] for s in
range(len(swing_val))]

for a in np.arange(0,2):
    df = round(historical_swings(df,_o,_h,_l,_c, dist= None, hurdle=
None),2)
    df = cleanup_latest_swing(df,shi,slo,rt_hi,rt_lo)
    ud, bs, bs_dt, _rt, _swg, hh_ll, hh_ll_dt =
latest_swing_variables(df,
            shi,slo,rt_hi,rt_lo,_h,_l, _c)
    vlty = round(average_true_range(df,_h,_l,_c, n= vlty_n)
[hh_ll_dt],2)
```

```
    dist_vol = 5 * vlty
    _sign = test_distance(ud,bs, hh_ll, dist_vol, dist_pct)
    df = retest_swing(df, _sign, _rt, hh_ll_dt, hh_ll, _c, _swg)
    retrace_vol = 2.5 * vlty
    df = retracement_swing(df, _sign, _swg, _c, hh_ll_dt, hh_ll, vlty,
retrace_vol, retrace_pct)
    stdev = df[_c].rolling(vlty_n).std(ddof=0)
    df = regime_floor_ceiling(df,_h,_l,_c,slo,
shi,flr,clg,rg,rg_ch,stdev,threshold)


    rohlc = ['rOpen','rHigh','rLow','rClose']
    _o,_h,_l,_c = [rohlc[h] for h in range(len(rohlc)) ]
    rswing_val = ['rrg','rL1','rH1','rL3','rH3','rclg','rflr','rrg_ch']
    rg,rt_lo,rt_hi,slo,shi,clg,flr,rg_ch = [rswing_val[s] for s in
range(len(rswing_val))]
```

We explained all these functions previously. Now, the sequence is packaged in one block of code. In the appendix, we will re-package this a bit more elegantly with a single function. Finally, we print colorful charts to represent the regimes both in absolute and relative:

```
ma_st = ma_mt = ma_lt = lt_lo = lt_hi = st_lo = st_hi = 0

rg_combo = ['Close','rg','Lo3','Hi3','Lo3','Hi3','clg','flr','rg_ch']
_c,rg,lo,hi,slo,shi,clg,flr,rg_ch =[rg_combo[r] for r in
range(len(rg_combo)) ]
graph_regime_combo(ticker,df,_c,rg,lo,hi,slo,shi,clg,flr,rg_ch,
ma_st,ma_mt,ma_lt,lt_lo,lt_hi,st_lo,st_hi)

rrg_combo =
['rClose','rrg','rL3','rH3','rL3','rH3','rclg','rflr','rrg_ch']
_c,rg,lo,hi,slo,shi,clg,flr,rg_ch =[rrg_combo[r] for r in
range(len(rrg_combo)) ]
graph_regime_combo(ticker,df,_c,rg,lo,hi,slo,shi,clg,flr,rg_ch,
ma_st,ma_mt,ma_lt,lt_lo,lt_hi,st_lo,st_hi)
```

All other parameters have been muted. The code will print two charts. We only want to look at the floor/ceiling regimes in absolute and relative. First, we will print the absolute series:

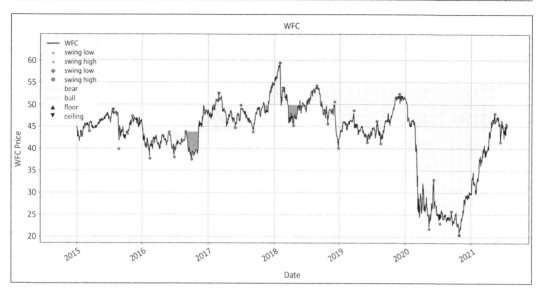

Figure 5.26: Wells Fargo floor/ceiling regime in absolute

This chart is a great example because it shows this regime is not a panacea. The floor/ceiling methodology is not a universal cure for randomness. There are loss-making periods on the long side. This simply means that regime definition is not a substitute for risk management. Next, we print Wells Fargo relative to the S&P500:

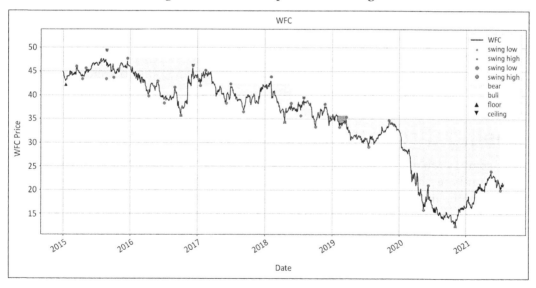

Figure 5.27: Wells Fargo floor/ceiling regime relative to the S&P 500

Again, Wells Fargo is not a perennial underperformer. It has its fleeting moments of glorious "rise and shine" in the sunset before slipping back into a long descent. As the last swing low suggests, the regime might even have turned bullish. Maybe this time around, outperformance may be more sustainable.

Timing the optimal entry point after the bottom or the peak

"Far more money has been lost by investors preparing for corrections, or trying to anticipate corrections, than has been lost in corrections themselves."

– Peter Lynch

The first problem is market participants who want to protect their gains by anticipating regime change tend to lose money in the long run. If some "expert" walked up to you and said, "you will fall sick next week. You will be ill for an average of three months. You will be cured on this precise day," you would probably think they had lost their L-size tin-foil hat!

Yet, in the markets, we pay attention to this constant chrematocoulrophony (remember our keyword from *Chapter 2, 10 Classic Myths about Short Selling*). Market gurus are excellent at timing tops and bottoms. In fact, they impeccably timed the last 2 bear markets 39 times in a row! However, predicting tops and bottoms is a fool's game. There are thousands of days between the day of the bottom and the peak. You can afford to miss the first 50 days and still catch the big move. The floor/ceiling method will not get you out at the peak. It will get you into a short position at the highest point possible with reasonable accuracy.

Seeing through the fundamental news flow

The second problem comes when the fundamental news flow catches up with the tape. Fundamental information looks strong around the top and weak around the bottom of the market. It reports past numbers, such as monthly sales, orders, and so on. Meanwhile, markets tend to look forward. Market participants fall prey to "confirmation bias": they have all the fundamental evidence they need to double-up their positions or throw in the towel.

This floor and ceiling method is an objective way to assess whether it is time to remain bullish or take a more defensive stance. This method has several advantages. First, stability brings reliability. For example, the regime for the S&P 500 switched from bull to sideways-bearish only twice in the ten plus years following the 2008 crisis. Each time, the regime reverted to bullish less than 3 months thereafter.

Compare this with the 20+ times when the price at close flip-flopped around the 200-day moving average. That level of stability brings superior confidence to market participants. Until the regime changes, every pullback is an opportunity to buy.

This method also brings clarity. It saves us from our rationalizing stupidity. At some point, we have all come across a stock where we thought: "This has gone up too much, time to short." Well, this tends to happen to stocks in a bull regime. Or, we might utter: "This has fallen way too much, time to buy." That also tends to happen to bearish stocks. The regime brings clarity: buy bull and hedge, sell bear and hedge.

Recognizing turning points

The strength of the floor/ceiling method comes around turning points. We grew up thinking that a bull needs to die for a bear to start and vice versa. With this method, bear markets start within dying bull markets and vice versa. The nuance is expensive. It allows market participants to position themselves as one regime transitions to the next.

Euphoric market participants often remain bulled up past the peak and depressed past the bottom. In the screaming match between our left and right earlobes, we often fail to listen to what the market quietly whispers.

The hardest thing to determine is when to liquidate a profitable position. This method is robust enough to keep Ulysses tied to the mast of reason while he sails past the sirens of the markets. The good news is that this method is logically accurate. Bear markets start when new advances retreat below the ceilings. Bull markets start when new lows remain above the floor.

Let the market regime dictate the best strategy

> *"When you have eliminated all which is impossible, then whatever remains, however improbable, must be the truth."*
>
> *– Sir Arthur Conan Doyle*

Over the years, I have come to believe that the two primary determinants of performance are position sizing and market regime. Trade too big and you could be out of business. Trade too small and you do not have a business. Secondly, seasoned market participants usually have several strategies to cope with different market types.

The difficulty is which strategy to use when and more importantly when to fade them. This comes down to regime definition. The floor/ceiling method could potentially change the way you trade markets.

There are two types of strategy: mean reversion and trend following. Mean reversion works best in range-bound markets. The price oscillates around a mean in a semi-predictable fashion. Mean reversion strategies perform poorly in trending markets. Trend-following strategies work well in bull or bear markets but end up giving back their gains in sideways markets.

At the end of a bull run, when a ceiling is found, the market can either go sideways or bear. All the summer bulls are not going to wake up with their winter bear clothes on the same day. Assume the market will be sideways, until it dawns upon the "golden traders" (laggards whose intellectual density is thicker than gold) that the bears are in charge. Conversely, when a floor is found, it will take time to process the traumatic experience of the bear market and be positioned for a nascent bull market.

Once a floor or a ceiling is found, assume that markets go sideways, or trade in a range, until there is evidence it goes bearish or resumes its bull trend. Pause trend trading and step into mean reversion. Once there is evidence a new trend has emerged, and the market makes lower highs/higher lows or breaks out of the range, re-activate trend trading and pause mean reversion.

Symmetry is usually a foreign concept to market participants coming from the long-only side. Market participants all start with the ideal of symmetry but quickly realise that their long-side rules do not work well on the short side. After all, the long side is slow moving and generally quiet while the short side is fast paced and volatile. They then proceed to develop two sets of rules to contend with each side separately. As usual, it all works well in theory until it needs to work in practice. Problems arise when both rules are simultaneously valid, and stocks could be either long or short. This usually happens at the worst time: when performance starts to suffer. Dwindling performance is not conducive to clarity. At this point, market participants resort to conviction, stories, or complicated risk management. Symmetry avoids conflicting rules. It is either a long or short, never both.

Let the market regime dictate the strategy. The floor/ceiling method gives an objective start and ending point for each of those regime changes: ceiling, range, and floor. Once you know if the broader regime should be bullish, bearish, or sideways, it is easier to design strategies that fit into each bucket. With proper regime definition and position sizing, even a mediocre strategy can have a positive edge.

Summary

We have examined a few regime methodologies that will help you pick up on signals that a market is going up or down. Regime breakouts and moving average crossovers are staples in the arsenal of trend-following traders. Duration is as much a function of style as what the market happens to reward. Then, we introduced the floor/ceiling methodology. This regime definition method works on absolute and relative series. It is symmetrical and above all more stable than any other methodology. It therefore supersedes everything else.

However, regime definition methodologies are not mutually exclusive. For example, the floor/ceiling method could be used to determine the direction of trades, long or short. Then, regime breakout could be used to enter after consolidation or sideways markets. Finally, the moving average crossover could be used to exit positions.

Having a signal is one thing. Turning it into a profitable strategy with a robust statistical edge is another. There is no profitable equivalent the "buy-and-hold" mentality on the short side. Short selling is like mixed martial arts. That belt will claim its pound of flesh. For this reason, we will spend the rest of *Part II, The Outer Game: Developing a Robust Trading Edge* working on how to do just that; build a robust trading edge.

6

The Trading Edge is a Number, and Here is the Formula

In this chapter, we will unveil one of the most well-guarded secrets in the finance industry: behind the curtain is not an old man, but a simple formula. Then, we will decompose this formula into two distinct modules: signal and money management.

Within the signal module, we will explore how to time entries and exits, and the properties of the two strategy types that seem to provide a trading edge; trend following and mean reversion. We will continue this discussion in *Chapter 7, Improve Your Trading Edge*, before covering the money management module in more depth in *Chapter 8, Position Sizing: Money is Made in the Money Management Module*.

Along the way, we will cover the following topics:

- Importing libraries
- The trading edge formula: arithmetic and geometric gain expectancy
- A trading edge is not a story
- Regardless of the asset class, there are only two strategies

You can access color versions of all images in this chapter via the following link: https://static.packt-cdn.com/downloads/9781801815192_ColorImages.pdf. You can also access source code for this chapter via the book's GitHub repository: https://github.com/PacktPublishing/Algorithmic-Short-Selling-with-Python-Published-by-Packt

Importing libraries

For this chapter and the rest of the book, we will be working with the pandas, numpy, yfinance, and matplotlib libraries. So, please remember to import them first:

```
# Import Libraries
import pandas as pd
import numpy as np
import yfinance as yf
%matplotlib inline
import matplotlib.pyplot as plt
```

The trading edge formula

"Information is not knowledge."

– Albert Einstein, patent clerk

Who said that science fiction hasn't found its way into the austere world of finance? Ask any hedge fund manager about their edge and you will enter a world of crusaders against corporate cabals, financial Sherlock Holmeses patiently piecing the information puzzle together, and visionaries investing in the next new [insert the next disruptive technological buzzword here…].

Everyone in the trading business will say that you need an edge to make money. Yet, they will never tell you how to build a sustainable one, presumably for fear that dissemination could erode theirs. Understandably, the trading edge has been this mysterious secret sauce.

There are only three common types of edge: technological, information, and statistical, which will be considered over the next few sections.

Technological edge

Any retail trader today has access to more information and computing power than any top-tier institutional investor 10 years ago. Anyone with a little bit of Python skill can scrape data off the internet and process it via machine learning or artificial intelligence much faster than any traditional research department. A hedge fund-grade cloud infrastructure costs less than 50 dollars per month. Anyone can learn how to code, analyze data, trade, invest, and manage a portfolio for free on YouTube, Quora, or any other learning platform. Technology has brought democracy to the world of finance.

Everyone wants to be Jim Simons, but no one wants to take care of the plumbing. As shown in *Figure 6.1*, when asked what the number-one problem facing programmatic traders is, a third of responses were relating to data processing and storage and server management. This shows that the main hurdle remains technology for many aspiring algorithmic traders, who need an entire engineering team to automate their trading. Market participants need to be expert system engineers to ensure continuous connectivity. Then, they have to polish their development skills to write code that not only machines but more importantly humans can read.

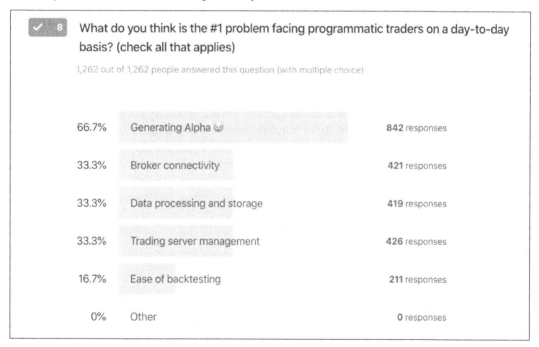

Figure 6.1: Bottlenecks to trading automation: for many aspiring algorithmic traders, the main hurdle continues to be technology

The first iteration of a strategy is like the stone imprisoning Michelangelo's David. It takes a lot of patient carving to reveal the ephebe. When written poorly, it takes a lot more time to disentangle the other Italian cultural heritage: spaghetti. After all this is taken care of, market participants can finally focus on designing alpha-generating strategies. Then come a whole other set of difficulties: scaling in/out, risk management, all the juicy stuff this book is about. The transmutation of billion-dollar ideas into bug-free code is still a daunting technological hurdle. Bottom line, it takes enormous work to make money work for you.

A simple analogy would be the personal computer industry circa Apple 1. Everyone wanted to play Space Invaders. Only a rare die-hard bunch of people were willing to build their own computers to play games. Today, every other Bitcoin enthusiast wants to learn algorithmic trading. Very few people are willing to put in the sweat, blood, and tears to build their own platform. This book will give you the building blocks to build your own strategy.

Information edge

The industry has traditionally operated on the belief that information gives an edge. This has been either privileged information, like getting access to top management and better treatment by analysts, or its more sinister cousin, inside information. Any information edge gets arbitraged away fast.

The information edge never really made a difference in the first place. If all it took to beat the Street was a better information edge, then, in theory, the animal kingdom of big trading houses with their parliaments of analysts, schools of Ph.D.s, prides of fund managers, murders of traders, drifts of sell-side researchers, herds of brokers, and kaleidoscopes of expert opinions, with corporate access on speed-dial and enough money to bail out half a continent would consistently outperform the market. In practice, venerable institutions have limped behind low-tech, plain-vanilla index funds for every year on record. Information gives only a temporary edge that gets arbitraged increasingly quickly over time. Information wants to be democratized.

Statistical edge

A statistical edge does not get arbitraged away easily. It exists and persists by design. It is not "what" but "how" you trade that matters. In the next sections, we will look at ways to build a robust statistical trading edge. We will not try and tell you how to pick stocks differently, but how to squeeze more juice out of those you have already picked.

A trading edge is not a story

"If you can't measure it, you can't improve it."

– Peter Drucker

A trading edge is not a story. A trading edge is a number, and the formula is composed of a few functions:

1. Arithmetic gain expectancy: In execution trader English, this is how often you win multiplied by how much you make on average minus how often you lose times how much you lose on average. This function is the classic arithmetic expectancy, present in every middle school introduction to statistics and absent in a Finance MBA. When talking about trading edges or gain expectancy, market participants default to the arithmetic gain expectancy. It is easy to grasp and calculate. The simplicity of this formula imposes itself, even to those who do not understand its sophistication.

    ```
    # Expectancy formula, win_rate is your Hit ratio, avg_win is the
    average gain per trade, and avg_loss is the average loss per
    trade

    def expectancy(win_rate, avg_win, avg_loss):
        # win% * avg_win% - loss% * abs(avg_loss%)
        return win_rate * avg_win + (1-win_rate) * avg_loss
    ```

2. Geometric gain expectancy (George): Profits and losses compound geometrically. Geometric gain expectancy is mathematically closer to the expected robustness of a strategy.

    ```
    def george(win_rate,avg_win,avg_loss):
        # (1+ avg_win%)** win% * (1- abs(avg_loss%)) ** loss%  -1
        return (1+avg_win) ** win_rate * (1 + avg_loss) ** (1 - win_
    rate) - 1
    ```

3. The Kelly criterion is a position sizing algorithm that optimizes the geometric growth rate of a portfolio. Kelly has a fascinating history, starting with the 18th century mathematician Daniel Bernoulli, re-discovered by J.L. Kelly Jr., and popularized by the legendary Edward Thorp. Kelly uses the same ingredients as the previous expectancies but cooks them a bit differently.

    ```
    def kelly(win_rate,avg_win,avg_loss):
        # Kelly = win% / abs(avg_loss%) - loss% / avg_win%
        return win_rate / np.abs(avg_loss) - (1-win_rate) / avg_win
    ```

Over this chapter and the next one, we will use a rudimentary strategy to show how the formulae work. Think of it as Turtle Trader for dummies. Firstly, we recycle the 50/20 turtle with Softbank (9984.T) without simulating slippage or transaction costs. The code is recycled from *Chapter 5, Regime Definition*. First, we redefine some functions.

```
def regime_breakout(df,_h,_l,window):
    hl =  np.where(df[_h] == df[_h].rolling(window).max(),1,
                              np.where(df[_l] == df[_l].
rolling(window).min(), -1,np.nan))
    roll_hl = pd.Series(index= df.index, data= hl).fillna(method=
'ffill')
    return roll_hl


def turtle_trader(df, _h, _l, slow, fast):
    '''

    _slow: Long/Short direction
    _fast: trailing stop loss
    '''

    _slow = regime_breakout(df,_h,_l,window = slow)
    _fast = regime_breakout(df,_h,_l,window = fast)
    turtle = pd. Series(index= df.index,
                        data = np.where(_slow == 1,np.where(_fast ==
1,1,0),
                                      np.where(_slow == -1, np.where(_fast
==-1,-1,0),0)))
    return turtle
```

We then run Softbank through the Turtle for dummies strategy, calculate returns, and print out two charts.

```
ticker = '9984.T' # Softbank
start = '2017-12-31'
end = None
df =  round(yf.download(tickers= ticker,start= start, end = end,
                        interval = "1d",group_by = 'column',
                        auto_adjust = True, prepost = True,
                        treads = True, proxy = None),0)
slow = 50
fast = 20
```

```
df['tt'] = turtle_trader(df, _h= 'High', _l= 'Low', slow= slow,fast=
fast)
df['stop_loss'] = np.where(df['tt'] == 1, df['Low'].rolling(fast).
min(),
                    np.where(df['tt'] == -1, df['High'].rolling(fast).
max(),np.nan))


df['tt_chg1D'] = df['Close'].diff() * df['tt'].shift()
df['tt_PL_cum'] = df['tt_chg1D'].cumsum()


df['tt_returns'] = df['Close'].pct_change() * df['tt'].shift()
tt_log_returns = np.log(df['Close']/df['Close'].shift()) * df['tt'].
shift()
df['tt_cumul'] = tt_log_returns.cumsum().apply(np.exp) - 1



df[['Close','stop_loss','tt','tt_cumul']].plot(secondary_y=['tt','tt_
cumul'],
                                    figsize=(20,8),style= ['k','r--
','b:','b'],
                        title= str(ticker)+' Close Price, Turtle L/S
entries, cumulative returns')


df[['tt_PL_cum','tt_chg1D']].plot(secondary_y=['tt_chg1D'],
                            figsize=(20,8),style= ['b','c:'],
                            title= str(ticker) +' Daily P&L &
Cumulative P&L')
```

The code takes the following steps:

1. Use logarithmic returns: Log returns are easier to manipulate than arithmetic ones. Arithmetic sums do not compound, whereas logarithmic ones do. The cumulative returns are calculated with the apply(np.exp) method.

2. Strategy entry/exit: Entries and exits are delayed by one bar using the shift() method.

The following chart shows the closing price in black and the trailing stop loss in a red dashed line. On a secondary axis, we have the long/short positions: –1 for short and +1 for long positions. The solid blue line is the cumulative returns:

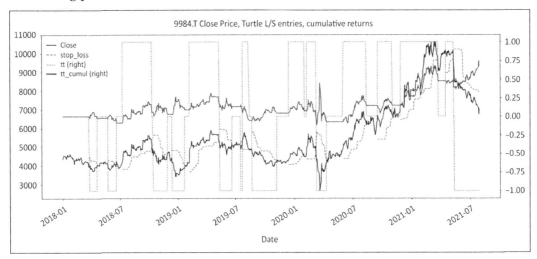

Figure 6.2: Turtle for dummies: long and short entries, cumulative returns

This strategy seems to be working in its primitive format. The second chart shows the daily and cumulative profits and losses. Flat lines are when there is no active position:

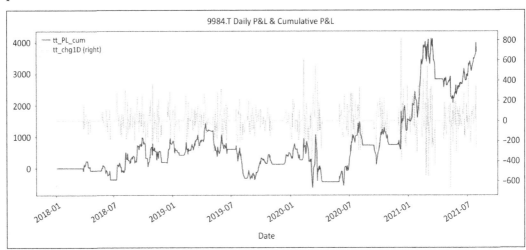

Figure 6.3: Softbank daily and cumulative profit and loss (P&L)

Next, we will calculate the rolling profits, losses, and expectancies and plot them in a graph.

```
# Separate profits from losses
loss_roll = tt_log_returns.copy()
loss_roll[loss_roll > 0] = np.nan
win_roll = tt_log_returns.copy()
win_roll[win_roll < 0] = np.nan

# Calculate rolling win/loss rates and averages
window= 100
win_rate = win_roll.rolling(window).count() / window
loss_rate = loss_roll.rolling(window).count() / window
avg_win = win_roll.fillna(0).rolling(window).mean()
avg_loss = loss_roll.fillna(0).rolling(window).mean()

# Calculate expectancies
df['trading_edge'] = expectancy(win_rate,avg_win,avg_loss).
fillna(method='ffill')
df['geometric_expectancy'] = george(win_rate,avg_win,avg_loss).
fillna(method='ffill')
df['kelly'] = kelly(win_rate,avg_win,avg_loss).fillna(method='ffill')

df[window*2:][['trading_edge', 'geometric_expectancy', 'kelly']].plot(
    secondary_y = ['kelly'], figsize=(20,6),style=['b','y','g'],
    title= 'trading_edge, geometric_expectancy, kelly')
```

1. Copy the daily returns in `win_roll` and `loss_roll` to have a uniform-length series. Assign N/A to the losses on the `win_roll` series and vice versa with profits for the `loss_roll` series.

2. Instantiate the window size and rolling count to calculate both the win rate and loss rate.

3. The rolling sum method does not accommodate missing values. So, we use the `fillna(0)` method to replace missing values with 0 to calculate moving averages. Populate the dataframe and plot.

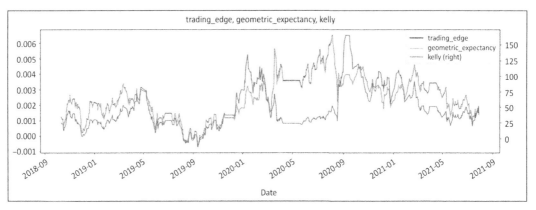

Figure 6.4: Softbank rolling trading edge, geometric expectancy, Kelly

The strategy has a positive trading edge, but once again please do not try this at home—it is too simplistic to be deployed in real-money production and is for educational purposes only. Those three lines on the chart are a variation on the same theme. The ingredients are the same, but the cooking is a bit different. The key takeaway is: nothing happens until the gain expectancy turns positive. Sharpe, Sortino, Jensen, Treynor, and information ratios are all well and good, but they come after the gain expectancy is positive.

All of these formulae can be decomposed into two modules:

- **Signal module**: Win/loss rate. These are the returns generated from entry and exit signals.
- **Money management module**: Average profit/loss. These are contributions generated from returns multiplied by bet sizes.

This demystifies the trading edge as something that can be engineered from the ground up. Market participants pretend they have superior knowledge of the future thanks to their analytical superpowers and machine learning crystal balls. Meanwhile, casinos publicly advertise randomness. Still, the former have lumpy returns, and the latter consistently print money day-in, day-out. This is not a coincidence. The former believe knowledge is an edge, while casinos engineer their edge. The job of every market participant is therefore to optimize their trading edge. Over the next few chapters, we will consider how to engineer these modules and maximize the trading edge, starting with the signal module, before moving onto the money management module and position sizing in *Chapter 8, Position Sizing: Money is Made in the Money Management Module*.

So, without further ado, let's start with the signal module.

Signal module: entries and exits

"You've got to know when to hold 'em,

know when to fold 'em,

know when to walk away,

and know when to run."

– Kenny Rogers, The Gambler

Let's start gently by strangling a classical myth once and for all: "you will make money as long as you are right 51% of the time." Wrong. By their own admission, the industry's top performers with decades-long track records often claim unimpressive long-term win rates. Conversely, LTCM boasted an exceptionally high win rate until its liquidation and dissolution in 2000.

You will make money so long as you have a positive trading edge. The first thing we need to engineer is the signal module. As we saw in *Chapter 1, The Stock Market Game,* false positives cannot be eradicated. Randomness is here to stay. Every basket comes with a few bad apples. The key is to design policies to spot those bad apples, deal with them before they spoil the basket, and move on.

Entries: stock picking is vastly overrated

"The beatings will continue until the morale improves."

– Captain Bligh, HMS Bounty

The stock market is the only competitive sport where people like to hand out medals before the race starts. The industry is built on the cult of the stock picker. Everyone loves to talk about their top stock picks. 90% of the energy of market participants is focused on making the right calls. Unfortunately, the same 90% of market participants will fail to beat their benchmark 5 years in a row.

In quants trader jargon, this is called correlation. When correlation endures year after year for every year on record, r-squared, *causality* in quants vernacular, goes to 1. In execution trader English, insanity is when the average frustrated market participant puts more and more energy and resources into stock picking and yet consistently fails year after year. Bottom line, 90% of market participants predictably fail because they consistently focus on the wrong thing: entry. Maybe it is time we entertained the possibility of a different approach.

According to Professor Jeremy Siegel, the long-term average return of the stock market is +7%. That leaves little room for pleasantries on the short side. Ideas are cheap and plentiful. Every single human being has a bag full of million-dollar ideas. The difference between ideas and profits is called execution. As we saw in *Part I, The Inner Game: Demystifying Short Selling*, many market participants fail on the short side because they enter when ideas germinate, not when they are fully ripe for the picking. Underperformance is the financial equivalent of the indigestion we get when we eat fruits that have not ripened yet.

This book will not give you a silver bullet methodology. The purpose of this book is to introduce a probabilistic view of the markets so that you can become a statistically better version of yourself. This book is merely a cookbook for the ingredients you bring to the table. Fundamental, technical, and quantitative short-sellers have all made money, but they could not have succeeded without getting probabilities on their side first.

There are two times when you need to be cognizant of probabilities: stock selection and entry. In execution trader English, this means there are two times when you should listen to what the markets have to say before pulling the trigger.

- First, you need to short stocks that are either in sideways or bear regimes. Shorting stocks in a bull regime is like standing on the tracks expecting freight trains to stop one after the other. In *Chapter 5, Regime Definition*, we learned an objective way to reclassify stocks according to their regime. Since short selling is a relative game (stocks' prices dropping in absolute is a laggard indicator), regime change often takes the form of sector rotation in the equities market. Yesterday's darlings are tomorrow's dogs.

- The second time when you need to be aware of probabilities is entry. Market participants coming from the long side like to buy on breakouts. The same logic does not translate well on the short side. Remember that almost all market participants are in the markets to buy long. Some people have been waiting on the sideline for an opportunity to buy on dips. Fast-falling markets are often followed by rapid bear market rallies. There is a short window when probabilities are in favor of short sellers.

The best time to enter a short position is when a bear market rally rolls over. We will go over the aikido of the short squeeze in *Part III*, *The Long/Short Game: Building a Long/Short Product*.

We saw earlier a visual representation of gain expectancy. In the following chapters, we will look at techniques designed to increase your trading edge. They extend beyond short selling. Some may not apply to your style or strategy.

Exits: the transmutation of paper profits into real money

The only soldiers who walk into battle without an exit strategy are called kamikaze soldiers. They do not expect to come back alive. Since you probably do not expect your trading to look like a suicide mission, the best time to develop an exit strategy is before you "get boxed in," by entering a position.

In the financial services industry, the only thing cheaper than toilet paper are back-tests and simulation print-outs. This is just paper money. No one gets hurt. Real money is the only thing that matters. Let's take the idea one step further. The only time when you know how much "real money" was made, or lost, is after closing a trade. Anything before that is called paper profit. Bottom line: exits matter.

We have all been conditioned to believe that our initial choices are what matter the most. If we have the right internship, graduate from the right university, or choose the right first job, then our careers will be smooth. Life, however, is what happens to us when we have other plans. We often underestimate the role of luck in our lives. Being at the right place at the right time has made a lot of lucky people rich. Those individuals however rarely succeed on their first attempt. They try, fail, and pivot until something finally clicks.

Since market participants like to buy and hold, marriage is arguably a sensible metaphor. Every marriage starts with an optimistic "happily ever after," yet roughly half of them end up as a divorce statistic. Getting married is easy. Getting divorced is a life-altering event. If you have not considered the eventuality before getting married, then it will be emotionally and financially devastating. Bad marriages can be saved. Bad divorces can't. Bad entries can be salvaged. Bad exits can't. This is when the P&L gets printed.

As you will see in the coming chapters, 5 of the 7 steps to increase your trading edge deal with losses. Another good analogy is personal finance. There are two ways you can increase your savings. Either you maintain your current spending and go for a better-paying job, or you restrict your expenses and save the difference. The former works well if you have a stable high salary.

If your earnings are entirely variable, then you would be wiser to maintain a low fixed cost base and pocket whatever difference you glean from the markets. You will get the same big paydays as the other players, but the difference is you will not need them to stay afloat. In financial creole, this focus on expenses is called "cutting your losses short."

Regardless of the asset class, there are only two strategies

Jack Schwager often points out that there is no universal holy grail. Market wizards come in all shapes and forms, sometimes even with contradicting strategies. They have one thing in common though. They excel at managing risk and controlling losses. They consistently focus on the downside. Winning positions take care of themselves. Market participants' job is to take care of losers.

Market participants usually define themselves by "what" they trade (asset class, markets, time horizon), rarely "*how*" they trade. Regardless of the asset class, there are only two types of strategies: trend following and mean reversion. The reason why there are only two strategies is not entries but exits. How you choose to close a trade determines your dominant trading style. The mean reversion camp closes early when inefficiencies are corrected. The trend-following crowd loves to ride their winners. A classic example is value versus growth. Value investors buy undervalued stocks and then pass the baton to growth investors who ride them into the sunset.

For example, a mean reversion market participant would buy a stock at a **Price to Book Ratio (PBR)** of 0.5, close the position when PBR reverts back to 1, and move on. A trend follower would buy the same name at the same valuation but would ride it deep into euphoric territory. They would eventually close the position after this once-obscure, under-researched name would finally make it to the "Strong Buy" lists of tier 1 investment banks and predictably underperform thereafter.

Some readers may argue that value investors are more the mean reversion kind and growth managers the trend following type. That is usually true but not always the case. The best counterexample and probably the ultimate value trend follower is Warren Buffett. He invests in undervalued businesses that he intends to hold ad perpetuum. Your positions are not Philippe Patek watches. You do not hold them for future generations. At some point, you will close your positions. Only three things can happen: the price goes up, down, or nowhere. You either lose, make, or waste money. You need a scenario for each case. You need a plan to realize profits, mitigate losses, and deal with freeloaders. Our objective is to engineer a better statistical trading edge. If there are only two strategy types, then it is important to spend time understanding how they behave, their payoffs, and risks, and whether they are mutually exclusive or compatible.

Trend following

"Money is made in the sitting and waiting."

– Jesse Livermore

Trend following strategies rely on the capital appreciation of a few big winners. systematic **Commodities Trading Advisors (CTAs)** look for breakouts and place protective trailing stop losses. Technical analysts look for entry points and ride the upside. Even fundamental stock pickers qualify as trend followers. Instead of price action, they follow improvement in fundamentals, earnings momentum, or even news flow. Bottom line, whether they consciously admit it or not, the default mode for market participants is trend following. Since trend following is the dominant model for market participants, we use a rudimentary trend following strategy (turtle for dummies) in this book.

This is what the P&L distribution of trend followers looks like:

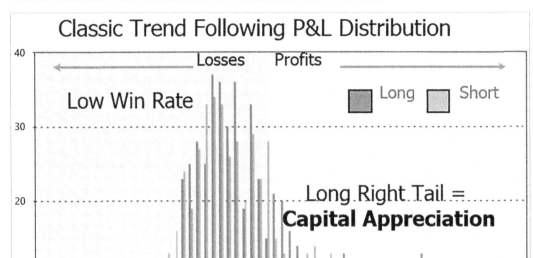

Figure 6.5: Classic trend-following long/short P&L distribution

We can observe the following properties:

- **Low win rate**: Somewhere between 30 to 50%. The mode, the peak number of trades, is in the loss-making section of the distribution. For every Alphabet, Amazon, or Apple, there are countless Nestcapes, Ataris, or MySpaces.

- **Alpha generation**: Trend-following strategies rely on the capital appreciation of a few winners to offset numerous small losses. This introduces a lag between profits unfolding over time, and losses promptly denting the equity curve. Losses are quickly dealt with while winners take time to mature.

- **Positive skew**: A right-tailed P&L distribution gives a favorable tail ratio. Winners are bigger than losers. The above chart is a visual representation of the time-honored "cut your losers, ride your winners." Again, it takes time to achieve those outsized returns. Meanwhile, the equity curve has to deal with the frog smudge along the way.

- **Cyclicality**: Markets do not trend all the time. Styles come in and out of favor. When a style does not work, losses start mounting. Successful trend followers are prompt to recognize their mistakes and keep individual losses small. When their style is in favor, they ride the trends into the sunset.

- **Relatively low turnover**: Turnover is a function of cyclicality. When markets are trending up or down, there is no need to do anything. Money is made in the sitting and waiting, as legendary trader Jesse Livermore used to say. When a style goes out of favor, turnover will increase as more frogs will be churned.

- **Volatility**: This is a consequence of cyclicality. Market participants go through periods of lackluster returns.

Trend followers kiss a lot of frogs. The risk is that the cumulative smudge of all the delicious batrachians may not outweigh the fairness of a few princesses. The risk with trend-following strategies is in the aggregate weight of losses over profits.

The most pertinent risk metric for trend-following strategies is to compare cumulative profits and losses. This is the gain-to-pain ratio, also commonly known as the profit factor or profitability factor, favored by the prophet Jack Schwager. It states that when cumulative profits in the numerator exceed losses, the ratio is above 1, and vice versa for loss-making strategies. This is yet another version of the arithmetic gain expectancy, as a ratio instead of a delta.

```
def rolling_profits(returns,window):
    profit_roll = returns.copy()
    profit_roll[profit_roll < 0] = 0
    profit_roll_sum = profit_roll.rolling(window).sum().
fillna(method='ffill')
    return profit_roll_sum

def rolling_losses(returns,window):
    loss_roll = returns.copy()
    loss_roll[loss_roll > 0] = 0
    loss_roll_sum = loss_roll.rolling(window).sum().
fillna(method='ffill')
    return loss_roll_sum

def expanding_profits(returns):
    profit_roll = returns.copy()
    profit_roll[profit_roll < 0] = 0
    profit_roll_sum = profit_roll.expanding().sum().
fillna(method='ffill')
```

```
        return profit_roll_sum

    def expanding_losses(returns):
        loss_roll = returns.copy()
        loss_roll[loss_roll > 0] = 0
        loss_roll_sum =    loss_roll.expanding().sum().
    fillna(method='ffill')
        return loss_roll_sum

    def profit_ratio(profits, losses):
        pr = profits.fillna(method='ffill') / abs(losses.
    fillna(method='ffill'))
        return pr

    window = 252
    df['pr_roll'] = profit_ratio(profits= rolling_profits(returns = tt_log_
    returns,window = window),
                                 losses= rolling_losses(returns = tt_log_
    returns,window = window))
    df['pr'] = profit_ratio(profits= expanding_profits(returns= tt_log_
    returns),
                                 losses= expanding_losses(returns = tt_log_
    returns))

    df[window:] [['tt_cumul','pr_roll','pr'] ].plot(figsize =
    (20,8),secondary_y= ['tt_cumul'],
                                 style = ['b','m-.','m'],
       title = str(ticker)+' cumulative returns, Profit Ratio, cumulative &
    rolling '+str(window)+' days')
```

The above code calculates the rolling and cumulative gain-to-pain/profit ratio. The structure is symmetrical, so let's concentrate on rolling profits.

1. Instantiate a `profit_roll` dataframe by copying the returns series. Assign 0 to losses. This will preserve the shape of the dataframe.

2. Calculate a rolling sum using the `rolling` method. Fill #N/A missing values using the `fillna` method.

3. From the `rolling_profits` and `rolling_losses` functions, calculate `profit_ratio`.

4. The `rolling` functions are followed by the cumulative versions. The `expanding()` method does synthetically the same thing as the popular `cumsum()` method. The only difference is that `expanding()` does not reset to 0 when stumbling upon missing values, unlike `cumsum()`.

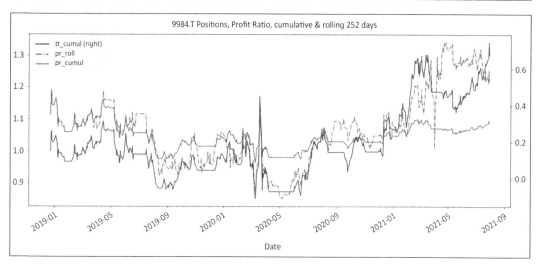

Figure 6.6: Softbank cumulative returns and profit ratios: rolling and cumulative

The above chart plots the rolling and cumulative profit ratios side by side with the signals. The profit ratio nosedives as signals are choppy. Conversely, the profit ratio rises in trending markets.

Trend-following strategies post impressive but volatile performance. They go through long periods of underwhelming performance, which take their toll on the emotional capital of managers and investors. Their main challenge is to keep cumulative losses small. Profits only look big to the extent that losses are kept small.

To illustrate this phenomenon, one of the original turtle traders used to say that, with a 30%+ win rate, they took on positions expecting them to fail. This subtle shift in mindset made them more vigilant about risk management.

Mean reversion

Mean reversion strategies compound numerous small profits. They rely on the premise that extremes eventually revert to the mean. They arbitrage market inefficiencies. Mean reversion strategies essentially capture the time it takes for inefficiencies to correct. For example, the price of a warrant may look cheap compared to its underlying stock. Over time, prices will converge, and the gap will close. They often have low-volatility, consistent performance. They perform well during established markets: bull, bear, or sideways. The markets of predilection for mean reversion strategies are typically sideways phases where prices oscillate in semi-predictable fashions. They may find bull or bear phases more challenging, but there is ample empirical evidence of talented managers performing in those markets. Again, risk management is what separates the pros from the tourists.

Mean reversion strategies perform poorly during regime changes. For example, long high beta, short low beta will do wonders in a bull market but will give back a lot of performance as the regime transitions to sideways and bear. The darlings of the last bull market sometimes lead the way down in the ensuing bear market. They also perform poorly during tail events. Short gamma funds performed well for years until they spectacularly blew up in three weeks during the 2008 GFC.

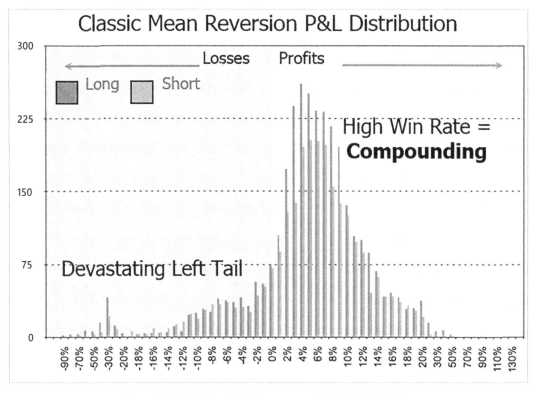

Figure 6.7: Classic long/short mean reversion P&L distribution

The characteristics of mean reversion strategies are:

- **Alpha generation**: Mean reversion strategies have high turnovers. They **compound** small profits quickly.

- **Negative skew**: Left-tailed P&L distribution. Unfavorable tail ratio: losers are bigger than winners. The above chart is a visual representation of the time-honored adage "you can't go broke taking profits." It turns out you probably can if losses are too big. Mean reversion strategies arbitrage inefficiencies. Trades are closed when inefficiencies are corrected. Sometimes, those inefficiencies persist. Since the original premise is that inefficiencies are bound to correct anyways, stop losses are not enforced. This leads to rare but devastating blows.

- **High win rate**: Often above 50%. Markets are not efficient all the time on all time frames.

- **Moderate to high turnover**: In practice, inefficiencies appear more frequently than the **Efficient Market Hypothesis (EMH)** and subsequent academic theories generally suggest.

- **Consistent low-volatility small profits**: Mean reversion strategies arbitrage multiple small inefficiencies during stable market regimes.

- **Potentially devastating left-tail losses**: Mean reversion strategies perform in established markets where inefficiencies correct. They fail during regime changes when past inefficiencies persist. Interestingly enough, trend-following strategies start to perform well right around the time mean reversion strategies falter.

- **Slow recovery**: Mean reversion strategies bank small profits but post big losses. It takes a lot of small wins to offset a few big losses.

As we saw earlier, mean reversion strategies post consistent small profits but suffer rare but game-ending setbacks. The risk for mean reversion strategies is in the tail. A few devastating losses have the power to sink the ship. After all, the captain of the Titanic had a 99% win rate. The most relevant measure of risk is therefore the ratio of the biggest profits to the worst losses, or tail ratio:

```
def rolling_tail_ratio(cumul_returns, window, percentile,limit):
    left_tail = np.abs(cumul_returns.rolling(window).
quantile(percentile))
    right_tail = cumul_returns.rolling(window).quantile(1-percentile)
    np.seterr(all='ignore')
    tail = np.maximum(np.minimum(right_tail / left_tail,limit),-limit)
    return tail

def expanding_tail_ratio(cumul_returns, percentile,limit):
    left_tail = np.abs(cumul_returns.expanding().quantile(percentile))
    right_tail = cumul_returns.expanding().quantile(1 - percentile)
    np.seterr(all='ignore')
    tail = np.maximum(np.minimum(right_tail / left_tail,limit),-limit)
    return tail

df['tr_roll'] = rolling_tail_ratio(cumul_returns= df['tt_cumul'],
                        window= window, percentile= 0.05,limit=5)
df['tr'] = expanding_tail_ratio(cumul_returns= df['tt_cumul'],
percentile= 0.05,limit=5)
```

```
df[window:] [['tt_cumul','tr_roll','tr'] ].plot(secondary_y= ['tt_
cumul'],style = ['b','g-.','g'], figsize = (20,8),
    title= str(ticker)+' cumulative returns, Tail Ratios: cumulative &
rolling '+str(window)+ ' days')
```

The code includes the following steps:

1. cumul_returns: In this function, returns refer to the log returns np.log(px/ px.shift()). Calculate the cumulative returns using the cumsum() method and fill the missing values.

2. Calculate rolling left and right tails using the quantile method.

3. This series is a bit jumpy — 0 in the denominator returns an error, hence the error setting to ignore.

4. Set upper and lower bounds to avoid infinite numbers on each side.

The resulting chart shows cumulative returns and the rolling and cumulative tail ratios.

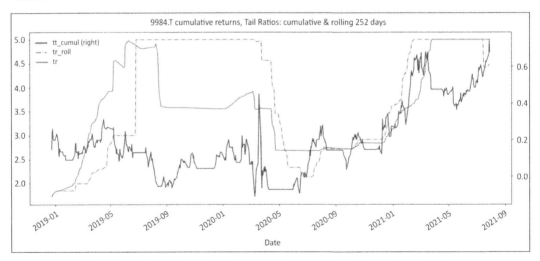

Figure 6.8: Softbank, cumulative returns, and tail ratios: rolling and cumulative

As you can see, we calculated a 5% tail ratio both on a cumulative and rolling basis. As you can see, the tail ratio can veer to infinity or zero quite quickly. This is why it should be range-bound via the limit. Note that the tail ratio is a lot less responsive than the profit ratio we saw earlier. This ratio does not apply to trend following strategies. It is so consistently high that the limit had to be lowered to the 5th and 95th percentile to be visible. This goes to illustrate that those strategies really have different risk profiles.

Summary

Let's recap. The mysterious, mystical, mythical, magical trading edge is nothing but a little formula we learned back in school called gain expectancy. Now, it turns out that strategies with a positive trading edge tend to fall into two buckets. This happens regardless of time frames, asset classes, instrument, and market phases. Market participants expect inefficiencies to either correct and revert to the mean, or to persist and form trends. Those strategies are mutually exclusive. They have opposite payoffs and risk profiles.

We then took time to understand the properties of each strategy type so that we can come up with better ways to engineer a superior trading edge. Now that we understand how those strategies behave, the next step is to roll up our sleeves, pop the hood, and tune up the signal engine.

7

Improve Your Trading Edge

"I never buy at the bottom and I always sell too soon."

– Baron Nathaniel de Rothschild

Usain Bolt and Roger Bannister both run fast. The former is a sprinter. The latter ran a mile. Same sport, different disciplines. The equivalency here is that you have a dominant style: either mean reversion or trend following. The best way to sharpen your trading edge is to improve upon your dominant style. The first step is to start with what an optimal strategy would look like and then gradually nudge your style in that direction.

Building a statistically robust trading edge is about taking control back. You cannot control where the market might end up a week or a year from now, but you have complete control over what is going on in your portfolio today. The following chapters are an invitation to think differently about your dominant style and how you could build a better version of your trading edge.

By now, we know that the trading edge has two modules: signal and money management. We also have a clear visual representation of what trend following or mean reversion positive trading edges look like. Next, we will break the **Profit and Loss (P&L)** distribution into two parts. First, we will go through all the steps you can take to control losses. Then, we will look at the steps you can take to increase profits. Finally, we will look at an innovative bet sizing strategy.

Along the way, we will cover the following topics:

- Blending trading styles
- The psychology of the stop loss
- The science of the stop loss
- Techniques to improve your trading edge
- How to tilt your trading edge if your dominant style is mean reversion

 You can access color versions of all images in this chapter via the following link: <add url of online colour image pack here>.

Blending trading styles

As we discovered in *Chapter 6, The Trading Edge is a Number, and Here is the Formula,* mean reversion strategies have a negative skew. A few titanic losses will sink the ship. Trend following strategies have a positive skew. A few princes will make up for all the frogs. Both strategies have good and bad attributes that can be summarized in the following table:

	Mean Reversion	Trend Following	Hybrid
Win Rate	High	Low	High
Volatility	Low	High	Low
Left Tail	Long	Short	Short
Right Tail	Short	Long	Long
Skew	Negative	Positive	Positive

An ideal strategy would combine the positive attributes and minimize the shortcomings of both styles. It would be a hybrid with a high win rate, low volatility, and short left and long right tails. A hybrid P&L distribution would look like this:

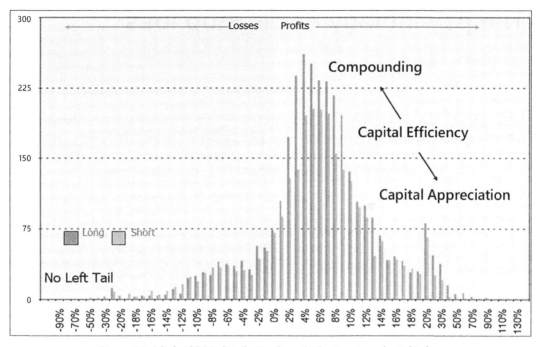

Figure 7.1: A hybrid P&L distribution has a high win rate and a right skew

Mean reversion market participants and trend followers operate from different belief systems. The former believe that inefficiencies eventually revert to the mean, while the latter expect them to persist. While those belief systems are irreconcilable, it is still possible to blend your dominant style with some attributes of the opposite system.

The techniques outlined in the following sections will sustainably improve performance. Yet, as we all know, the difference between top athletes and the rest is not the physical outer game. It is the quality of their inner dialog, their inner game. None of the techniques will work if we do not acknowledge the elephant in the room.

What separates professional short sellers from tourists is the ability to set, and more importantly the fortitude to honor, stop losses.

The psychology of the stop loss

"Hope is a mistake."

– *Mad Max, post-apocalyptic Aussie philosopher*

In the US alone, the weight-loss industry is worth 64 billion dollars. Yet, obesity rates have increased by 30% from the year 1999 to 2016. The weight-loss industry is a commercial success, but a practical failure, simply because it tries to solve the wrong problem. This has a lot to teach us about stop-loss psychology.

The cause of our collective obesity is not the food we ingest. It's how we relate to food. If instead of "eat your hamburger, it will make you strong", your parents told you, "supersize those carcinogenic genetically modified proteins, pumped full of antibiotics, they will triple your risk of cardiovascular health problems," then you might feel a little less inclined to partake in the consumption of the flesh of the holy cow.

 The following Scientific American report discusses the health risks associated with livestock being fed antibiotics: `https://www.scientificamerican.com/article/most-us-antibiotics-fed-t/`.

Everyone knows the recipe to make money in the markets: "cut your losers, ride your winners." Cutting losers is not rocket science. The math is somewhere between elementary and middle school level arithmetic. And yet, it is how we relate to losses that makes honoring stop losses insurmountable. The need to be right supersedes the imperative to make money.

When people say, "I don't believe in stop losses," what they really mean is, "I don't like to admit that I was wrong." They are often acutely aware that something is wrong. Yet their egos are willing to endure more pain, hoping that things will turn around and that they will eventually be vindicated. Pride supersedes profit every single time. Nobel laureates Daniel Kahneman and Amos Tversky have called our risk-seeking attitude to losses and risk aversion with profits the endowment effect.

If being profitable equals being right, then, logically speaking, losing money means being wrong. Any loss is therefore a direct attack on our self-image. The ego feels the need to be right but does not feel obligated to make money, and will default to defense mechanisms—denial and deflection—in order to protect itself. This drives us to sacrifice profits, endure excruciating pain for long stretches of time, and jeopardize our jobs, our reputations, and even our families. Reputations, companies, and nations have fallen before egos have surrendered.

The bottom line is that overly educated, ferociously competitive, and supremely sophisticated 40-year-old hedge fund managers still subconsciously operate on a 5-year-old child operating system. They just got better at crafting elaborate rationalizations.

The public debacle of Bill Ackman and Valeant (VRX) illustrates the primacy of ego over profits. When VRX dropped 50% from its peak, the alternative was simple: stick to the process or stick to the stock. Prudent stewardship of other people's money (OPM) dictates closing all or part of the position, since the stock price would have had to rally 100% just to make it back to the previous level. The alternative is to assume that the analysis is correct, but "the market is wrong" and call the market's bluff. Mr. Ackman patriotically chose to immolate another tranche of OPM by buying an additional 2 million shares at $104. The need to be right superseded the fiduciary duty to prudently manage risk for his investors.

Then, Valeant took another dive, a total decline 92% from its peak. At this point, the price would have to rally by a multiple of 11 just to break even. The position was liquidated at around $11 per share. Sometimes we win, and sometimes we learn. In his 2016 letter to shareholders, Mr. Ackman reiterated the importance of humility: *"in order to be a great investor one needs to first have the confidence to invest without perfect information at a time when others are highly skeptical about the opportunity you are pursuing. This confidence, however, has to be carefully balanced by the humility to recognize when you are wrong."*

This leads us to the fate of our winners. Kanneman and Tversky have demonstrated that we are risk-averse when it comes to profits. We are not born eager to take profits early, quite the contrary in fact. *Beginner's luck* is another phrase for taking big risks on low probability events, something no seasoned player would ever dare. We are not born risk-averse. Babies stumble and fall all the time. They pick themselves up and march on.

We become risk-averse only after a few traumatic losses. Once we experience the pain of losses, we rush to protect whatever profits are left whenever they start evaporating before our eyes. If we never experienced losses, we would not feel the need to be risk-averse with profits. We would gladly embrace the riskiest strategies if it was not for the painful lessons we have learned through losses. Bottom line: it is in our nature to run losers and then cut winners. Making money in the markets goes against our nature.

If we want to succeed in this fight against nature, we need to rewire our association with losses. As long as we maintain an outcome-oriented perspective, then nature, our amygdala, will beat reason, our prefrontal cortex.

In execution-trader English, as long as we think making money equals being right and losing money is for losers, we will find excuses not to take those losses. We need to associate being right with doing the right thing, regardless of the outcome.

Here is a six-step process to completely transform your association with stop losses.

Step 1: Accountability

"Business is a form of procrastination."

– Tim Ferriss

The job of the ego is to protect itself at all costs, at all times. Perhaps you've concluded by now that you are immune to the influence of a toxic ego but have witnessed it in other market participants. Well, if those thoughts have just crossed your mind, then your ego has just played a trick on you. According to Daniel Goleman, self-deception is a deeply-seated, built-in mechanism that covers its own tracks. Below are two examples that will help you see for yourself just how good your subconscious mind is at deceiving you.

Example 1: What did you do the last time there was a large loss in your portfolio? Did you read every analyst report? Did you call or visit the company or analyst? Did you update your earnings model? Did you get color on the stock, a code term for *is it a popular short*? Did you vent with your peers on forums? Did you get drunk, blame someone else, or take it out on your family? Or, did you just stop-loss it and move on?

Recent studies on procrastination in academia show that ahead of exams, students engage in important activities that register positively with the brain, like tidying up their room, cleaning up their desk, or calling their parents, but not essential ones like studying for the exam. They practice a form of mental accounting: by doing good deeds, they hope they will compensate for failing to do the essential ones. Market participants are no different. When positions go sour, we engage in tasks that register positively: updating earnings models or calling analysts, experts, and companies, but delay the inevitable: cutting losers.

Example 2: Let's bring it closer to home with the impact on performance. In one of my previous jobs, I was fortunate enough to have access to all the trades of several managers. I proceeded to analyze them, hoping to glean some lessons from such brilliant minds. The biggest finding was a counterintuitive game changer. Had the three worst-performing stocks been excluded from every portfolio, every single manager would have outperformed the benchmark (before cost) every single year throughout the entire sampled period. However, had the three best-performing stocks been excluded, not everyone would have outperformed. Moreover, outperformance would have not been consistent.

Every single market participant has delayed closing a loss-making position expecting the price to come back just a little more to exit at a more favorable quote. Unfortunately, one day morphs into a week, a month, and so on. Bad losses do not happen overnight. They fester and gangrene. The first step is to keep a neat trading journal. Always have in mind your average and worst losses. Next time someone asks about your trading edge, your default response should be something like: "Which side: long, short, or consolidated?" This will avoid delayed responses to market events due to the resistance of your own ego.

Step 2: Rewire your association with losses

Let's revisit weight loss for a moment. Healthy food choices are like sell-side maintenance research: insipid and boring. We know that sticking to a diet will get us in shape. So, we soldier on and shed those layers of prosperity. But what happens once we have reached our weight-loss goal? The overwhelming majority relapses. Some people hop from one diet to the next, hoping that one day something will finally click. We fail because we only address the physical aspect of dieting: weight loss. We go through the motions but we forget the lesson. We eat the right things in the right amounts for the duration of the diet, yet we maintain the underlying unhealthy associations that will eventually drive us back to poor eating habits. Food is not the problem. Often, weight loss is not a physical issue, it is a mental one.

The same holds true for stop losses. We intellectually understand they are important. When we go through a rough patch, we diligently cut losers. But then comes this particular position: "If we give it just one more day, one more week at most, it will turn around. This is just temporary." Our inner idiot handles the negotiation with our psychopathic alter-ego, homo economicus. The foregone conclusion is this exception: "Just this one time, we can override the stop loss." Next thing we know, the portfolio looks like an orchard of rotten apples. As long as we associate being right with being profitable on a trade-by-trade basis, we operate from an outcome-oriented perspective.

We cannot fight our need to be right, but we can change what we choose to be right about. Rather than making money, we can associate being right with sticking to the disciplined adherence to an investment process. We shift from an outcome over which we frankly have no control, to a process-oriented perspective.

This accomplishes two things:

- Success becomes quantifiable and measurable. One trade is random. One hundred trades is a data sample. Trying to control individual outcomes is futile. It is however entirely possible to measure the adherence to the investment process. The good news is that in every culture throughout history, and particularly in our industry, discipline is a virtue.

- The temptation to cheat naturally fades away. Being right is no longer about the outcome of discrete series. You can repeatedly lose money and still be right. When you consistently operate from this perspective, you literally rewrite the neural pathways in such a way that it reshapes your identity.

An advanced version is to gamify this process mindset. Here is a little personal story. Back in late 2012, prime minister Shinzo Abe decided to reinvigorate the Japanese economy. The market regime instantly changed from dull bear to raging bull. Every time a stock would hit a stop loss, I would play the first notes of James Brown's *I Feel Good* on YouTube and do a little impersonation of Robin Williams in *Good Morning, Vietnam*. At some point, one colleague walked up to me and said: "You really like James Brown, don't you?" My response was, "Well, I have just taken a stop loss today."

The anecdote might be silly, but there was a little bit of science there. The brain hates taking stop losses. It also craves instant gratification. That little jingle brought that jolt of dopamine. Over time, it overpowered the reluctance to honor those stop losses and rewired the association with losses. By the 30th consecutive stop loss, I had become immune and could have stomached the next hundred without breaking a sweat. Try and see for yourself. Start small. Reward yourself immediately after executing a stop loss. After a few rounds, you may notice that your brain has started to crave stop losses. That primitive part of your brain will do anything for its jolt of dopamine. Your job is to figure out what to attach the reward to.

Disciplined fund management should be as boring as dental hygiene. People seldom get excited about flossing. Yet, the brain craves excitement and novelty. It is therefore difficult to build habits that stick if there is no fun in it. One way to build the habit of hygienic fund management is to introduce a reward. Here is how it can be done in practice:

1. Score your adherence to your system on a weekly or monthly basis.
2. Decide on a reward that will make you feel good. It could be anything. For example, the principal of my first hedge fund would buy a bottle of wine, the price of which would relate to cumulative performance. Everyone looked forward to that Friday stress release.
3. Every time you beat your high score, reward yourself immediately.

Gamification effortlessly accomplishes two things. It keeps us engaged in profitable activities and drives us to beat our high score.

Step 3: When to set a stop loss

There is a reason marriage contracts are called prenuptial and not postnuptial agreements. As soon as we enter a position, emotions kick in. We are no longer spectators. We are in the race and our inner idiot is in the driver's seat. The best time to set a stop loss is five minutes before entering a trade. Secondly, the risk budget determines the position size. The stop loss is a variable in the equation. If you do not set a limit on how much you can afford to lose, you will probably end up losing a lot more than you should.

A stop loss is not a story. Some discretionary market participants claim they will change their view when the story changes. The problem is that we are not impartial judges. We always strive to align our actions with our beliefs. Discomfort arises when our actions cease to match our thoughts. This is called *cognitive dissonance*. We are left with a simple alternative: re-align our actions with our beliefs, or change our views to match the new facts. While the former is the logical choice, we regrettably often opt for the latter. When the price goes against us, the easier alternative is to change the story we tell ourselves. By the time the story changes, our original thesis has long gone down the wrong path of evolution. A simple manifestation of this phenomenon is our attitude toward loss-making positions. We intellectually know that roughly half our trades will fail, yet we emotionally behave as if we must be 100% right all the time. In execution-trader English, this is called hubris.

An effective nudge for discretionary market participants is to assign a budget to each trade at the onset of a trade. Past that budget, commit to halving the position. If the trade subsequently works, profits will compensate realized losses. If it continues to deteriorate, it becomes easier to deal with a small position than a high stake one. A stop loss is a budget management exercise. Therefore, it is a price. Commit to writing it down alongside entry cost and price. Do not trust your brain with keeping score. Your inner idiot will renegotiate and trick you into making a stupid mistake.

Step 4: Pre-mortem: the vaccine against overconfidence

Post-mortem analysis is a popular topic in the financial services industry. In financial creole, it usually refers to the bureaucratically sterile ritual of management going through your past trades with the impeccable accuracy of hindsight. If there are two takeaways from this entire book, pre-mortems should be one of them. A pre-mortem is the ultimate antidote to overconfidence. A technique invented by psychologist Gary Klein, the pre-mortem method involves moving forward in time and visualizing the decision you are about to make as ending in failure.

Optimism usually peaks before entry. No-one thinks about divorce while proudly walking up to the altar. As we place an order, our inner idiot sings some toxic rationalization like: "Of course it is going to be a winner, otherwise, why would I make that trade in the first place? Am I that stupid?" Unfortunately, the cold statistical reality confirms that, "Yes, we are that stupid." Even though our long-term win rate is below 50%, we predictably behave as if every trade is going to be a winner.

Practice this exercise for every trade: Just before placing an order, imagine it will be a loser that will have to be stopped out. Visualize yourself closing the trade at a loss. Feel the drain on your emotional capital. Use all your senses to make this visualization as vivid as possible: a bad taste in your mouth, tunnel vision, sweaty palms, helplessness, a deadly inner dialog. Now, what would you do differently? Adjust your position size and send the order. This technique may seem masochistic, but it accomplishes two things:

- It ensures conservative position-sizing: If you enter a trade expecting it to fail, you will take smaller bets. You will also stay away from illiquid stock picks. You will be a better risk manager.

- It allows us to pre-process our grief. We normally expect trades to work. When they don't, we grieve our way to liquidation. Following Elisabeth Kübler-Ross's classic five stages of grief, we waste time, energy, and money bargaining with the inevitable. If you make a trade expecting it to work and it does not, it reinforces learned helplessness. If you expect every trade to fail, those that work will be pleasant surprises. Those that fail will perform as expected. Thus, the pre-mortem removes the emotional toll. Pre-packaging your grief allows you to be more surgical about losses.

As much as the secret to a happy life is to accept death as a daily companion, the paradox of making money in the markets is to accept losses and move on.

Step 5: Executing stop losses: forgiving ourselves for mistakes

"Pain is inevitable, suffering is optional."

– *Rande Howell*

A stop loss is just like any other trade. The meaning we assign to it can however be devastating. Every time you beat yourself up over a stop loss, you deprive yourself of the lesson.

Recent studies on self-forgiveness suggest that students who were taught self-forgiveness techniques improved their learning capabilities and did better over time. People who forgive themselves when they have trespassed their own boundaries tend to learn from their mistakes. Those who do not forgive themselves deny themselves the benefit of learning from their mistakes. The paradox is that by punishing our fallibility, we condemn ourselves to repeat our mistakes. Instead, be kind to yourself. Soothe yourself as if you were talking to your child.

Here's how it helps:

- The more you forgive yourself, the less daunting executing stop losses becomes.
- The easier it is to execute stop losses, the easier it is to make new trades.
- The smoother the execution, the better the performance.

Bottom line: Forgive your mistakes, and you'll be a better portfolio manager, and better at enduring the hardship of the markets.

Step 6: What the Zeigarnik effect can teach us about executing stop losses

Bluma Zeigarnik was a psychologist living in Vienna in the early part of the 20th century. As she was enjoying a coffee, she noticed a waiter who could remember the orders of all patrons with impressive accuracy. On the way home, she realized she had forgotten her scarf and returned to the establishment. However, while the waiter could effortlessly memorize all outstanding orders, he did not recall seeing her half an hour ago. This led her to a momentous discovery of how our brain deals with incomplete tasks. Unfinished business (in this case, a pending order) tends to linger on our mind while completed tasks (a customer who has paid and left) quickly get forgotten.

At any point in time, our portfolios have problem children. Those always occupy more mental space than their fair share. They always linger on our minds until we finally muster the courage to kick them out. Now, have you ever noticed that a week or two later, you can barely remember the names of the positions that bothered you so much? This is the Zeigarnik effect applied to portfolio management: out of sight, out of mind. Swiftly dealing with problem children accomplishes two things: it protects your financial capital from further erosion. More importantly, it frees up mental space and protects your emotional capital from spiraling down into self-flagellation.

The Zeigarnik effect is a powerful incentive to execute stop losses. The last thing you want is to allow small losses to gangrene into full-scale blow-ups. Executing a stop loss is never an easy decision. If you look back at all the losses along the way, you can safely conclude that nothing catastrophic happened. In fact, you are still there, partly because you made those difficult decisions. So, next time you hesitate to pull the trigger, tell yourself that it may seem difficult now, but you will get over it and feel refreshed by next week.

Now that we have upgraded our inner game, let's work on our outer game and make those statistics look good!

The science of the stop loss

"Profits look big only to the extent losses are kept small."

– Michael Martin

Most market participants have some vague idea that losses hurt the bottom line. They have just never really visualized the damage. Losses work geometrically against you. A 50% drawdown means you will have to make 100% profit just to get back to break even. As an example: someone buys a stock at 100. You take the other side of the trade and escort it down to 50. The tourist holds on all this time because the long-term story is still intact. That obstinate amateur will have to clock 100% to make it back to break-even.

The innocuous graph below shows something powerful enough to convince any rational market participant that keeping losses small is the only way to go. The lower line represents drawdowns from peak to -90%. The upper line represents the percentage growth needed to recoup those drawdowns. At -10% drawdown, the account must grow 11.2% to get back to par. At -20%, it takes 25% to make those losses back. At -90%, it takes 10 times growth to recoup losses. Therefore, most of the techniques we will see in the coming chapters have to do with losses, which geometrically deplete the account. Next time you want to hold on to a loser, pull up this chart as a reminder that the price to pay for being right is going broke:

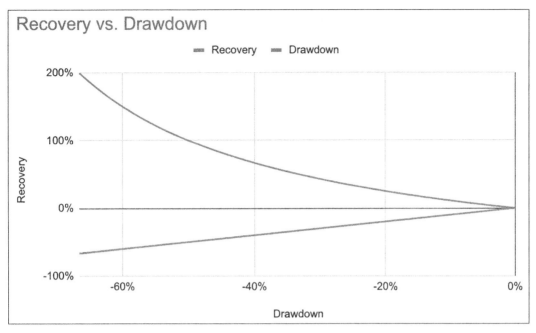

Figure 7.2: Drawdown levels and the percentage gains required to recoup losses

The ability to set and honor stop losses is what separates professional short sellers from tourists. It takes practice to know how to place a stop loss so as to minimize whipsaws and maximize risk-reward. It takes humility and courage to honor stop loss after stop loss and still take the next trade.

The stop loss is the most important variable in the trading edge formula. It has a direct impact on three variables: win rate %, loss rate %, and average loss %. By comparison, entry directly affects none of these variables. Stop loss also plays a vital role in bet-sizing and trading frequency: the tighter the stop loss, the bigger the bets, but also the higher the trading frequency.

Market participants are sometimes skeptical of stop losses. However, stop losses are like sushi knives. You will cut yourself if you do not know how to use them. No-one in their right mind would ever blame a sushi knife for a self-inflicted cut. By the same token, the only people who cut themselves with stop losses are tourists who have not done their homework. Here are three simple principles.

Stop losses are a logical signal-to-noise issue

Stop losses are vastly misunderstood. They are not part of daily trading decisions. Waiting for a stop loss to be triggered is a highly inefficient way to exit a position. You do not want your airbag to burst at every traffic light. Ideally, you would like to reduce, exit, or even reverse a position before a stop loss is triggered.

Think of a stop loss as the signal and volatility as noise. If you place your signal within the noise band, all you are going to get in return is noise. Markets are noisy. There are usually a few false starts before a major move. If you place your stop loss in the volatility band, you are likely to get whipsawed a few times before getting it right. This will rapidly erode your capital base. You will need big moves to make up for all the previous small losses.

You want to place your stop loss at a point where there is a clear signal that either your thesis is invalidated, or that there could be a valid entry on the other side. This can be done using volatility measures such as **average true range** (**ATR**) or standard deviation. These signals can also be logical inflections like a few bid/ask spreads above or below a high/low.

Stop losses are a statistical issue

Novice traders like to protect their profits, so they set tight stop losses. The tighter the stop loss, the smaller the distance to the stop loss, therefore a bigger position size can be afforded for the same risk budget. This results in a large average position size and a low average loss, but a high loss rate. Tight stop losses tend to be easily triggered. This also increases trading frequency. Failure comes from the accumulation of small losses. For example, if it takes three trials to get it right, then the price has to move three times the distance to the stop loss just to maintain a positive **gain expectancy** (**GE**).

Veteran traders get the privilege from a good night's sleep. They have come to understand that the markets need wiggle room. They set their stop losses a bit wider. This results in smaller average position size, larger average losses, higher win rates, lower loss rates, and lower trading frequency. The table below summarises the effect of stop losses on GE:

	Tight	**Loose**
Win Rate	Lower	Higher
Loss Rate	Higher	Lower
Trading Frequency	Higher	Lower
Position Size	Bigger	Smaller

The stop loss is by far the single most important variable in the GE equation. Knowing how to place a stop loss will therefore have a formidable impact on any strategy. In comparison, stock picking (that is, entry) only has an indirect impact on win rate and loss rate.

Moral of the story: give the market enough wiggle room to stretch its legs, but not too much to run away. There may be a mathematical optimum, but again market conditions vary over time. Volatility is not uniform.

Stop losses are a budgetary issue

Stop losses are used to calculate position size. The farther away from entry cost, the smaller the position should be and vice versa. This will have implications on performance, volatility, and stock selection.

Wide stop losses warrant small positions. Those will generate lower performance with lower volatility. Volatile stocks tend to have wide stop losses, which lead to small positions. When it is time to rank signals by position size to allocate capital, low-volatility stocks will systematically be prioritized.

When switching sides from long to short, it is fair to expect some pushback from the market. Anchoring a stop loss at a level that would invalidate your thesis is the equivalent of taking a small exploratory position. If it does not pan out, the damage will be minimal. If it works, this small position will finance subsequent campaigns.

Techniques to improve your trading edge

Next, we will look at techniques to improve your trading edge, which is the main focus of this chapter. We will start by considering how we shorten the left tail, and bring the peak of losses closer to breaking even.

Technique 1: The game of two halves: how to cut losers, ride winners, and maintain conviction while improving your trading edge

There is an unwritten rule in every hospital around the world: surgeons should not operate on their own family. There is no such thing as professional detachment when it comes to your own child. In the investment realm, however, fundamental discretionary market participants struggle with the idea of stop losses.

They are consistently asked to defend their convictions, yet expected to be surgical about their losses. They are forced to lose impartiality, but still required to maintain professional detachment. If they want to master the short selling game, discretionary participants will have to overcome their reluctance.

This powerful technique will help you achieve the impossible: cut your losers, run your winners, and maintain your conviction, while mechanically improving your trading edge. It is specifically designed for discretionary market participants who struggle with the idea of stop losses.

Dealing with today's losers is a lot easier than predicting tomorrow's winners. GE remains positive as long as losers are kept smaller than winners in aggregate. If you halve the losers that have lost half the average contribution, mechanically you win. In practice, this is how it is done:

1. Separate all positions between contributors and detractors.
2. Calculate the aggregate average contribution or average profit. Market participants with unusually long right tails may want to use the median instead of the mean.
3. Halve the weight of all detractors once they have lost half of the average contribution.

With the remaining open positions, only two things can happen:

1. Stocks turn around and start contributing. This will offset losses. Add a new tranche.
2. Positions continue to hurt. They only detract half as much and half as fast. More importantly, it is easier to be clinically detached with a smaller position than a big one.

The game of two halves offers a simple elegant solution to the oldest problem in fundamental investing. There is a fine line between conviction and obstination. Investors want managers to have conviction. Yet, they do not forgive obstination. Maritime gallantry is not in their pedigree. They do not want to sink with the ship. The game of two halves reconciles the demand for conviction with the need for action if a position starts to hurt. You display both conviction by keeping a portion open, and humility by paring down risk.

Secondly, this method follows the cycle of performance. When your style works, your average profit increases. You can afford more risk, taking on bigger positions and tolerating bigger losses too. When your style goes out of favor, average profit shrinks, thereby allowing for smaller losses, that is, smaller positions.

Thirdly, the trading edge mechanically improves: losses are kept smaller relative to profits. This method tilts the loss distribution into a right skew. It brings the mode, the peak of loss-making trades, closer to breaking even. In execution-trader English, when profits dwindle, shrink losses faster. Finally, it changes the definition of being right. This is no longer a binary outcome on the profitability of each individual idea. Being right is the observance of a process that will lead to higher aggregate profitability. In short, it no longer triggers the fight, flight, or freeze instinct, but activates the thinking brain. In this way, the game of two halves reduces stress and improves profitability.

Technique 2: Mitigate losses with a trailing stop

"You should always have a worst-case point. The only choice should be to get out quicker."

– Richard Dennis, turtle farmer

Positions are most vulnerable immediately after entry. Profitable trades take time to mature. Meanwhile, unprofitable ones are generally quick to crater. This time lag results in an erosion of the account balance. You may not be able to reduce the number of false positives, but you can still limit the damage by inserting a loss mitigation exit before reaching a stop loss. This is where a trailing stop loss comes in handy. A trailing stop is a mobile stop loss that moves along with the price. There are two objectives:

1. Reduce risk as the price moves favorably.
2. Give back as little profit as possible when the price starts to move in the other direction.

Trailing stop losses are not a panacea. They are effective for protecting profits but counterproductive for capturing long-term trends. This is especially true on the short side. A trailing stop loss might shake you out of a position prematurely before the market resumes its downward journey. Trailing stop losses should be used judiciously to rapidly reduce risk when trades are most vulnerable. The objective here is to take advantage of every favorable price move to reduce risk. This may adversely affect the win rate but it will result in lower average losses and smaller cumulative losses. This will tilt the mode of losses closer to breaking even.

Let's take a numerical example to illustrate the impact of a logical stop loss on position size, loss mitigation, trading edge, and the overall equity curve. Let's say the market prints another local high at 100, below the all-time high of 108. This looks like a ceiling. The current price level is around 98. You decide to enter a short position.

Let's draft a standard battle plan:

1. Set a fixed stop loss at the ceiling: If the market takes the all-time high, then it is obviously bullish.

2. Set a trailing stop loss: As a seasoned trader, you expect the high of 100 to be retested, so you initialize your trailing stop at 101, just above the local high.

3. Choose a stop loss to calculate your position size: You have the choice between the fixed and the trailing stop losses to calculate your position size.

4. Calculate your position size: Your current position sizing algorithm spits out a risk budget $100,000, which divided by the distance to the stop loss returns a number of shares. We will consider position sizing in more detail in the next chapter.

5. Set a target price for risk reduction: You detected the local high after it was printed and including slippage and transaction costs, your average price is 98. You set a target price at 95, at which point you will exit 3/4 of the position (to maintain a positive expectancy) and let the remainder go risk free. Should the market rally hard, you would still have time to cover.

Now, let's choose which stop loss to anchor your position size. Cases 1, 2, and 3 rely on the same signal. Case 1 assumes a signal is valid and will hold the position until proven wrong. Case 2 uses the trailing stop loss to aggressively capture profit. Case 3 assumes the signal is right but expects whipsaws:

- Case 1: No trailing stop loss: You set your stop loss at 108: 10,000 shares short. You assume that anything in between is noise and do not want to trade in and out.

- Case 2: Aggressive trailing stop: You calculate your position size from the 101-trailing stop: 33,000 shares short. You assume the signal is valid enough and want to capture as much profit as possible.

- Case 3: Exploratory position: You calculate your position size from 108 but set a trailing stop loss at 101: 10,000 shares short. Since there is little evidence that the market has turned bearish, as a prudent risk manager, you use the fixed stop loss to calculate your position size but use a trailing stop loss to protect your capital base.

It is fair to say that most market participants would choose either case 1 or case 2. Either set a stop and let the position run its course or work the trade are the two obvious choices. Let's say you entered at 98. Now that we are set, let's look at price action. The market nicely comes down to 96 before changing her mind and decides to push through the 108 level. The trailing stop loss has moved down to 99, therefore in cases 2 and 3, you close your position at 99. In case 1, you close at 108.

	Case 1	Case 2	Case 3
Risk Budget	100,000	100,000	100,000
Cost	98	98	98
Position Stop Loss	108	101	108
Shares	-10,000	-33,333	-10,000
Exit Price	108	99	99
P&L	-100,000	-33,333	-10,000

Let's analyze all cases:

- Case 1: This is the base case. The signal was effectively a false positive. You win some, you learn some. *C'est la vie.*

- Case 2: When calculating position size from the trailing stop, the stop loss is effectively anchored within the noise band. It is an assumption on both the statistical validity of the signal and the market regime. For the strategy to be effective, the market must trend down. Should the market trade sideways, there will be quite a few failed attempts, which as a cumulative effect will erode the capital base.

- Case 3: First, the fixed stop loss was set at a logical position. If the price makes a new high, then the market has obviously decided to move back into bull territory. This is congruent with case 1. Secondly, the trailing stop loss protects the position when it is most vulnerable. Every favorable price move reduces risk. When it does not work, a big portion of the risk is crystallized into a small loss close to break-even. It does not develop into a full-blown loss as in case 1. Thirdly, when sizing the position against the ceiling, you have effectively taken a small exploratory position. You have put a chip on the table, but you are not ready to call the market's bluff just yet. If it correctly detects a trend, the initial position can be topped up. If not, losses will be contained. Case 3 is an effective way to deal with randomness and protect capital. By comparison, in case 2, every failed attempt will dent your capital. Case 2 is precisely the reason why trend followers end up giving back their gains in sideways markets.

There is no right and wrong here. The objective is not to impart you with a strategy you could just code away, but to make you think in terms of P&L distribution. The preceding example is one of the many ways to deal with randomness, that is, reducing the drag of false positives. The objective is to bring the peak of losses as close as possible to break even. For discretionary market participants, the "game of two halves" outlined in future chapters is a systematic way to keep losses small versus profits.

Technique 3: the game of two-thirds: time exit and how to trim freeloaders

If you were the landlord of a building, would you allow some tenants to go rent-free? After a few delinquent months, you would evict the freeloaders as it hurts profitability. This common-sense approach does not transfer to the stock market. Every portfolio has its fair share of stale positions that are late on rent.

A classic misconception is that performance tanks because of a few big blow-ups. Deeper analysis reveals that the cumulative weight of freeloaders puts a drag on performance that eventually fails to compensate for a few hits. A "sub-optimal alpha" often happens because a bunch of "has-beens" still clog the portfolio.

The most common type is the "once we were warriors" veterans. They used to contribute but have gone nowhere for a while. They are particularly difficult to spot because of the embedded P&L and emotional attachment. This is an interesting and arguably perverse manifestation of the anchoring bias. When entry cost is far from the current price, we dismiss the current lackluster returns as temporary. In many cases, we should nurture this detachment for all the stocks in the portfolio. Yet, the same "laissez-faire" attitude breeds dangerous complacency. Market participants sometimes end up giving back a lot of their paper profits before taking action.

A simple solution is to introduce time-weighted returns. If a stock has failed to earn its keep over a period of time, its weight should be reduced. This is a simple three-step process:

1. Decide on the duration. When in doubt, calculate the annual turnover and divide it by 3, taking the first third as the duration. For example, a turnover of 1 would yield a 4-month period.

2. Calculate stock returns (not performance attribution) over the period in step 1. Divide it into four quartiles. Concentrate on the third quartile. The first and fourth quartiles stand out. So, they will be dealt with either way. Stocks in the second quartile are not stellar contributors, but they still pay their rent. The problem with stocks in the third quartile is they do not stand out. They are dead money walking, slowly dragging performance down.

3. Halve the weight of all the stocks in the third quartile. Complicated rules are easily transgressed. So, keep it simple: no contribution, halve the allocation.

Two things can happen thereafter:

1. Stocks start to perform again: add a new tranche.
2. Stocks continue to languish or even underperform. Realized profit will appear prescient. It is always easier to deal with a smaller position.

Think of your portfolio as your house. The longer you live in one place, the more stuff you accumulate over time. There are always small things you keep for sentimental value. If you are superstitious or sentimentally attached to your baggy old university sweater, for instance, chances are you also a "sentimental value" investor in your professional capacity. The longer stocks have been in a portfolio, the stickier they become. Our inner idiot always finds ways to rationalize old positions with mental shortcuts such as "what do I buy instead?", or "this has been such a great performer, it will come back." This game provides objective rules to overcome the initial reluctance. The first step is always the hardest. Reducing a stale position once makes it easier to deal with it the next time.

Secondly, it fluidifies the portfolio. As the market adage goes, "you are only as good as your next idea." Forcing stale positions out makes room for fresh ideas. Market participants subject to **First In, First Out (FIFO)** rules are understandably reluctant to let go of old positions. Another way to deal with stale positions is to use options strategies over the underlying cash positions. Bear in mind that over time you will be wrong more often than right, so dealing with today's losses will make tomorrow's profits look a lot bigger. Winners take care of themselves. Your job is to take care of losers. Now that we have dealt with the losing side of the distribution, we will next consider the profit side of the equation.

Technique 4: The profit side: reduce risk and compound returns by taking small profits

"That all you got, George?"

– Muhammad Ali, The Greatest of All Time

The idea of closing a portion of a position to reduce risk is somewhat foreign to market participants coming from the long side. They want to ride their winners through "ups and downs." On the short side, "ups" are called bear market rallies and short squeezes. One day, market participants sit comfortably on a short, humming "never let you go" with the rich baritone voice of Barry White.

The next day, they are squeezed on their tiptoes whistling "staying alive" through their teeth with the high falsetto pitch of Barry Gibb. The following technique goes one step beyond immunity to bear market rallies. Unlike tourist short sellers, this technique will teach you how to welcome short squeezes.

If you do not take money off the table, you will be psychologically on your back foot when the inevitable bear market rally hits. Profits will quickly evaporate, and your inner idiot will trick you into covering the position to protect whatever profit is left. By doing so, a short cover will add fuel to the rally, thereby warranting an unfavorable execution. On the other hand, if you reduce your exposure in advance, you will be in a much better position to weather the rally. You will have realized some profit, reduced your risk, and are guaranteed to break even on the trade even if it hits your original stop loss. The toll on your emotional capital is in direct proportion to position size. Now, you have money in the bank. You have a small bet that barely dents the P&L and may finance subsequent campaigns.

Taking money off the table may reduce risk, yet it also cuts profit potential short. Meanwhile, trades stopped out cost a full risk unit each time. If not done properly, GE is bound to rapidly turn negative.

Let's go back to GE to solve this equation:

$$Expectancy = win\_rate \times avg\_win - (1 - win\_rate) \times abs(avg\_loss)$$

Next, let's remove the win and loss rates and focus solely on break even, when *R = cost – stop loss*, *X = price – cost*, and *N = fraction of the position to be closed*:

$$avg\_win - abs(avg\_loss) = 0$$

$$avg\_win = abs(avg\_loss)$$

$$X \times N \times R = R$$

$$N = 1/X$$

The portion of the position to be closed to achieve break even is the inverse of the distance to cost expressed in R (distance from cost to stop loss). If the price has traveled 1.1R, 1.5R, or 2R, then close 91%, 67%, or 50%, of your position respectively:

Figure 7.3: Fraction of the position to be closed as price moves favorably

Simply said, the earlier a position is reduced, the bigger the portion that needs to be closed out and vice versa. It then becomes a dance with chance: should we let positions run a little longer or should we cash in while we can? When we reintroduce the win rate using this fractional exit, the GE equation now looks like this:

$$GE = X \times N \times R \times win\% - 1 \times R \times loss\%$$

$$GE = X \times 1/X \times R \times win\% - 1 \times R \times loss\%$$

$$GE = win\% - loss\%$$

We originally removed *win%* and *loss%* to concentrate on breaking even. This simply says that the earlier a position is closed, the smaller the remainder. Now, the market is not always kind to its participants. Think of every position as two separate trades: one big coupon and one small lottery ticket. The first trade needs to have a high probability of >50%. It is short in duration and distance. The second one is a risk-free lottery. Sometimes it will go on forever, sometimes it will be closed at a cost.

Here is an additional tip, also learned the hard way. The win rate is not constant. In order to break even and maintain at least a neutral trading edge, you can either take out a bigger portion, or close earlier. You take out 75% instead of 67% or you cover at 1.5R instead of 2R. The break-even formula then becomes:

$$GE = X \times win\%/loss\%$$

If *loss%* > *win%*, simply close a bigger portion or bail early. Making money is now reduced to having a win rate higher than the loss rate. Now that we know the relationship between distance and partial exit, let's compare the GE between a single exit and scaling out.

Let's take a simple numerical example. Let's assume our strategy has a 60% win rate at 1R, or 100% of the distance from cost to stop loss. For the sake of the exercise, let's pretend the win rate decreases by 1% for every 0.1R increase: the bigger the move, the lower the frequency. This is the black line in the chart below. The decrease in the win rate is linear (1% for every 0.1R):

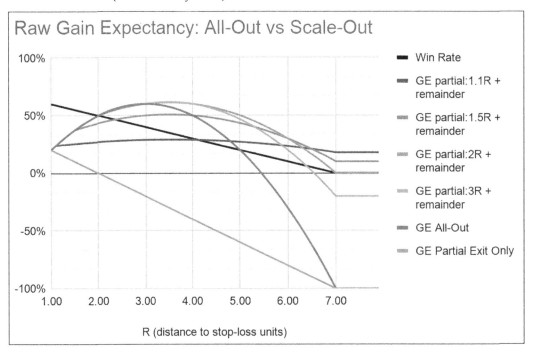

Figure 7.4: Scale-out GE

Let's calculate GE, assuming we close 100% of the position. This is the long arc line labeled GE All-Out. GE follows an arc. Big moves are rare, and eventually fail to compensate for losses. In this case, break even stands at a 16% win rate with a 5.4R risk/reward ratio.

Next, let's calculate GE for the fraction of the trade closed. This is the GE Partial Exit Only line. It follows the win rate in a linear fashion. The probability of success drops below 50% as the price moves beyond 2R. GE of the sole partial exit mechanically turns negative. Note that this partial exit is there solely as a visual reference as the remainder is indefinitely open. Trend-following strategies generally have a default negative GE. Big moves are rare. Loss control is really the only way to ensure long-term GE remains positive.

Finally let's calculate GE with one partial exit and the remainder. We set four target prices at 1.1R, 1.5R, 2R, and 3R. We close 91%, 67%, 50%, and 33%, respectively. The remainder is closed. A partial exit significantly improves GE. The 1.1R is the most conservative. It has the lowest return potential, but it has a built-in robust GE. 1.5R has a higher return potential but a lower residual GE. 2R and 3R have terminal negative GE in this example. Past a certain point, the remainder is akin to a lottery ticket.

Risk reduction follows two rules:

1. Win rate > loss rate: there will be times when the win rate is temporarily lower. Then, either close earlier to improve the win rate, or close a bigger portion to reduce the risk.
2. Target price > 1R: Profits must be bigger than losses.

The moral of the story is that market participants are better off closing a bigger portion below 2R. This provides a robust GE. Robust expectancies warrant bigger position sizes.

However, this form of guerilla trading does not come to mind naturally when designing robust strategies. The counterargument to a partial exit is that stop losses are bound to be costly. Closing a trade early cuts its profit potential. Meanwhile, a failure will cost a full risk budget. It seems like the trading edge is bound to be negative. Besides, scaling out intuitively feels like leaving money on the table. In fact, the vast majority of market participants would rather concentrate on improving their signal than work on their order management.

Most market participants operate from an all-in/all-out mode. They stroll in, sometimes top up, and then stampede out all at once, so exiting is a single event. Market participants may find themselves unwilling to drastically reduce their positions just as they start to work. Remember that we are playing an infinite game. The objective is to engineer a robust GE. This leads us to a variation on the scale-out technique called Kelly scale-out combo (for the lack of better word). A more aggressive variation on this theme is to take advantage of the high win rate to supersize positions.

As we saw throughout the book, the exit policy determines the strategy type. Trend followers who let their stocks run have infrequent big wins. Contrarians have frequent small wins. Since the exit determines the shape of the distribution, it is possible to combine the attributes of both by simply scaling out.

	Mean Reversion	Trend Following	Hybrid
Win Rate	High	Low	High
Volatility	Low	High	Low
Left Tail	Long	Short	Short
Right Tail	Short	Long	Long
Skew	Negative	Positive	Positive

The concept is to enter big, close a big portion of the trade, and let the remainder run risk free. A high-probability early partial exit brings the mode, the peak number of trades, to the profit side. With a win rate above 50%, the position size could even be supersized using a formula like a **fractional Kelly**, or Ralph Vince's **Optimal F**. Optimal F is another powerful position sizing algorithm that takes into account the largest drawdown. This warrants big position sizes. These are quick trades. They rapidly compound profits at a geometric rate. This means we get in big, make a quick buck, close a big chunk, then put that money back in circulation for the next trade, and so on.

Let's go back to our hypothetical example to explain the process. The assumption is that the win rate recedes by 1% for every additional 0.1 gain. The Kelly criterion is a bet-sizing algorithm that we will soon revisit in the next chapter. Exiting at 1.1R, the win rate is 59%, which warrants 18% risk per trade.

R (Distance to Stop Loss Units)	Win Rate	Kelly All-Out	Partial Exit Quantity	Remainder
1.00	60%	20%	100%	0%
1.10	59%	18%	91%	9%
1.20	58%	16%	83%	17%
1.30	57%	14%	77%	23%
1.40	56%	12%	71%	29%
1.50	55%	10%	67%	33%
1.60	54%	8%	63%	38%
1.70	53%	6%	59%	41%
1.80	52%	4%	56%	44%

1.90	51%	2%	53%	47%
2.00	50%	0%	50%	50%
2.10	49%	-2%	48%	52%

Let those percentages sink in for one second. What if "go big AND go home... early" was a winning strategy after all? For example, suppose you set a target price at 1.5R. The win rate is a comfortable 55%, so according to the Kelly column in the preceding table, you can afford 10% risk per trade. All you have to do is close 67% of the position at 1.5R, then reset the stop loss to cost. The remaining 33% is a risk-free lottery ticket. Sometimes you clock 2R, sometimes you pocket 5R. Worst case scenario, you close at cost.

Let's recap to reinforce the argument. The first trade is a short-duration, high win rate, big-size position, that will mimic the mean reversion distribution. This trade feels like clipping coupons, hence its name. The second trade is a small lottery ticket. Once the first trade is closed, reset the stop loss to cost (absolute or relative) and ride it into the sunset. This trade inherently has more random returns, hence its nickname, the lottery ticket.

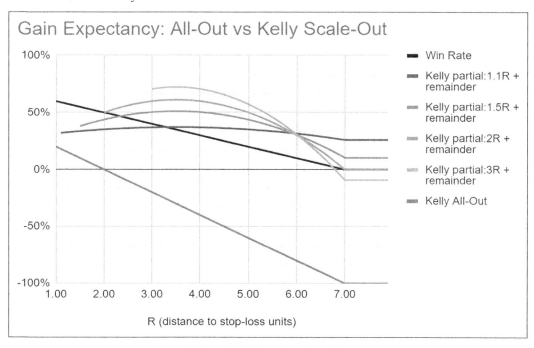

Figure 7.5: Kelly scale-out combo

This graph builds on the previous one. It includes the position size. Remember that investors will always subconsciously react to drawdowns even though they consciously say they want returns. So, closing early is not only prudent, it is the key to raising assets under management. The shape of the P&L distribution of a combined mean reversion and trend-following strategy looks like this:

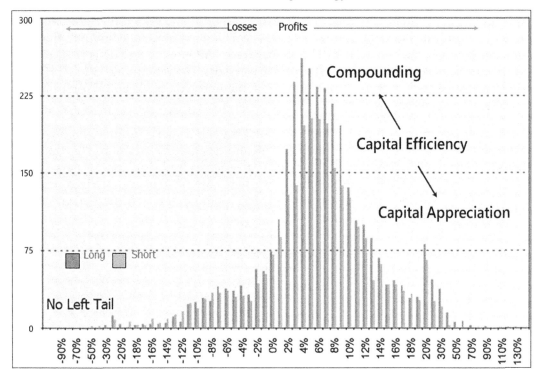

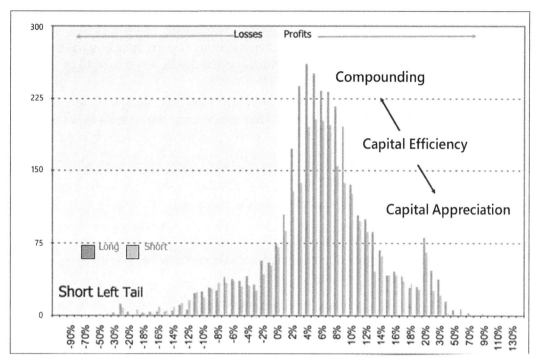

Figure 7.6: Combined mean reversion and trend-following strategy P&L graph

The mode of trades is on the profit side (the win rate is high). This is consistent with a mean reversion strategy. The distribution of trades is skewed to the right. This is the right-tail lottery ticket of trend followers.

This is a powerful way to exploit a high win rate and the law of large numbers. This compounds the capital base, mops up failures, and subsidizes future trading campaigns. Since there are losing streaks, exposure constraints, and above all else investors' peaceful sleep to preserve, it is not advisable to trade big Kelly sizes. As we saw earlier, investors pay less attention to returns than drawdowns, so it is always wise to err on the conservative side. In the following chapters, we will see a dynamic fractional Kelly that will help mitigate drawdown risk.

Let's recap what scaling-out, that is, disciplined profit-taking, accomplishes:

- Compound small profits: mean reversion market participants make their money by compounding small profits. Risk reduction synthetically does the same thing. Small profits compound quickly.

- Secondly, partisans of the "Short and Hope" strategy always claim they can see past short-term volatility. That is true until their first encounter with volatility. If you have closed a portion of the position, reduced risk, crystallized some profit, and ensured that you will break even on the trade, you will be in a much better mental state to weather a bear market rally. In practice, you will probably be relieved to finally see a bear market rally to get back in the game and slap on another tranche.

- Thirdly, it gives another mode and a positive skew to the profit side of the P&L distribution. This profit mode is there to compensate for the mode on the loss side. In other words, those cumulative small profits are there to absorb the bulk of the losses.

This is probably not what you had in mind when you were thinking about building a trading edge. Clipping coupons is laborious and unsexy, but it is also an efficient way to tilt a trading edge in your favor, and rapidly compound profits.

In fact, if you diligently practice this risk-reduction method enough times, you will train your brain to look forward to those bear market rallies as opportunities to ride your winners. You will effectively be on the offensive when everyone else plays defense.

Technique 5: Elongate the right tail

"You don't have to swing hard to hit a home run. If you got the timing, it will go."

– Yogi Berra

Trailing stop losses are great to protect capital, but they only work in perfect conditions. As such, they have a limited shelf life. Once risk is reduced, keeping a trailing stop loss on might trigger a premature exit. The objective of a trailing stop loss is only to tilt the P&L distribution closer to break even. Now that the remainder runs risk free, you might want to deactivate the trailing stop and rely on your fixed stop loss. Volatility is high on the short side. Give some wiggle room to the market until it is time to re-enter.

We all struggle with the final goodbye. We become "sentimental value investors" with our winners. We are all inclined to delay the inevitable. Besides, the fundamental news flow remains supportive of our thesis long after the price action has started to move in the opposite direction. Round trips are not uncommon.

What market participants really need is an objective signal that the trend has ended. The Floor/Ceiling approach is stable enough to keep market participants firmly saddled through markets rodeos. As a general principle, the final exit should be a reversal of the trend: the stocks stay in the portfolio, just switching sides.

Conventional wisdom says that you cannot write the "book of exits" until you have written the "book of entries." Experience on the short side suggests otherwise. If you build your escape routes first, then entries are just sliding probabilities. For example, entering after a bear market rally rolls over has both a higher probability of success and a bigger position size than if you wait for a new low. Exits are when paper profits turn to real money. However, in our look at the final technique, we will discuss everyone's favorite topic: entry.

Technique 6: Re-entry: Ride your winners by laddering your positions

"You, me, or nobody is gonna hit as hard as life. But it ain't about how hard you hit. It's about how hard you can get hit and keep moving forward."

– Rocky Balboa, the Italian Stallion

In the early 1980s, turtle traders made hundreds of millions despite a paltry 34% win rate. Their secret sauce: they added to their winners. One of the major differences between long-only participants and short sellers is the necessity to periodically replenish successful positions. Shorts shrink as they become profitable. So, the all-in/all-out methodology that prevails on the long side fails on the short one. At some point, you will need to replenish your successful shorts. When you top up your winners, your win rate and average wins go up, which mechanically improves your trading edge.

Re-entry is really where the strategy reveals its acceleration potential. You have already qualified winners, banked some money, and reduced risk. The bear market rally has rolled over below your stop loss. Buying pressure is exhausted. There is now sufficient evidence that a bearish trend is under way. Tourists have been flushed out. Borrow might even be marginally easier to locate. The stars are aligned for a glorious round 2.

Unfortunately, scaling in and out of cash positions is not possible for market participants who are guilty of **TWA**, "**Trading While American**." The US has put in place an inventory valuation method known as the FIFO rule, which specifies that all positions must be depleted from the oldest to the newest one. This effectively deters US participants from trading around their positions.

Before we go any further, here's an important note on scaling in during a bear sell-off. As the market tanks, it is tempting to scale in. However, most market participants are in this game to buy, not sell. This puts short sellers at a natural disadvantage. Assume that someone somewhere has been waiting for this weakness as an opportunity to buy. This means that once selling pressure is exhausted, long participants will push prices up and trigger short stop losses. Second tranches at a lower price are likely to get caught in the crossfire. The good news is: if a short position is validated, then the market will give you another chance to enter when the next bear rally rolls over. Patience is a profitable virtue.

First things first, reset your fixed stop loss on the original position. There are several logical places. The more aggressive version is to place it above the peak of the current bear market rally level. That will protect profits but will be vulnerable to volatility shocks. The most conservative version is to place the stop loss at the previous cost. Somewhere in between is the "French stop loss." Markets go up and down in swing highs and lows. This gives the market some additional wiggle room. It will warrant a smaller position size. You might even give up a bigger portion of your profits if the trend reverts, but you will sleep much better at night. This stop loss delayed by one swing is fashionably late, hence its nickname, the "French stop loss."

Once risk is reduced on the first tranche, it is time to re-enter using the same strategy as before. The best time to re-enter a short position is after a bear market rally or a short squeeze. Tourists have been forced to cover. Buying pressure is exhausting. If the current top is lower than the one preceding the previous entry, then sellers are still in charge. Conditions for re-entry do not need to be as stringent as for the initial entry. Three criteria must however be met for reentry:

1. The trend is your friend: the current entry price must be lower than the previous one. Market participants are sometimes tempted to re-enter at a higher cost than the previous entry. This is greed rearing its ugly face. It will work until it does not. One day, it will feel like the morning after tequila shots: "At the time, it seemed like a good idea." A higher entry price may be an early indication that the market is about to consolidate or reverse.

2. Borrow utilization must be below 50%: Borrow utilization is defined as the shares available for borrowing divided by shares already borrowed. It is the simplest canary in the coalmine and most robust expression of supply and demand. As long holders liquidate, the supply of shares available for borrowing dries up. Meanwhile, as short sellers pile in, demand increases. Short sellers make money by riding the tail of long sellers. When borrow utilization rises above 50%, it means that long holders have left the building and that the only players left are tourists. Adding another tranche as a trade gets crowded is asking for trouble. Instead of riding the tail of long sellers, you will be trapped in a petri dish of short sellers. On the long side, fresh buyers bid the price up. On the short side, the supply of new short sellers is limited by the availability of borrow. They therefore do not have the ability to push prices down, but they add to the selling pressure, making stocks prone to short squeezes.

3. Depreciate risk for every new position: Adding to an existing position is called pyramiding. Remember that trends revert eventually. The probability of trend reversal increases as trends mature.

Reset the fixed stop loss for all open positions to a "French stop loss," that is, somewhere close to the cost of the previous entry. When you lower the stop loss on older positions, no matter what happens next, they will be profitable. This embedded P&L will subsidize newer and riskier positions. Adding to successful positions increases both the win rate and average win.

All good things eventually come to an end. It would be a pity to work so hard on a trade, only to be squeezed or shaken out.

Final exit: the right tail

Trend followers would love to ride their positions into the sunset. Sometimes they do, on the long side. On the short side, it takes a little more finesse to clock a 2-3 bagger when downside potential is capped at 100%.

The hardest task is to let go of a successful trade. There is always this nagging thought that this could be temporary and there could be more juice. There is also the fear of giving back too much performance. This can be broken down into two separate problems. Market participants need to have an objective way of knowing when a trend has ended. Secondly, if the wobbliness was just temporary, then they need a way to get back in.

In *Chapter 5*, *Regime Definition*, we described the floor and ceiling method. The rationale is simple. A bull market ends when all swing highs are below the peak (ceiling). A bear market ends when swing lows are above the trough (floor). The floor and ceiling method is an objective way to define when a trend has ended. Exit all your short positions when a new floor is printed. Remember that you will give back some performance. With this method, you are not trying to time the top, but you are paying for confirmation that a trend has ended.

Re-entry after a final exit

Markets do not always behave as expected, and sometimes you will be shaken out of a position. If markets start to perform desirably again, you will want to get back in. The conditions imposed for the initial entry are unlikely to be met again. For example, if you shorted an expensive **Price to Book** (**PBR**) of 2, current valuations might have come down to just about fair by now. Consequently, you would not enter the trade. You therefore need something simple and robust enough to get back in.

This is where the floor and ceiling method comes in. If you were shaken out because the price printed a floor, but then subsequently made a ceiling, then get in. Set your stop loss at the ceiling level, verify that borrowing is still reasonably priced, and off you go. The big takeaway about shorts is that their descent is not always linear. Stocks drop from overpriced to fair valuations. They sometimes lure long participants, only to resume their descent into the short selling heaven of value traps. Give yourself the flexibility to re-enter.

Trend followers account for the overwhelming majority of market participants. Next, let's see how mean reversion participants are a rare breed with their own set of challenges.

How to tilt your trading edge if your dominant style is mean reversion

"Grant me the serenity to cut the losers,
The courage to ride the winners,
And the wisdom to know the difference."

– The trader's serenity prayer

Mean reversion strategies have a negative skew with a mode on the profit side: short right and long left tails. The solution is to shorten the left tail and elongate the right one.

Mean reversion market participants are naturally gifted at short selling. They short on a high and cover at a low. They are also better equipped to deal with sideways markets. The main danger however is to ignore the regime. While it is tempting to short rich valuations, or overbought RSI, stocks on an uptrend will often continue on their ascending trajectory. For example, RSI will travel from 40 to 80 on bullish stocks, and 60 to 20 on bearish ones. Overbought and oversold conditions are usually signs of continuation.

The solution is to wait for the regime to rotate from bullish to sideways or bearish to start shorting. Incorporate regime definition methods such as Floor/Ceiling or moving average crossover in the analysis to reduce false positives.

Losses

The risk associated with mean reversion strategies is in the tails: a few titanic losses. Mean reversion market participants do not like stop losses. They are sometimes triggered before stocks start to behave as expected. The win rate drops, average loss rises, expectancy tanks. One approach is to have wider stop losses. They will warrant smaller positions but they will also prevent devastating losses.

Mean reversion market participants are often tempted to add to losing positions on the premise that they will eventually revert. For example, if a stock was expected to revert at 2.5 standard deviations from the mean, at 4 standard deviations, it would even be more attractive. This may work most of the time, but when it does not, losses can be devastating. LTCM tried that. Martingale works until it does not.

A statistically more robust yet counterintuitive approach is to reduce size when market participants would feel like adding. Assume that past a certain point, inefficiencies will not correct but persist. If instead of adding to a loser at 4 standard deviations, the position was reduced, then either it would revert and offset the losses or it would detract less thereafter. Either way, it would tilt the skew of losses toward breaking even.

Another practical reason why market participants should reduce instead of adding to losing positions is the deterioration of GE. Adding to a loser directly increases the loss rate and average loss. It generally works until it breaks.

Profits

Mean reversion market participants eject prematurely. Deep value investors often pass the baton to growth managers who then ride stocks deep into euphoric territory. They leave money on the table.

More importantly, they have an unfavorable tail ratio. It takes a lot of small wins to make up for one big loss. Mean reversion market participants need to elongate their right tail.

The solution is therefore to close a fraction of the position and let the remainder run with a different exit mechanism.

Partial exit

Use the partial exit formula ($N = 1/X$) shown earlier to calculate the exact amount you need to close for the trade to break even. When in doubt, close between two thirds and three quarters of the positions. The high win rate coupled with above 50% profit taking keeps the money-making engine humming.

The impact on the distribution will be a mode closer to break even on the profit side. The win rate does not get impacted, only average win.

Exits

Trend followers need to be convinced of the need to take profits along the way. Mean reversion market participants need to be persuaded they should delay their final exit. The problem is that value investors are not wired to rationalize growth. After a partial exit, the remainder will be closed at a later date using a different exit mechanism. Here are two methods:

- Inefficiencies around the mean: Mean reversion implies oscillations around a mean. It is therefore unnecessarily conservative and somewhat illogical to close a position at the mean. Wait for the price to overshoot in the other direction before closing a position. This overshoot does not have to be symmetrical. For example, a 2.5 standard deviation move might warrant an entry, but full exit might occur somewhere between 1 and 1.5 standard deviations. When valuations drop, they often do not stop at the market average. They overshoot on the downside before stabilizing. This method is more congruent with the mindset of mean reversion market participants. Inefficiencies exist on both sides.

- Volatility trailing stop loss: The first one is to set a volatility trailing stop loss, often referred to as a chandelier stop. Add a number of average true ranges to the lowest low. Close the position when the price closes above the stop loss. This technique is borrowed from trend-following strategies.

Think of right tail elongation as an antidote to those devastating losses. The more you allow your positions to run a little bit longer, the less time it will take to recover next time.

Summary

Randomness cannot be eradicated. So, stop fooling yourself by pretending to predict anything. When the markets throw lemons, those who learn to make lemonade for their investors stay business.

In this chapter, we started by considering the psychological impact of exiting a position, and some steps to overcome your unwillingness to cut losses. We then explored six techniques that will improve your trading edge. Five of them deal with exits, one with entry, the objective being to shorten the left tail and elongate the right one. This is accomplished by trimming losers and letting winners run beyond your comfort zone.

Next, we will consider another important part of any strategy—position sizing.

8
Position Sizing: Money is Made in the Money Management Module

Legendary investors have always emphasized the same thing: risk management is the key to long-term superior returns. Stock picking is sexy, but vastly overrated. Risk management is boring but vastly underappreciated. In execution trader English, where market gurus focus on picking the right ingredients, market wizards concentrate on getting the right recipe.

At the end of the day, the primary determinant of long-term geometric returns is position sizing. The expanding nature of longs does not compel market participants to think about position sizing. After all, one good AAPL can make a basket of rotten apples look good. They can survive despite bad position-sizing algorithms. Short sellers do not have the luxury of logarithmic price declines. In this chapter, we will consider some classic examples of bad position-sizing algorithms. Those are the four horsemen of apocalyptic position sizing.

After we have taken a close look at common pitfalls, we will consider a strategy that not only works, but minimizes the devastating effects of bad decision-making.

We will cover the following topics:

- Importing libraries
- The four horsemen of apocalyptic position sizing

- Position sizing is the link between emotional and financial capital
- Comparing position-sizing algorithms
- Refining your risk budget

 You can access color versions of all images in this chapter via the following link: `https://static.packt-cdn.com/downloads/9781801815192_ColorImages.pdf`. You can also access the source code for this chapter via the book's GitHub repository: `https://github.com/PacktPublishing/Algorithmic-Short-Selling-with-Python-Published-by-Packt`

Importing libraries

For this chapter and the rest of the book, we will be working with the pandas, numpy, yfinance, and matplotlib libraries. So, please remember to import them first:

```
# Import Libraries
import pandas as pd
import numpy as np
import yfinance as yf
%matplotlib inline
import matplotlib.pyplot as plt
```

The four horsemen of apocalyptic position sizing

"Only listen to advice from people you want to look like."

– *Gilbert Bernut, father, superhero, unsung 20th-century philosopher*

Whilst at Fidelity, I used to run my algorithm across other managers' portfolios. My unbridled ambition was to help my colleagues improve their performance by a whopping 0.01% at a time. Whilst it does not look like much, 1 basis point even on every other trade compounded over a year would be enough to lift a ranking from the second quartile to the rarefied atmosphere of top-decile performers.

It soon dawned upon me that the same stocks kept popping up across all portfolios. Put smart, passionate people together in a collegial atmosphere, and healthy cross-pollination naturally ensues.

What was more intriguing was the disparity in performance despite the low dispersion in holdings. One would expect similar holdings to generate similar performance. There were, however, differences in both performance and tracking errors, that is, the volatility of returns versus the benchmark. Since the same issues were present in most portfolios, stock picking was clearly not the primary driver of performance. The difference that really made the difference was position sizing. Money is made in the money management module.

Now, the paradox of making money on the markets is this: the module that will generate money is also the most boring part of a strategy. Everyone wants to shout out to the world that they bought Netflix or Amazon years ago. Yet, no-one will admit they only had marginal positions, and did not know how many they should have bought. And then, they wonder why they keep underperforming despite those exceptional stock picks.

Consequently, the discipline of money management has been relegated to a distant afterthought, some chore that needs to be done, like taking out the garbage or paying the utility bills. This has led market participants to promote disastrous money management practices. In execution trader English, all the potential gains made by picking the right stocks are wiped out because of ignorant bet sizes.

Let us look at four of the most damaging money management techniques currently embraced by the industry.

Horseman 1: Liquidity is the currency of bear markets

> *"You can check out anytime you want, but you can never leave."*
>
> *– Don Henley, Hotel California*

Large positions in illiquid stocks have sunk many a talented fund manager. Small caps and illiquid stocks are like boats and luxury toys. You can buy anytime you want, but you can never leave. If you can't get out of a position without damaging market impact, you don't own it. It owns you.

Liquidity is the currency of bear markets. When the "redemption song" starts playing, managers are forced to liquidate whatever they can, not necessarily what they would like to.

This leaves them with illiquid debris, which perpetuates the vicious cycle of redemption. Small caps are particularly vulnerable in bear markets. Liquidity evaporates, the bid/ask spread widens. Those who tried to cash out of illiquid assets during the Great Financial Crisis (GFC) quickly realized that the bid/ask spread was wide enough to dock a supertanker without a scratch.

A side note on capacity. One of the first questions from investors is about capacity: how many assets a manager can take on before returns start to dwindle. Investors know that the strongest returns happen in the earlier years, when funds are small and managers hungry. Yet, they want to see some track record before pulling the trigger. So, they wait and see as much as possible, but not too much to make sure they will still enjoy some decent returns. More than a mathematical approximation, a real-life acid test is inertia. When managers start to pass up trades because of market impact, they have reached their saturation point. As my mentor June-Yon Kim always said: "capacity sets in when inertia creeps in." If you find yourself passing up signals because of inertia, and this seems like the right thing to do, either you are lazy, or your asset size is too big. Either way, it is a wake-up call.

Horseman 2: Averaging down

"Losers average losers."

– Paul Tudor Jones

Averaging down is still a popular method amongst fundamental market participants. As prices come down, valuations look cheaper, so they add to their existing loss-making positions. Adding to a losing position worsens three of the four variables in the trading edge formula: loss rate and average loss increase, win rate goes down. The only variable that remains unaffected is average win, something which no-one has any beginning of control over anyhow. Moreover, additional capital allocated to losers has to come from somewhere. It either comes from fresh infusions of cash or profit-making positions cut short. In summary, averaging down can be summarized as: "cut your winners, run your losers." Wasn't the secret to success: "cut your losers, run your winners"?

The financial services industry is replete with arcane theories supported by batteries of back-tests, optimizations, and soporific white papers. Rather than staying in the abstract world, a simple way to assess their validity is to draw parallels with the real world. In the gambling world, averaging down is known as a **martingale**. Every rookie gambler has come up with an iteration supposed to break the casino. Double your bet size after each loss, then you will eventually get your money back. First, this strategy ignores the theory of runs.

Over the long run, coin tosses have 50% probability. Yet, it is not a neat succession of heads and tails. Every turn is independent of the previous one. Sometimes heads can come up 8, 9, or 10 times in a row. This presupposes infinite capital. Secondly, the most favorable outcome is break even. This means that any outcome before that has an interesting statistical property called **certainty of ruin**. Bottom line, there is a reason why casinos have marble, paintings, and free booze, and rookie gamblers go home broke in their busted cars.

If averaging down is demonstrably statistically bankrupt, then why is it still so popular among professional investors? In his fascinating autobiography *A Man for All Markets*, Edward Thorp describes averaging down as anchoring bias. Market participants anchor an assumption about the value of a stock at the moment they enter a position. Value is the subjective meaning they ascribe to valuation, or as Warren Buffett said: "Price is what you pay. Value is what you get." Subsequently, their judgement will always be colored by the initial cost. If a stock looked cheap when they first bought at $10, it must be a bargain at $9. Market participants assume that their analysis is right and the market temporarily wrong. Adding another tranche before the market corrects this inefficiency could potentially lead to bigger profits. In theory, it makes sense.

In practice, "it's complicated." When bets are small, emotional involvement remains minimal. Adding another tranche increases the stress level. The brain suddenly jumps from a $1 buy-in to the high roller table. A whole slew of emotions that did not exist before hijack the thinking brain. Stakes are high now, and the ego cannot afford to be wrong. As we saw in *Chapter 7, Improve Your Trading Edge*, with the psychology of the stop loss, ego that manifests here as the "need to be right" invariably supersedes the obligation to be profitable.

Legendary investors emphasize the importance of risk management. They also talk about humility before the markets. Market wizards are synthetically long math and short ego. Partisans of the martingale follow a statistically bankrupt method; short stats. They also call Mr. Market's bluff by doubling down. Short math, long ego sounds like a recipe for a short career in the financial services industry.

Horseman 3: High conviction

"I feel good!"

– James Brown, Godfather

Conviction is a position-sizing algorithm practiced by both the worst and the best investors. The worst investors develop an investment thesis. They then broadcast their conviction to the world with some "chutzpah" bet: "go big or go home."

Unfortunately, t-stat, a measure of statistical robustness, does not provide mental robustness. When market participants take on big bets, they lose impartiality. Their ego craves validation. High conviction is a "feel-good" bet size with no statistical validity. Sure enough, obvious trades that feel good are rarely the most profitable ones.

Now, the most successful investors also take big, high-conviction bets. The difference is they express conviction in units of risk. This means that they develop a thesis, quantify risk first, and then size positions accordingly. George Soros is famous for taking on massive bets. Whilst everyone remembers the short pound trade, few people know about the **Long-Term Capital Management** (**LTCM**) story. According to legendary trader Victor Niederhoffer, who was working in Mr Soros' shop at the time, he made a lot of traders' bonuses by cutting his losses during the LTCM debacle. Those are calculated units of risk.

Horseman 4: Equal weight

Equal weight is a staple among fundamental stock pickers. They rely on their stock-picking ability to generate performance. All stock picks are roughly equally good, so they do not perceive the need to size positions differently.

Portfolio management is not an exercise in democracy. Equal opportunity will not bring about ruin, but it may prevent you from achieving your long-term objectives. Not all stocks have the same beta. Sleepy utilities do not have the same volatility signature as racy internet stocks. By ignoring beta at the position sizing level, volatility resurfaces at the portfolio level. Volatile stocks will drive the overall portfolio volatility. Since investors react to volatility, it is therefore advisable to size positions according to their volatility or Beta. In execution trader English, remember that if you give equal rights to your ideas, this will come with equal lefts to your equity curve.

This leads us down an interesting path. Is there an optimal position-sizing algorithm that institutional investors are aware of?

Position sizing is the link between emotional and financial capital

"This is a great experiment for many reasons. It ought to become part of the basic education of anyone interested in finance or gambling."

– Edward Thorp, a (super)man for all markets

Victor Haghani, founder of Elm and former trader at LTCM, conducted an experiment on 61 volunteers, bright students in finance and sophisticated investment professionals. Participants were given $25 starting capital and were told to flip a virtual coin for 30 minutes, being told, "the coin is biased to come up heads with a 60% probability, and you can bet as much as you like on heads or tails on each flip." How much would you bet? It appears there is a formula to calculate the optimal bet size that would maximize long-term geometric returns. The Kelly criterion formula is:

```
def kelly(win_rate,avg_win,avg_loss):
    # Kelly = win% / abs(avg_loss%) - loss% / avg_win%
    return win_rate / np.abs(avg_loss) - (1-win_rate) / avg_win
```

Despite the pedigree and alleged sophistication of the participants, results were vastly ... underwhelming. Only 21% of the players hit the maximum cap. Despite odds of 60% in their favour, a whopping 28% of those fearless sharp financial professionals managed to go bust! Some people are destined to seek asylum in the sanctuary of bankrupt fund managers called **management**...

Now, let's play the same game, but up the ante this time. Let's start with your entire lifetime savings. Last time, the expected return on a meagre $25 was north of $3 million after 300 flips. Now, you know the odds and the formula. This time, betting your life savings should put you well ahead of Bill Gates, Warren Buffett, and Jeff Bezos.

If it is so easy, why does no-one get that rich that quickly? There is a catch: losing streaks. Coin tosses have no memory. Every flip is independent from the previous one. Even though the long-term probability is 60%, there will be some streaks of consecutive losses in a row.

This is what your life savings would look like in a losing streak, if you were to bet 20% of your capital each flip.

Figure 8.1: Capital depletion when risking 20% on each bet

After 3 losses, your lifetime savings would have halved. After 5 losses, only a third would remain. Will you still stick with the mathematically correct plan after half of your hard-earned life savings (or ill-acquired gains in the case of finance professionals) have been erased in less than 1 minute? More likely than not, at some point, your brain will say stop.

There are four important lessons here:

1. Only 5 out of 61 participants knew about the Kelly criterion. This raises disturbing questions about the curriculum in finance. How can students be expected to win a probabilistic game called the stock market if they have never been taught how to bet? Teaching something like the **Efficient Market Hypothesis** (**EMH**) is like teaching Hippocratic body humors to medical students long after the discovery of penicillin. As Edward Thorp, hedge fund manager with a stellar track record and vocal critic of the EMH, wrote: "This is a great experiment for many reasons. It ought to become part of the basic education of anyone interested in finance or gambling."

2. Position size determines the long-term geometric return of any strategy. Bet too conservatively and you end up making less money than you could. Bet too aggressively and you end up losing a lot more than you should. In execution trader English, bet too small and you don't have a business. Bet too big and you will lose your business.

3. The Kelly criterion or *optimal f* may be the position-sizing algorithms that will yield the highest long-term geometric return. It does not mean professional fund managers should be adopting them unconditionally. Formula 1 cars might be the fastest vehicles, but they are not made to fetch milk at the local grocery store. As we will see in *Part III, The Long/Short Game: Building a Long/Short Product*, investors trade performance for returns. Consequently, market participants usually trade using a fractional Kelly or even less sophisticated algorithms.

4. Position sizing is not just a mathematical exercise. Position sizing is the critical articulation between financial and emotional capital. Deplete the former and it will take time and effort to rebuild capital. It is a complicated problem, but not a complex one. There is an optimal solution. On the other hand, break the latter and *Game Over*. In practice, psychology supersedes mathematics. Every market participant has encountered the "fear of pulling the trigger" or taken one big bet too many before the plunge. Capital preservation is paramount, especially the emotional side of it.

This neatly leads us into the next section.

A position size your brain can trade

"I am not afraid, I was born to do this."

— *Joan of Arc, freedom fighter*

Position-sizing algorithms are designed by mathematicians for functioning psychopaths. They fail to appreciate the inner idiot in the driver seat. The reason why we drift away from rational bet sizing has nothing to do with logic. In the biased coin game at the beginning of the chapter, you probably would have bet your life savings more conservatively after the second consecutive loss, even though the rational choice would have been to soldier on throughout the entire experiment.

Joan of Arc was a French freedom fighter and the original inventor of Brexit. At the tender age of 16, she had the idea of booting the English out of the kingdom of France. In the French collective imagination, Joan of Arc is remembered for two things. The first one is so tragic it continues to haunt the French psyche.

She was captured, tortured, and eventually roasted in a public place in Rouen. Not nice, but again the Middle Ages are known to be somewhat medieval. Secondly, she is famous for hearing voices. When stocks start drilling holes deep enough to strike shale gas in the portfolio, our inner Joan of Arc awakes. We start hearing voices. We get paralyzed by fear. Cortisol floods the prefrontal cortex, or "thinking brain," and we pass up even "free money" trades.

Bottom line, our inner idiot understands only two position sizes: too little or too much. When everything works fine, there is never enough of a good thing. When nothing seems to work, there is always too much of a bad thing.

This leads us to a first important point: risk must have boundaries.

Establishing risk bands

Risk needs to oscillate between a minimum and a maximum. Those bounds can be a fraction of Kelly for the upper band, such as 30-50%. The pro of a variable upper band is fluidity. You don't know how much risk your system can tolerate unless you take it for a spin. Maybe you are taking too much or too little risk. Two considerations: volatility is a function of concentration, the number of positions, which itself is a function of risk-per-trade. If your objective is to have a diversified low-volatility portfolio, it might be wise to cap the upper bound as well.

On the other hand, the lower band can be a strict minimum such as 0.10%-0.15%. Make sure your system continues to trade during losing streaks. A variable lower band can lead to negative position sizing. This leads to trading suspension. If the system cannot generate new trades, it cannot trade itself out of a hole.

Our inner idiot always tricks us into gambling a little too much around the top and risking too little around the bottom. We have all been there. The way to stop the madness is to involve the thinking brain before the inner idiot wakes up. The way to do this is to set boundaries:

- **Minimum risk**: Winning the lottery is not going to be easy if you don't buy at least one ticket. You must continue trading to get out of a drawdown. The classic "fear of pulling the trigger" is essentially a position size issue. There is a size small enough where you will be saying "hey, why not?" Minimum risk is somewhere between the minimum size for the system to run and the maximum size before "fear of pulling the trigger" kicks in.

- **Maximum risk**: This is a function of the risk appetite of your investors. When they say they can stomach a -20% drop, what they really mean is you will enter a Bob Marley market, that is, a "redemption song", after a -10% drawdown.

Whatever you think your investors tolerance might be, a third of that number is a decent approximation. Maximum risk is also a function of the number of stocks you run and your average win rate.

Your strategy will be safe if it stays within those confines. The next step is to build a transmission that will allow you to shift gears btween minimum and maximum risk.

At this juncture, we understand the need to incorporate some feedback mechanism from the markets into our risk appetite, which leads us to the next section.

Equity curve oscillator – avoiding the binary effect of classic equity curve trading

What would you think of someone who drives their car in first gear only? Hardly Nobel Prize material. Welcome to the financial services industry, where geniuses drive their portfolios in either first or fifth gear through bull and bear markets alike. Constant risk is as efficient as a Lamborghini stuck in first gear. When your style works, take more calculated risks. When it doesn't, focus on capital protection.

Modulating risk according to performance is called **equity curve trading**. Classic equity curve trading uses methods such as moving average crossover or breakouts. As the equity curve crosses over a moving average or makes a new high, risk abruptly jumps from timid to bold.

This approach lags the market. It measures the advance from an equity base level. For example, when the equity level raises from 100 to 105, then an additional 0.1% risk can be added. To illustrate this mechanism, imagine taking someone on a date in a car with only two gears, first and fifth. Once you have been on a straight line in first gear for a while, you would switch into fifth gear, probably just in time for the next curve.

If you want to improve your chances of passing down your genes, you and your traveling companion might appreciate a smoother ride. The oscillator in the simplified convex position-sizing algorithm is the automatic gearbox that will ensure a smooth and comfortable transition from minimum to maximum risk.

Lag is the main problem with classic equity curve trading. The simplest way to avoid lag is to measure drawdown from peak, not advance from base. Basically, you would be driving the portfolio at optimum speed the whole time but only slow down when necessary.

The methodology is as follows:

- **Drawdown tolerance**: This is the minimal fraction of capital that would be deployed if there was a drawdown of $X\%$. For example, a famous hedge fund has a -5% drawdown tolerance after which assets under management are reduced by 50%. Allocating a fraction of capital is synthetically like taking less risk. Either the system takes less risk, or it deploys less money. The result is synthetically the same.

- **Drawdown oscillator**: Rebase the drawdown using the above tolerance. Build an oscillator that tracks the current equity curve versus its peak and a trailing trough...

- **Shape of the oscillator**: Concave or convex. Think of this little jewel of sophistication as the equivalent of automatic transmission in a car. There is an inherent lag in classic equity curve trading. Risk does not drop fast enough to reduce shock. Conversely, it is slow to recover after a drawdown.

Convexity and concavity accelerate both drop and recovery as shown in the theoretical example below:

```python
def concave(ddr, floor):
    '''
    For demo purpose only
    '''
    if floor == 0:
        concave = ddr
    else:
        concave = ddr ** (floor)
    return concave


# obtuse
def convex(ddr, floor):
    '''
    obtuse = 1 - acute
    '''
    if floor == 0:
```

```
            convex = ddr
        else:
            convex = ddr ** (1/floor)
        return convex

# instantiate minimum Kapital
floor = np.arange(0,1,0.125)
# print('floor', floor)

x = -np.linspace(0, 1, 100)

fig, ax = plt.subplots()
for i,f in enumerate(floor):
    y = concave(ddr=-x, floor=f)
    current_label = f' concave f = {f:.3}'
    ax.plot(x, y, linewidth=2, alpha=0.6, label=current_label)

ax.legend()
plt.ylabel('Concave Oscillator')
plt.xlabel('Equity Curve From Trailing Trough To Peak')
ax.set_ylim(ax.get_ylim()[::-1])
plt.show()

fig, ax = plt.subplots()
for i,f in enumerate(floor):
    y = convex(ddr=-x, floor=f)
    current_label = f' convex f = {f*10:.3}'
    ax.plot(x, y, linewidth=2, alpha=0.6, label=current_label)
ax.legend()

plt.ylabel('Convex Oscillator')
plt.xlabel('Equity Curve From Trailing Trough To Peak')
ax.set_ylim(ax.get_ylim()[::-1])
plt.figure(figsize=(20,8))
plt.show()
```

The output of this function is graphs like the following:

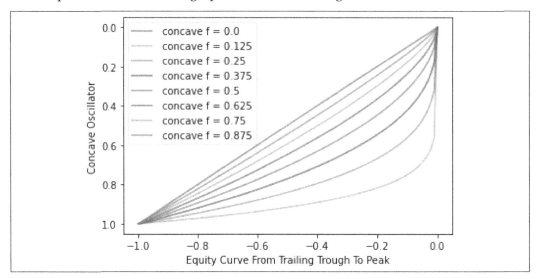

Figure 8.2: Concave oscillator at various levels

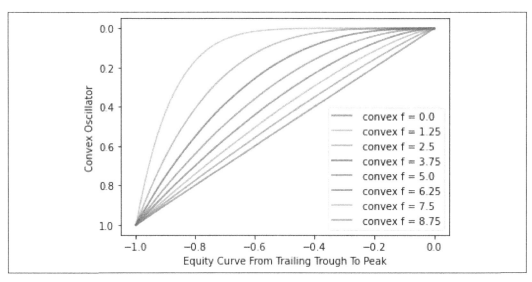

Figure 8.3: Convex oscillator at various levels

Convex is above and concave below the diagonal line. This 45-degree line is the linear drop. It is good enough when coupled with drawdown tolerance. Concavity and convexity really deliver when the ratio of minimum over maximum risk is high. For example, if minimum risk is –0.25% and maximum –1%, then either concavity or convexity would help in the transmission.

Next, let's illustrate how this oscillator works in practice. We will simulate an equity curve by downloading the adjusted close of the German DAX index using Yahoo Finance. Next, we instantiate a dataframe, and calculate peak equity using the cummax() method. We proceed to calculate drawdown from the peak.

dd_tolerance is the drawdown tolerance we are willing to tolerate before slamming risk down. For good measure, we plot the dataframe. This gives us a good starting basis to work with:

```
ticker = '^GDAXI'
dd_tolerance = -0.1

equity = pd.DataFrame()
start = '2017-12-31'
end = None
equity['equity'] = yf.download(tickers= ticker,start= start, end = end,
                    interval = "1d",group_by = 'column',
                    auto_adjust = True, prepost = True,
                    treads = True, proxy = None)['Close']

equity['peak_equity'] = equity['equity'].cummax()
equity['tolerance'] = equity['peak_equity'] * (1 + dd_tolerance )
equity['drawdown'] = equity['equity'] /equity['equity'].cummax() -1

equity.plot(style = ['k','g-.','r-.','m:'] ,
            secondary_y=['drawdown'], figsize=(20,8),grid=True)
equity.columns
```

You should observe a chart like the following:

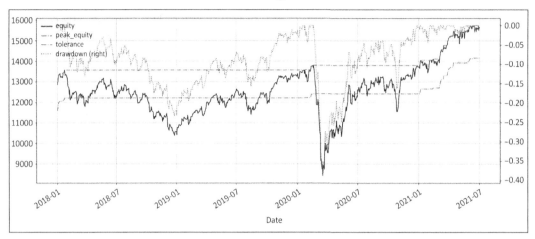

Figure 8.4: The equity curve, peak equity, drawdown, and drawdown tolerance band

One observation imposes itself right out the gate. If this equity curve is anywhere near your real equity curve, then stick to barbecues on Sundays, writing newsletters to gullible tourists, or teaching **Efficient Market Hypothesis (EMH)** to bored rich kids. This chart screams impostor syndrome.

The dotted line at the top of the chart is the drawdown. It is painted on the secondary *y* axis. The two dotted lines above and below the equity curve are peak equity and drawdown tolerance. If the equity curve drops below the lower line, then risk should be reduced. As the lower dotted line shows, the equity curve spends a considerable amount of time below the tolerance curve. We therefore expect to be trading at minimum risk for a while.

Next, we will calculate how much risk we should be taking along this equity curve. From the preceding theoretical discussion, risk is range bound between a minimum and maximum. This next little function is the best sleeping pill for experienced traders. It is worth multiple times the value of this book:

```
def risk_appetite(eqty, tolerance, mn, mx, span, shape):
    '''

    eqty: equity curve series
    tolerance: tolerance for drawdown (<0)
    mn: min risk
    mx: max risk
    span: exponential moving average to smoothe the risk_appetite
    shape: convex (>45 deg diagonal) = 1, concave (<diagonal) = -1,
else: simple risk_appetite
```

`...`

```
# drawdown rebased
eqty = pd.Series(eqty)
watermark = eqty.expanding().max()
# all-time-high peak equity
drawdown = eqty / watermark - 1
# drawdown from peak
ddr = 1 - np.minimum(drawdown / tolerance,1)
# drawdown rebased to tolerance from 0 to 1
avg_ddr = ddr.ewm(span = span).mean()
# span rebased drawdown

# Shape of the curve
if shape == 1: #
    _power = mx/mn # convex
elif shape == -1 :
    _power = mn/mx # concave
else:
    _power = 1 # raw, straight line
ddr_power = avg_ddr ** _power # ddr

# mn + adjusted delta
risk_appetite = mn + (mx - mn) * ddr_power

return risk_appetite
```

This is how it works:

1. Calculate peak equity, watermark in financial creole, from the eqty series.
2. Calculate drawdown and rebased drawdown using drawdown tolerance. Smooth the average rebased drawdown using an exponential moving average.
3. Choose the shape of the curve: concave (-1), convex (1), or linear (anything else).
4. Calculate the risk appetite oscillator.

Next, we run a few lines of code through the equity curve to compute the risk budget throughout the period. The risk budget is the fraction of the equity we are ready to risk. For example, if we use a constant equity at risk of –0.50%, it would be the current equity multiplied by –0.50%.

In the example below, we use three levels of risk: minimum at –0.25, maximum at –0.75%, and average at –0.50%. For the purpose of the exercise, the average risk is the constant equity at risk. Below is the source code:

```
eqty= equity['equity']
tolerance= dd_tolerance
mn= -0.0025
mx= -0.0075
avg = (mn + mx)/2
span= 5
shape = 1
equity['constant_risk'] = -equity['equity'] * avg
equity['convex_risk'] = -risk_appetite(eqty, tolerance, mn, mx, span,
shape=1) * equity['peak_equity']
equity['concave_risk'] = -risk_appetite(eqty, tolerance, mn, mx, span,
shape=-1) * equity['peak_equity']

equity[['equity', 'peak_equity', 'tolerance',
        'constant_risk','convex_risk','concave_risk']].plot(figsize=
(20,8),grid=True,
    secondary_y=['constant_risk','convex_risk','concave_risk'],
    style= ['k','g-.','r-.','b:','y-.', 'orange'])

equity[['drawdown','constant_risk','convex_risk','concave_risk']].
plot(grid=True,
    secondary_y=['drawdown'],style= ['m--','b:','y-.', 'orange'],
figsize= (20,8) )
```

 Note that constant risk is multiplied by the current equity level whereas both concave and convex use peak equity. The last two incorporate drawdown in their calculation.

We have the same equity curve as before along with peak and tolerance. Then, we have two risk budget charts.

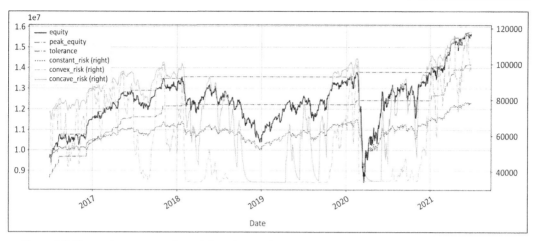

Figure 8.5: The equity curve, peak, and drawdown tolerance. Concave, convex, and constant equity at risk

Concave, the solid line, is by far the most responsive risk budget. It mirrors the equity curve. Convex, the dashed line, is the most conservative of the three. It will stay longer at minimal risk but will react positively in a sustained uptrend. The constant risk, the dotted line, does not fluctuate much at all. Whilst it may not seem like a bad thing on the surface, it can cause some severe damage to the equity curve. For example, the middle section would tend to be more pronounced. At the end of the day, choosing not to reduce risk when things go wrong is also a risk management decision, just not a good one.

The next chart plots the risk budget along with the drawdown.

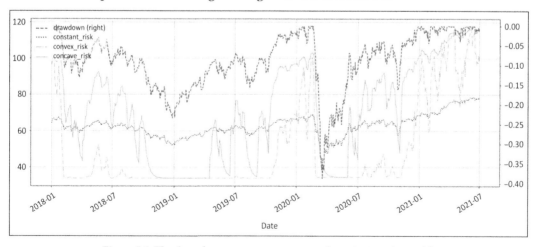

Figure 8.6: The drawdown, concave, convex, and constant equity at risk

The above chart shows how the oscillator responds to drawdown. In comparison, constant equity at risk looks blunt and unsophisticated. As the drawdown in the middle section deepens and worsens, constant risk becomes too risky. Conversely, when drawdowns are minor, constant risk fails to capitalize on those opportunities. This position-sizing algorithm is not bad compared to equal weight or a martingale. It is just unsophisticated.

Now, should you go for concave or convex? The optimal mathematical answer may not be the right one for you. Are wines in Bordeaux, Burgundy, or northern Rhône better? There is no right or wrong answer to those deep existential issues that have agitated mankind since the dawn of time.

Comparing position-sizing algorithms

Let's take an example to further illustrate the principle. Let's use the exact same signals and starting capital. Then, let's use various position-sizing algorithms. Let's compute the equity curve for each position-sizing algorithm. The objective is to see how much position sizing impacts returns.

For demonstration purposes, we will recycle our go-to Softbank in absolute with Turtle for dummies, along with our `regime_breakout()` function from *Chapter 5, Regime Definition*. Once again, please do not do this at home, as it is too simplistic to be deployed in a professional investment product:

```python
def regime_breakout(df,_h,_l,window):
    hl =  np.where(df[_h] == df[_h].rolling(window).max(),1,
                            np.where(df[_l] == df[_l].
rolling(window).min(), -1,np.nan))
    roll_hl = pd.Series(index= df.index, data= hl).fillna(method=
'ffill')
    return roll_hl

def turtle_trader(df, _h, _l, slow, fast):

#### removed for brevity: check GitHub repo for full code ####
    return turtle

# CHAPTER 8

ticker = '9984.T' # Softbank
start = '2017-12-31'
end = None
```

```
df =  round(yf.download(tickers= ticker,start= start, end = end,
                          interval = "1d",group_by =
'column',auto_adjust = True,
                                    prepost = True, treads = True, proxy =
None),0)

ccy_ticker = 'USDJPY=X'
ccy_name = 'JPY'
ccy_df = np.nan

df[ccy_name] =  round(yf.download(tickers= ccy_ticker,start= start, end
= end,
                          interval = "1d",group_by = 'column',auto_adjust
= True,
                                    prepost = True, treads = True, proxy =
None)['Close'],2)
df[ccy_name] = df[ccy_name].fillna(method='ffill')
slow = 50
fast = 20
df['tt'] = turtle_trader(df, _h= 'High', _l= 'Low', slow= slow,fast=
fast)
df['tt_chg1D'] = df['Close'].diff() * df['tt'].shift()
df['tt_chg1D_fx'] = df['Close'].diff() * df['tt'].shift() / df[ccy_
name]

df['tt_log_returns'] = np.log(df['Close'] / df['Close'].shift()) *
df['tt'].shift()
df['tt_cumul_returns'] = df['tt_log_returns'].cumsum().apply(np.exp) -
1

df['stop_loss'] = np.where(df['tt'] == 1, df['Low'].rolling(fast).
min(),
                    np.where(df['tt'] == -1, df['High'].rolling(fast).
max(),np.nan))# / df[ccy_name]
df['tt_PL_cum'] = df['tt_chg1D'].cumsum()
df['tt_PL_cum_fx'] = df['tt_chg1D_fx'].cumsum()

df[['Close','stop_loss','tt','tt_cumul_returns']].plot(secondary_
y=['tt','tt_cumul_returns'],
                                    figsize=(20,10),style= ['k','r--
','b:','b'],
                    title= str(ticker)+' Close Price, Turtle L/S
entries')

df[['tt_chg1D','tt_chg1D_fx']].plot(secondary_y=['tt_chg1D_fx'],
```

```
                                       figsize=(20,10),style= ['b','c'],
                                    title= str(ticker) +' Daily P&L Local
    & USD')

    df[['tt_PL_cum','tt_PL_cum_fx']].plot(secondary_y=['tt_PL_cum_fx'],
                                    figsize=(20,10),style= ['b','c'],
                                    title= str(ticker) +' Cumulative P&L
    Local & USD')
```

This is our go-to example. Typically, today we have a signal at the close of the day. Tomorrow we will enter or exit. Entries and exits lag signals by one day using the shift method. We calculate cumulative returns (tt_cumul_returns) and daily profit and loss (tt_chg1D). This gives us the following graphs:

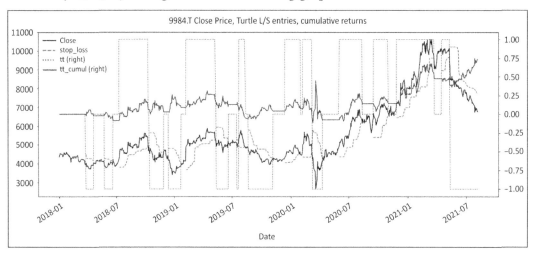

Figure 8.7: Softbank closing price, long/short positions, using Turtle for dummies on absolute series

The above chart sums up the strategy. With the black solid line, we have the closing price, closely followed by the red dashed stop loss line. We then have the +/-1 dotted line symbolizing long/short positions. Finally, the solid blue line represents cumulative returns.

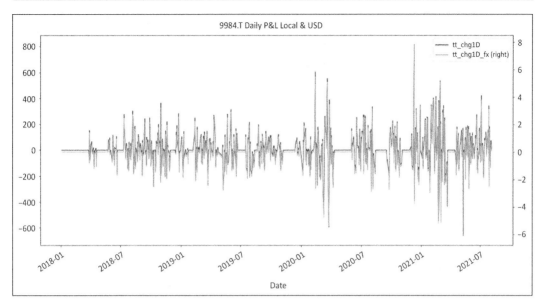

Figure 8.8: Strategy daily profit and loss in local currency and USD

The above chart represents the daily profit and loss in both local currency and adjusted to USD. The flat line shows when there is no active position.

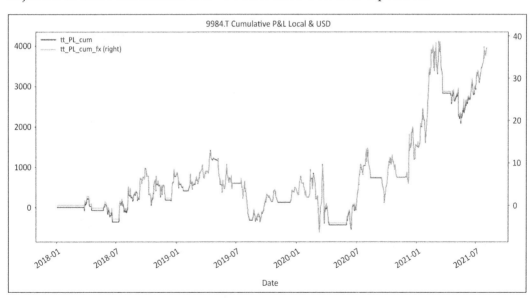

Figure 8.9: Strategy cumulative profit and loss in local currency and USD

The above chart represents the cumulative profit and loss in local currency and USD. We use the same strategy on the same instrument with no additional features such as benchmark or liquidity adjustment. Everything is rigorously identical. The only difference is the position-sizing algorithm.

Let's define a few standard position-sizing algorithms. Equal weight is not defined below as it is a numerical constant, of 3% of equity. Rather than complicate things with more exotic position-sizing algorithms, let's keep it simple. We will use two of the most popular position-sizing algorithms: equal weight and equity at risk. We will then compare them with this concave and convex equity at risk. The latter two are new to the game. First, the source code for equity at risk is as follows:

```
def eqty_risk_shares(px,sl,eqty,risk,fx,lot):
    r = sl - px
    if fx > 0:
        budget = eqty * risk * fx
    else:
        budget = eqty * risk
    shares = round(budget // (r *lot) * lot,0)
#    print(r,budget,round(budget/r,0))
    return shares


px = 2000
sl = 2222

eqty = 100000
risk = -0.005
fx = 110
lot = 100

eqty_risk_shares(px,sl,eqty,risk,fx,lot)
```

This produces the following output:

```
-300.0
```

The above function returns a number of shares using price (px), stop loss denominated in local currency (sl), equity (eqty), risk, fx in fund currency, the currency in which the fund operates, and lot size. In the above example, this would return -300 shares.

Next, we run the simulation with 4 position-sizing algorithms: equal weight, constant, concave, and convex equity at risk:

```
starting_capital = 1000000
lot = 100
mn = -0.0025
mx = -0.0075
avg = (mn + mx) / 2
tolerance= -0.1
equal_weight = 0.05
shs_fxd = shs_ccv = shs_cvx = shs_eql = 0
df.loc[df.index[0],'constant'] = df.loc[df.index[0],'concave'] =
starting_capital
df.loc[df.index[0],'convex'] = df.loc[df.index[0],'equal_weight'] =
starting_capital


for i in range(1,len(df)):
    df['equal_weight'].iat[i] = df['equal_weight'].iat[i-1] + df['tt_
chg1D_fx'][i] * shs_eql
    df['constant'].iat[i] = df['constant'].iat[i-1] + df['tt_chg1D_fx']
[i] * shs_fxd
    df['concave'].iat[i] = df['concave'].iat[i-1] + df['tt_chg1D_fx']
[i] * shs_ccv
    df['convex'].iat[i] = df['convex'].iat[i-1] + df['tt_chg1D_fx'][i]
* shs_cvx

    ccv = risk_appetite(eqty= df['concave'][:i], tolerance=tolerance,
                        mn= mn, mx=mx, span=5, shape=-1)
    cvx = risk_appetite(eqty= df['convex'][:i], tolerance=tolerance,
                        mn= mn, mx=mx, span=5, shape=1)

    if (df['tt'][i-1] ==0) & (df['tt'][i] !=0):
        px = df['Close'][i]
        sl = df['stop_loss'][i]
        fx  = df[ccy_name][i]
        shs_eql = (df['equal_weight'].iat[i]  * equal_weight
*fx//(px * lot)) * lot
        if px != sl:
            shs_fxd = eqty_risk_shares(px,sl,eqty=
df['constant'].iat[i],
                                        risk= avg,fx=fx,lot=100)
            shs_ccv = eqty_risk_shares(px,sl,eqty=
df['concave'].iat[i],
                                        risk=
ccv[-1],fx=fx,lot=100)
```

```
            shs_cvx = eqty_risk_shares(px,sl,eqty= df['convex'].iat[i],
                                    risk=
cvx[-1],fx=fx,lot=100)

df[['constant','concave','convex','equal_weight', 'tt_PL_cum_fx']].
plot(figsize = (20,10), grid=True,
    style=['y.-','m--','g-.','b:', 'b'],secondary_y='tt_PL_cum_fx',
title= 'cumulative P&L, concave, convex, constant equity at risk,
equal weight ')
```

The code takes the following steps:

1. First we instantiate parameters such as the starting capital, currency,
    minimum and maximum risk, drawdown tolerance and equal weight.

2. We initialize the number of shares for each posSizer. We initialize the
    starting capital for each posSizer as well.

3. We loop through every bar to recalculate every equity curve by adding the
    previous value to the current number of shares times daily profit.

4. We recalculate the concave and convex risk oscillator at each bar.

5. If there is an entry signal, we calculate the number of shares for each
    posSizer. The // operator is modulo. It returns the rounded integer of the
    division. This is a neat trick to quickly calculate round lots. Note that the
    only difference between concave and convex is the sign: –1 or +1.

We then print the equity curves and voila. The dashed line at the top is concave.
Below, the dash-dotted line is convex, followed by constant. The secondary vertical
axis represents the cumulative profit and loss before weight adjustment:

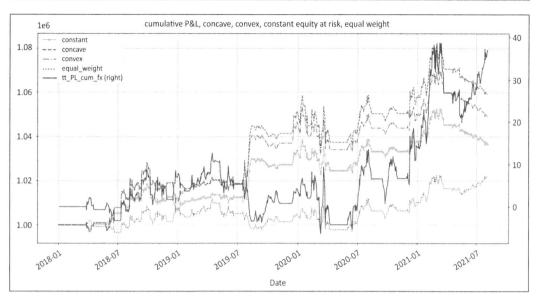

Figure 8.10: Equity curves using various position-sizing algorithms

Let's briefly recap here. We use the same strategy, in which cumulative returns adjusted for currency are represented by the solid blue line above. The only difference is money management. Trailing far away in a distant galaxy is the industry's standard equal weight. In this case, we use 5% of equity, a position size that seasoned institutional managers would call a "high-conviction" bet. A good second last is constant equity at risk. It is either first or fifth gear. Concave equity at risk surprisingly came first. Convex tends to perform better in choppy markets because of its responsiveness, while concave does well in trending markets.

The tectonic takeaway is that money is made in the money management module. How smart you bet determines how much you make. The best return on investment does not come from visiting one more company, making one more phone call, reading one more analyst report, or examining one more chart analysis. The best return on investment comes from polishing the money management module.

Refining your risk budget

A bit of finesse in the money management algorithm goes a long way. This leads us to small refinements in risk budget such as amortization and false positives.

Risk amortization

> *"Pyramiding instructions appear on a dollar bill. Add smaller and smaller on the way up. Keep your eyes open at the top."*
>
> *– Ed Seykota*

The short side has a unique set of challenges. Successful shorts shrink. Positions need to be periodically topped up. Adding to an existing position is called **pyramiding**. Pyramiding is a delicate business.

On the one hand, trends mature. The probability of reversal increases with the passage of time. Risk per trade should therefore be reduced with each additional position. On the other hand, news flow deterioration validates the original bearish stance. Market participants are often tempted to sizably increase their bets. In my personal experience, every time market commentators start to agree with my stance and I start to feel intelligent, there is invariably a nasty bear market rally round the corner.

A simple way to mitigate the risk of entering a mature trend is to amortize risk for each new position. The following snippet of code is a suggestion to market participants who usually add to their positions. As risk increases with the passage of time, positions should be reduced.

```
def pyramid(position, root=2):
    '''

    position is the number of positions
    power is root n.
    Conservative = 1, aggressive = position, default = 2
    '''

    return 1 / (1+position) ** (1/root)

def amortized_weight(raw_weight, amortization):
    '''
```

```
    raw_weight is the initial position size
    amortization is pyramid(position,root=2)
    '''

    return raw_weight * amortization

weight = 0.05
position = np.arange(1,4)

print('position', position)
print('linear',pyramid(position, root=1)* weight)
print('square root',pyramid(position, root=2)* weight)
print('position n',pyramid(position, root=position)* weight)
```

Following the formulae is a numerical example. We start with a position size (weight) of 5%. We re-enter three times using the np.arange method. We then calculate the suggested weight size of 3 additions to the original position using various amortizations, receiving the following results:

```
position [1 2 3]
linear [0.025      0.01666667 0.0125     ]
square root [0.03535534 0.02886751 0.025      ]
position n [0.025      0.02886751 0.03149803]
```

linear stands for no power. In the first additional tranche, the position size is 1/2 of the original position (0.025), the second tranche is 1/3, and so on. Using square root suggests a first additional tranche which is $1/\sqrt{2}$ times the size of the original position (0.3535), and a second position $1/\sqrt{3}$ times the size. position n suggests a first additional tranche of 1/2 times the size of the original position, the same as the linear tranche, and a second tranche $1/\sqrt{3}$ the size of the original position, the same as the square root amortization, and so on.

Square root is probably a good compromise. It allows market participants to take substantial risks without facing the risk of ruin. Again, selling short is a position-sizing exercise, not a stock-picking contest. Small positions do not contribute. Big positions are risky. There is an optimal number, to which our inner idiot will be completely unresponsive anyways. Once again, market participants have the choice between being conservative or aggressive. There are old traders and bold traders. There are very few old bold traders.

False positives

Not all trades work the first time. Sometimes, it takes two or three trials for a stock to finally behave as expected. This takes a toll on the equity curve. Market participants are often tempted to overhaul and tweak their signal engines to reduce the frequency of false positives. Whilst there may be some value in working on the blindspots that generated bad trades, it is unquestionably healthier to accept that false positives are part of the journey as well. Randomness cannot be eliminated.

We are generally good at dealing with disappointments in other areas of life. When something does not work, we invest less time and effort into it. Similarly, the solution may not be yet another tweak of the signal engine. When stocks refuse to behave as expected, keep trying, just invest less. This comes down to the risk amortization function defined above. Amortize risk for every failed attempt.

Order prioritization and trade rejection

At some point, you will have more signals than money to invest. You will have to make tough choices and prioritize signals. The simplest order prioritization algorithm is size: the bigger the size, the higher the risk/reward. Rank all positions by absolute size in descending order. It is not the case that just because you are seated at your desk and the markets are open that you should trade with abandon. Choosing not to trade is an important trading decision.

Trade rejection is an important tool in the arsenal of a short seller. On the long side, small holdings can mature into formidable positions. Bill Gates bought AAPL at $12 per stock in August 1997. On the other hand, on the short side, a drop of -10% on a -0.50% position will only contribute -0.05%. This is hardly the kind of return that attracts investors. When positions are too tiny to hurt, they are also too small to contribute.

Reasons that could lead to taking small positions could be either:

- Performance has hit a "soft patch"
- This particular strategy is out of favor now
- The side (long/short) is not working
- The instrument itself has a frustratingly low win rate
- There are already a few entries

Whatever the reason, this is not a fat pitch, so you want to keep your powder dry.

Game theory in position sizing

"You can observe a lot by watching."

– Yogi Berra, great American philosopher

Recent advances in computing technology have encouraged market participants to dabble in game theory, particularly at the stock selection level. Game theory is also well suited for position sizing. The difference is using game theory for entries comes down to a binary outcome: either in or not. There is little learning possible there because no-one keeps stats on the choices not made. Unless you are a creepy stalker, you do not keep tabs on the ex you did not marry.

One of the main causes of equity curve erosion is false positives. Some stocks may have two or three false starts before finally taking off. Then, it takes time to repay those false starts. Meanwhile, some stocks do well on their first trial. In the probabilistic game called the stock market, there is no way of knowing which is going to be which in advance. Reward those that do well and amortize risk for those that do not is a simple heuristic. This is where game theory and a cute little story comes in.

Here is the story behind the algorithm we use to reward well-behaving stocks. Once I showed up early at school to pick up my children. My daughter was having fun playing a game that we all played as kids, so I just sat there and watched. Interestingly enough, she ended up winning not because she tried to predict anything, but because she methodically reacted after each turn. She mirrored the behavior of each participant: nice to those who were nice to her and vice versa, tit for tat. This made me think of a simple game theory heuristic.

Fast-forward a few days of research on Google, it turned out that the tit-for-tat heuristic had repeatedly come first in game-theory algorithmic contests. Needless to say, this game theory module quickly found its way into our position-sizing approach, with the name of my daughter, "Alizee" (pronounced *Alizay*, French for *trade winds*). Tit-for-tat is a solid algorithm. Punish bad behavior and reward good behavior.

Summary

Everyone wants to pick the next [insert buzz stock ticker here…]. Stock picking is sexy. If however, you choose to be in the markets to make money, then be a student of the boring arts. Money is made in the money management module. In this chapter, we unveiled a small function that delegates risk setting to the markets, and will durably change the quality of sleep for seasoned market participants.

Next, we will explore risk. On the short side, the market does not cooperate. Market Darwinism dictates that surviving short sellers demonstrate superior risk management.

9
Risk is a Number

"Facts are stubborn, but statistics are more pliable."

– Mark Twain

At the end of the day, whether you trade U.S. equities, pork bellies, or colorful language with your significant other, you trade only one thing: risk. Academics build their careers on developing complicated abstract metrics with fancy names. The more arcane, the more likely they will land tenure somewhere. Proof by mathematical intimidation is an easy path to a cushy academic tenure. Unfortunately, those metrics ignore the experience of unsophisticated clients who stomach gut-wrenching drawdowns. When market participants and investors cannot reconcile abstract numbers with the reality of managing portfolios, they fall back on stories.

In this chapter, we will introduce three metrics: Grit Index, Common Sense Ratio, and t-stat of gain expectancy. The objective is to demystify risk and bring it back to something everyone can intuitively relate to.

We will cover the following topics:

- Importing libraries
- Interpreting risk
- Sharpe ratio: the right mathematical answer to the wrong question
- The Grit Index
- Common Sense Ratio
- Van Tharp's SQN
- Robustness score

You can access color versions of all images in this chapter via the following link: https://static.packt-cdn.com/downloads/9781801815192_ColorImages.pdf. You can also access source code for this chapter via the book's GitHub repository: https://github.com/PacktPublishing/Algorithmic-Short-Selling-with-Python-Published-by-Packt.

Importing libraries

For this chapter and the rest of the book, we will be working with the pandas, numpy, yfinance, and matplotlib libraries. So, please remember to import them first:

```
# Import Libraries
import pandas as pd
import numpy as np
import yfinance as yf
%matplotlib inline
import matplotlib.pyplot as plt
```

Interpreting risk

On the short side, the markets do not cooperate. Market Darwinism dictates that short sellers become exceptional risk managers. In the coming sections, we will explore three vastly underrated risk metrics and their source code. Calibrate risk using any or all of them, and you may have a long-term fighting chance. When asked about risk, market participants usually do one of two things.

The first one is to roll out a battery of metrics. They start with the Sharpe ratio, add a measure of tracking error, spice it up with Sortino, a teaspoon of Treynor, a drop of Jensen Alpha to make it look good, apply the finishing touch with information ratio, and it is ready to serve to a bunch of incredulous clients, who pretend to love the number "haute-cuisine." The indiscriminate proliferation of metrics tells us one thing: we are hardwired to not understand risk.

The second thing market participants do is to drop into dissertation mode. They tell stories about the Fed, quantitative easing, interest rates, technological disruption (the new synonym for trendy), and [insert laundry list of alarmist news flow here…].

In financial creole, the sum of all fears about a future over which no one has any control is called **the wall of worry**.

Risk is not the sum of all fears. Risk is not a story. Risk is a number. At the micro level, it is how much you can afford to lose on a single trade. At the portfolio level, it is how much drawdown as an aggregate you can withstand and still come out ahead. At the professional level, it is how much, how often, and how long you can afford to lose before someone unceremoniously yanks the plug. At the lifestyle level, it is how often you can jump from one shop to the next before teaching math to bored high school students.

No one can predict what happens in this world, but every market participant can control the vulnerability of their portfolio to shocks. In *Chapter 1*, *The Stock Market Game*, we considered finite versus infinite games. The objective of the infinite game is to stay in the game. If you want to play an infinite game, then you need to focus exclusively on the metrics that will unapologetically assess your ability to survive shocks and live to trade another day. The logical way to measure robustness is therefore to include drawdowns somewhere in the equation.

Sharpe ratio: the right mathematical answer to the wrong question

The Sharpe ratio is such an intricate part of life in the industry that a mundane greeting such as "how are you?" could easily be interchanged with "how is your Sharpe?" The question the ratio is trying to answer is conceptually simple: for every unit of volatility, how many units of excess returns over a risk-free asset do you receive in return? Now, all the problems derive not from the formula, but from the meaning people have ascribed to volatility. Is volatility bad, risky, or uncertain?

Here is the mathematical formula of the Sharpe ratio, where Rp is equal to asset returns, and Rf is equal to risk-free returns:

$$\frac{Rp - Rf}{stdev(Rp)}$$

This ratio looks at the annualized average excess returns over a risk-free asset divided by the standard deviation of those returns. Standard deviation measures the variance from the median returns. The more volatile the returns, the higher the standard deviation, and the lower the ratio (and vice versa). The excess returns over a risk-free asset is a simple test: for every additional unit of volatility, are you better off parking money with a specific manager or keeping it safe with T-bonds or money market funds?

Even the genius William Sharpe has become critical of the measure he created and that has now become the default industry standard: the Sharpe ratio. This metric served its purpose. There are two things it did really well:

1. **Cross-asset unified measure**: it is now widely accepted that the most critical component in alpha generation is asset allocation. The difficulty is to have a unified risk-adjusted measure of alpha across asset classes. This is where the Sharpe ratio did the job. It can be calculated across fixed income, equities, commodities, and so on.

2. **Uncertainty**: the human brain is hardwired to associate uncertainty with risk. It triggers the amygdala and activates the fight, flight, or freeze reflex.

Now, the Sharpe ratio was invented in 1966. It was revolutionary in revolutionary times: El Che Guevara and Fidel Castro were still fighting Batista in Cuba. As the pioneer William Sharpe himself said, it was good when computing power was still limited. But since then, times have changed. Doctors have stopped prescribing cigarettes to pregnant women, plastic has become the dominant marine species, and computers more powerful than those that sent people to the moon now fit in everyone's pocket.

First, let us take the example of our favorite *Turtle for dummies* strategy, and reuse the regime_breakout() and turtle_trader() functions. We will calculate the risk metrics on both rolling and cumulative series. This strategy is run on absolute series. It is here purely for education purposes.

```
def regime_breakout(df,_h,_l,window):
    hl =  np.where(df[_h] == df[_h].rolling(window).max(),1,
                              np.where(df[_l] == df[_l].
rolling(window).min(), -1,np.nan))
    roll_hl = pd.Series(index= df.index, data= hl).fillna(method=
'ffill')
    return roll_hl


def turtle_trader(df, _h, _l, slow, fast):
    _slow = regime_breakout(df,_h,_l,window = slow)
    _fast = regime_breakout(df,_h,_l,window = fast)
    turtle = pd. Series(index= df.index,
                        data = np.where(_slow == 1,np.where(_fast ==
1,1,0),
                                    np.where(_slow == -1, np.where(_fast
==-1,-1,0),0)))
    return turtle
```

```
ticker = '9984.T' # Softbank
start = '2017-12-31'
end = None
df =  round(yf.download(tickers= ticker,start= start, end = end,
        interval = "1d",group_by = 'column',auto_adjust = True,
prepost = True, treads = True, proxy = None),0)
slow = 50
fast = 20


#### removed for brevity: check GitHub page for full code ####

df[['Close','stop_loss','tt','tt_cumul']].plot(secondary_y=
['tt','tt_cumul'],
                                   figsize=(20,8),style= ['k','r--
','b:','b'],
                      title= str(ticker)+' Close Price, Turtle L/S
entries, cumulative returns')
```

Log returns are used instead of arithmetic ones. They are easier to manipulate. Cumulative returns are the sum of daily returns to which the np.exp method is applied.

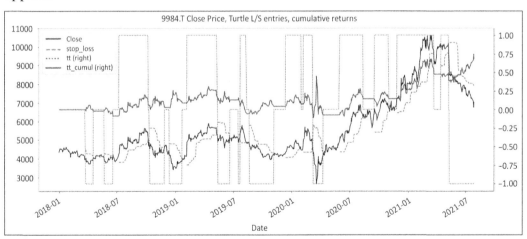

Figure 9.1: Softbank turtle for dummies, positions, and returns

This is also a graph we saw previously. It shows the closing price of Softbank, with a trailing stop loss above or below the close. It shows long and short positions and cumulative returns. Now that we have a strategy, let's run the risk metrics on both a rolling and cumulative basis.

We will get started with the Sharpe ratio. Risk-free return is set at an arbitrary one-tenth of a basis point.

```python
r_f = 0.00001 # risk free returns

def rolling_sharpe(returns, r_f, window):
    # Calculating average returns in a rolling window
    avg_returns = returns.rolling(window).mean()

    # Calculating the volatility of average returns in a rolling window
    std_returns = returns.rolling(window).std(ddof=0)

    # Rolling Sharpe ratio function
    return (avg_returns - r_f) / std_returns

def expanding_sharpe(returns, r_f):
    avg_returns = returns.expanding().mean()
    std_returns = returns.expanding().std(ddof=0)
    return (avg_returns - r_f) / std_returns

window = 252
df['sharpe_roll'] = rolling_sharpe(returns= tt_log_returns, r_f= r_f,
window= window) * 252**0.5

df['sharpe'] = expanding_sharpe(returns= tt_log_returns, r_f= r_f) *
252**0.5

df[window:][['tt_cumul','sharpe_roll','sharpe'] ].plot(figsize =
(20,8),style = ['b','c-.','c'],grid=True,
title = str(ticker)+' cumulative returns, Sharpe ratios: rolling &
cumulative')
```

There is no big mystery to the code. First, we calculate a rolling Sharpe, and then a cumulative one. Results are annualized using the standard formula: square root of 252 business days.

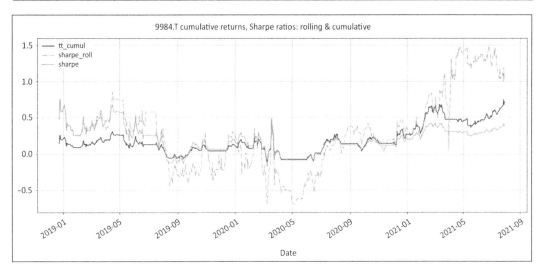

Figure 9.2: Softbank cumulative returns and Sharpe ratios: rolling and cumulative

The rolling Sharpe dash-dotted line is more volatile and responsive than the solid one representing cumulative Sharpe. This is simply due to the data sample size.

Risk is often equated to volatility. It makes up for agreeable formulas. In this context, the Sharpe ratio appears to be the perfect metric of risk-adjusted returns. The only problem is that in practice, volatility is not a measure of risk. To prove this point, let us bring up a few high Sharpe ratio strategies that hit an iceberg overnight, and a few low ones that have remarkably endured. Now, some low volatility strategies are extremely risky. Here are a few examples:

1. **Long Term Capital Management (LTCM)** had a fairly low volatility strategy until a few months before their demise. They were trading mean reversion strategies. Those strategies have consistent low volatility returns, which is conducive to high Sharpe ratios. They might have survived one Nobel prize, but two was too much.

2. **Short Gamma volatility funds**: pre-Great Financial Crisis, volatility funds were fashionable investment vehicles. Their strategy consisted of collecting premiums from selling **out-of-the-money** (**OTM**) options. Since the probability of those options expiring in the money was extremely low, they printed consistent low volatility performance. They had Sharpe ratios above the industry average. It all worked well until volatility spiked and options expired in the money. Losses mounted exponentially and years of accumulated returns were vaporized in weeks. Short Gamma is the financial equivalent of playing a statistical Russian roulette with a gigantic barrel. Nothing happens until the day you blow your brains out. In industry jargon, this is referred to as "picking pennies in front of a steam roller."

Conversely, some volatile strategies have exceptionally strong track records, despite awful Sharpe ratios. As a group, systematic trend-following **Commodity Trading Advisors (CTAs)** such as Paul Tudor Jones, Ed Seykota, Bill Dunn, and William Eckhardt have towered the alpha generation pyramid for decades. Returns are lumpy. Trend followers spend most of the year protecting their capital and harvest outsized returns only a few times a year.

Bottom line, with all humble respect due to its creator, the Sharpe ratio is the right mathematical answer to the wrong question. Is volatility the right measure of risk? The Sharpe ratio is a measure of volatility-adjusted returns. Volatility does not equate to risk, but reflects uncertainty. As much as uncertainty may trigger some alarms in our mammal brain, our job description as market participants clearly states: "get comfortable with discomfort."

Building a combined risk metric

The next three metrics are arguably closer approximations of risk and are more intuitive.

The Grit Index

"When I left the dining room after sitting next to Gladstone, I thought he was the cleverest man in England. But when I sat next to Disraeli, I left feeling that I was the cleverest woman."

– *Jennie Jerome, mother of Winston Churchill*

Investors often seem to act counterintuitively to their interests. They say they want returns, but they react to drawdowns. More specifically, they react to drawdowns in three ways:

- **Magnitude**: never test the stomach of your investors
- **Frequency**: never test the nerves of your investors
- **Period of recovery**: never test the patience of your investors

The **Grit Index** is arguably the most underrated metric in the entire finance multiverse. Less than a handful of metrics capture robustness so elegantly. Broadly speaking, it looks at downside risk by dividing performance by the entire surface of the losses over a period. The index has the rare privilege of a mathematical formulation so intuitive it can be visualized by anyone. The gut-wrenching time spent agonizing about the multitude and magnitude of losses seems so long ago that it feels like a long surface of pain.

The mathematical calculation of a surface is called an **integral**. Next, since those losses obviously weigh on the financial and emotional capitals, they should be in the denominator.

Returns are what investors end up perceiving in the end. The Grit Index is what investors end up getting in the end divided by all the agony of losses. This formula was originally invented by Peter G. Martin in 1987 and published as the **Ulcer Index** in his book *The Investor's Guide to Fidelity Funds*. Legendary trader Ed Seykota recycled it and renamed it the **Seykota Lake ratio**. These are the exact same formulas, just with a different name. Since Ulcer Index or Seykota Lake ratio may fail to draw the attention they truly deserve, how about renaming it the Grit Index?

The following is the source code:

```
def rolling_grit(cumul_returns, window):
    tt_rolling_peak = cumul_returns.rolling(window).max()
    drawdown_squared = (cumul_returns - tt_rolling_peak) ** 2
    ulcer = drawdown_squared.rolling(window).sum() ** 0.5
    return cumul_returns / ulcer


def expanding_grit(cumul_returns):
    tt_peak = cumul_returns.expanding().max()
    drawdown_squared = (cumul_returns - tt_peak) ** 2
    ulcer = drawdown_squared.expanding().sum() ** 0.5
    return cumul_returns / ulcer

window = 252
df['grit_roll'] = rolling_grit(cumul_returns= df['tt_cumul'] , window =
window)
df['grit'] = expanding_grit(cumul_returns= df['tt_cumul'])
df[window:][['tt_cumul','grit_roll', 'grit'] ].plot(figsize = (20,8),
                  secondary_y = 'tt_cumul',style =
['b','g-.','g'],grid=True,
    title = str(ticker) + ' cumulative returns & Grit Ratios: rolling &
cumulative '+ str(window) + ' days')
```

The Grit calculation sequence is as follows:

1. Calculate the peak cumulative returns using `rolling().max()` or `expanding().max()`

2. Calculate the squared drawdown by subtracting cumulative returns from the peak and squaring them

3. Calculate the least square sum by taking the square root of the squared drawdowns

4. Divide the cumulative returns by the ulcer

The code produces the following chart:

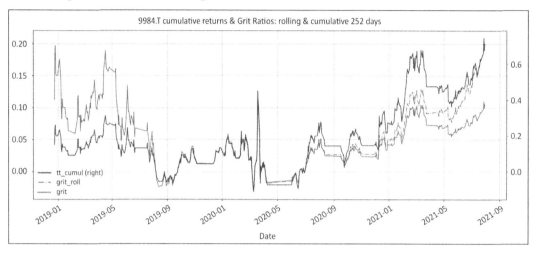

Figure 9.3: Softbank cumulative returns and Grit ratios: rolling and cumulative

Let's have a look at the progression across the chart. In the first half, the Grit Index mirrors performance. In the second half, performance jumps, but so do the magnitude and duration of drawdowns. The index trails behind the meteoric ascent. This strategy works but has some periods of drawdown, hence the lackluster index. This metric uses the only two variables that ever matter to investors: performance and drawdowns. If you think of performance as the end destination, then dividing it by the surface of losses shows the journey, and all the bumps along the road.

At the end of the day, human beings do not achieve greatness because of the absence of lofty goals. They give up along the way because of how hard the journey is. And this is precisely what this ratio does. This index accomplishes the same things as the Sharpe ratio while accounting for all the bumps along the road to great performance. It has the following advantages over the Sharpe ratio:

1. **Cross-asset unified measure**: it works uniformly across every asset class, every strategy, every time frame, in absolute and relative series.

2. **Uncertainty**: This metric focuses on the aspects of drawdowns that really matter to investors: magnitude, frequency, and a period of recovery. In contrast, the Sharpe ratio confuses uncertainty with fear. It punishes high volatility strategies, regardless of their profitability.

And it does more than the Sharpe ratio. The easiest way to reverse engineer a high Sharpe ratio is to dampen volatility. As long as volatility is compressed, even the most tepid returns look good. A tiny denominator will magnify any numerator, however mediocre. No wonder money flows to fixed income. Returns are pathetically mediocre, but predictably so.

On the other hand, the grit index focuses on cumulative instead of average returns. This is the number at the bottom of the bank statement the day after retirement. This metric therefore has a low tolerance for a fixed income type of stable mediocrity. Yet, this index will also penalize the only thing investors genuinely care about: the downside volatility. Upon retirement, pensioners only look at the total amount of money in their account. They do not care about the stability of the average daily returns. Stable daily returns are a feel-good measure for the fund managers, not the pensioners. When market participants allocate assets using Sharpe or the **Capital Asset Pricing Model (CAPM)**, they trade returns for stability. Fixed income has, by definition, a higher Sharpe ratio than equity. It also has asthmatic returns.

The privilege of the Grit metric is that it imposes itself, even to those who are completely financially illiterate. There is no better metaphor than life for this index. Performance is what you have accomplished. Life is what happened to you when you had other plans, with all the setbacks along the way. Divide your accomplishments by the obstacles and you have a pretty robust measure of grit. In practice, the robustness of the Grit Index means it could be used as an asset allocation key between strategies.

Common Sense Ratio

"Common sense is not so common."

– Voltaire, freedom fighter

Enter Jack Schwager. In my personal bucket list, having a one-on-one meeting with the author of the *Market Wizards* series is as close as it will ever get to a "thank you very much" from Elvis or a blood transfusion from James Brown. His books are as relevant now as they were when they were published decades ago.

I had the immense privilege of being instrumental to having Mr Schwager deliver a keynote speech at a CLSA conference in Tokyo. So, here we are discussing his underrated gem of wisdom, *Market Sense and Nonsense*. In it, he discusses the gain to pain ratio, better known as the **profit ratio**.

In essence, this is a fractional version of the trading edge/gain expectancy. Somewhere along the conversation, I introduced my homemade small metric, a blend of two ratios, to which his response was, "hmm, common sense." The master has spoken. I can die now, happy but somewhat perplexed. A couple of hours later back at the ranch, I unveil it to my boss and explain the rationale: "yeah dude, that is common sense," my boss vastly elaborated.

When two people for whom respect is plotted on a logarithmic scale reach the same conclusion... voilà: the **Common Sense Ratio** (**CSR**) is born. The rationale behind this metric is that there are two ways to lose a fight: either on points or by way of knock-out. There are two ways a strategy can fail: either with excess cumulative losses or by a few devastating blows. This goes back to the only two types of strategies ever traded: trend following or mean reversion. The risk associated with trend following is in the aggregates. The risk associated with mean reversion is in the tails.

Both strategies have different risk factors, aggregate or tail. They require different risk metrics. The rationale for the CSR is to come up with a unified measure. Back in elementary school, when my math skills had not yet reached a "permanently low plateau," there was this wonderful notion of transitivity of multiplication. The simplest way to combine those risk metrics for both strategies is to multiply the gain to pain (profit) ratio by the tail ratio. Here is a refresher of the original code from *Chapter 6, The Trading Edge is a Number, and Here is the Formula*, plus the CSR:

```python
def rolling_profits(returns,window):

#### removed for brevity: check GitHub repo for full code ####

def rolling_losses(returns,window):

#### removed for brevity: check GitHub repo for full code ####

def expanding_profits(returns):

#### removed for brevity: check GitHub repo for full code ####

def expanding_losses(returns):

#### removed for brevity: check GitHub repo for full code ####
```

```python
def profit_ratio(profits, losses):

#### removed for brevity: check GitHub repo for full code ####

def rolling_tail_ratio(cumul_returns, window, percentile,limit):
    left_tail = np.abs(cumul_returns.rolling(window).
quantile(percentile))
    right_tail = cumul_returns.rolling(window).quantile(1-percentile)
    np.seterr(all='ignore')
    tail = np.maximum(np.minimum(right_tail / left_tail,limit),-limit)
    return tail

def expanding_tail_ratio(cumul_returns, percentile,limit):
    left_tail = np.abs(cumul_returns.expanding().quantile(percentile))
    right_tail = cumul_returns.expanding().quantile(1 - percentile)
    np.seterr(all='ignore')
    tail = np.maximum(np.minimum(right_tail / left_tail,limit),-limit)
    return tail

def common_sense_ratio(pr,tr):
    return pr * tr

window = 252
df['pr_roll'] = profit_ratio(profits= rolling_profits(returns =
tt_log_returns,window = window),
                             losses= rolling_losses(returns =
tt_log_returns,window = window))
df['pr'] = profit_ratio(profits= expanding_profits(returns=
tt_log_returns),
                             losses= expanding_losses(returns =
tt_log_returns))

df[window:] [['tt_cumul','pr_roll','pr'] ].plot(figsize =
(20,8),secondary_y= ['tt_cumul'],
                             style = ['r','y','y:'],grid=True)
```

Here, we calculate rolling and cumulative ratios and print them:

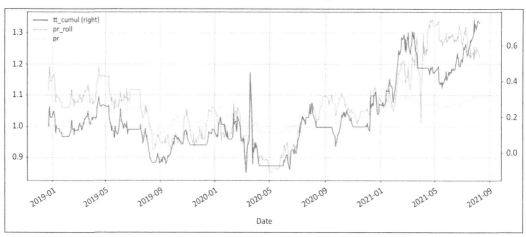

Figure 9.4: Cumulative returns and common sense ratios: cumulative and rolling

The profit ratio is the most appropriate risk measure for trend-following strategies. Risk is in the aggregates, as we saw in *Chapter 6, The Trading Edge is a Number, and Here is the Formula*, and *Chapter 8, Position Sizing: Money is Made in the Money Management Module*. The preceding chart shows a healthy but not spectacular profit ratio. In other words, the strategy, in its current pro-consul (the ancestor of the homo erectus) format, seems to work.

We will conclude with the CSR, which is the product of both the profit and tail ratios:

```
window = 252

df['tr_roll'] = rolling_tail_ratio(cumul_returns= df['tt_cumul'],
                        window= window, percentile= 0.05,limit=5)
df['tr'] = expanding_tail_ratio(cumul_returns= df['tt_cumul'],
percentile= 0.05,limit=5)

df['csr_roll'] = common_sense_ratio(pr= df['pr_roll'],tr= df['tr_
roll'])
df['csr'] = common_sense_ratio(pr= df['pr'],tr= df['tr'])

df[window:] [['tt_cumul','csr_roll','csr'] ].plot(secondary_y=
['tt_cumul'],style = ['b','r-.','r'], figsize = (20,8),
    title= str(ticker)+' cumulative returns, Common Sense Ratios:
cumulative &  rolling '+str(window)+ ' days')
```

The chart reflects a relatively healthy CSR, with no hidden surprises.

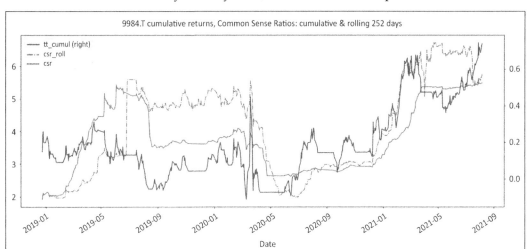

Figure 9.5: Cumulative returns and common sense ratios: cumulative and rolling

Patterns that would be a cause for concern for a trend-following strategy would be an increasingly heavy index value. As strategy progresses, the cumulative weight of losses would bear heavier on the profit ratio. Patterns that would be a cause for concern for a mean reversion strategy would be a steady low-value index with sudden drops. This would suggest that profits fail to compensate for losses.

The CSR recaptures risks associated with both strategies. It also gives powerful indications of the ability to recover from losses and the cyclicality of strategies. The following examples demonstrate how this metric works in practice.

Example 1: assume a strategy returns 10% per annum. The 95th percentile of best months has been at +0.6%, while the bottom 5th percentile of worst months has been at -2%. The following values can be calculated:

- Gain to pain ratio = 1.1
- Tail ratio = |0.6%/-2%| = 0.3
- CSR = 1.1* 0.3 = 0.33

A CSR below 1 means the strategy is vulnerable to shocks. A ratio below 0.5 means the strategy will probably fail to recover from serious shocks. The CSR is particularly efficient at identifying hidden risks with mean reversion strategies. Mean reversion strategies give the appearance of stability and robustness. Profits roll in with metronomic regularity. Yet, unpredictable left tail events derail this stability.

This strategy may seem like it generates a solid consistent profit of +10% per annum, but the tail ratio of 0.3 suggests it would take three times longer to recover from accidents. The only question that matters is: are investors going to be patient enough or will they cut their losses and look for alternative vehicles? The answer to this question might be found in the tale of the quants demise in 2007. Those strategies did well for years, but when they experienced unexpected drawdowns, relatively large to their monthly average returns, investors redeemed.

 We will consider some of the failures of previous strategies, and some pitfalls to avoid, in *Chapter 10, Refining the Investment Universe.*

Example 2: let's take a strategy that trails the benchmark by 2% over a complete cycle (GPR = 0.98). Assume winners are three times bigger than losers, or a tail ratio of 3. Again, calculate the necessary values from the previously defined functions:

- Gain to pain ratio = 0.98
- Tail ratio = 3
- CSR = 0.98 * 3 = 2.94

With a relative gain to pain ratio of 0.98, you may be thinking, "Why invest in a vehicle that loses money over time?" Welcome to your average **mutual fund**. Over time, fees eat performance away, causing mutual funds to underperform their benchmark. Yet, performance is cyclical. Sometimes, managers shoot the ball out of the park. The CSR is a simple way to time entry and, more importantly, exit. A high CSR combined with a subpar profit/gain to pain ratio is evidence of strong seasonality. Those products work very well some of the time but fail in the long run. In *Chapter 5, Regime Definition*, we saw several regime definition methodologies, which should help when identifying seasonality.

Van Tharp's SQN

This statistical measure was brought back to fame by Dr Van Tharp. System Quality Number SQN® is a brilliant interpretation of the time-honored t-stat. It has all the ingredients necessary to measure robustness. Firstly, a strategy is viable only if it has a trading edge. Nothing happens until gain expectancy turns positive.

Secondly, it incorporates trading frequency. Making money is one thing, trading on the appointment is another. The more a strategy can trade while maintaining a positive gain expectancy, the faster returns compound. Time is the variable that immediately jumps to mind.

Market participants should lower their time frames as long as they can maintain a positive gain expectancy. For example, a strategy viable on daily and 4-hour bars will generate more signals on the lower time frame. Besides, shorter time frames mean tighter stop losses and bigger positions, but also noisier signals.

Thirdly, results are normalized. They are expressed in standard deviations, which, in this case, means trading edge volatility. When it comes to returns, everyone likes the peaks, but no one likes the valleys. Last but not least, the code is straightforward to implement:

```python
def expectancy(win_rate,avg_win,avg_loss):
    # win% * avg_win% - loss% * abs(avg_loss%)
    return win_rate * avg_win + (1-win_rate) * avg_loss

def t_stat(signal_count, trading_edge):
    sqn = (signal_count ** 0.5) * trading_edge / trading_edge.std(ddof=0)
    return sqn

# Trade Count
df['trades'] = df.loc[(df['tt'].diff() !=0) & (pd.notnull(df['tt'])),'tt'].abs().cumsum()
signal_count = df['trades'].fillna(method='ffill')
signal_roll = signal_count.diff(window)

# Rolling t_stat

#### removed for brevity: check GitHub repo for full code ####

# Cumulative t-stat

#### removed for brevity: check GitHub repo for full code ####

df[window:][['tt_cumul','sqn','sqn_roll'] ].plot(figsize = (20,8),
                secondary_y= ['tt_cumul'], grid= True,style =
['b','y','y-.'],
                title= str(ticker)+' Cumulative Returns and SQN:
cumulative & rolling'+ str(window)+' days')
```

This is how the code works:

1. The number of signals needs to be disentangled from the regime. `.diff()` identifies when there is a change in regime: from 0 to 1 and vice versa. The `notnull()` method ensures that signals are counted once upon entry. From there, `abs()` counts all trades as one. The cumulative sum is done via `cumsum()`. Then, the `fillna` method fills all the missing values forward. `.diff(window)` applied to the trades column returns the rolling number of trades.

2. Next, we calculate the rolling series. Copy the daily returns and assign N/A to losing days. This leaves positive returns. We calculate a moving average count and divide it by the window. Similarly, we calculate rolling profits and losses and divide them by the window.

3. The cumulative calculation works a bit differently. Calculate the cumulative count of returns using the expanding method. Calculate the cumulative count of positive returns the same way. Then, calculate the win rate, average win, and loss.

4. We reuse the code for gain expectancy in *Chapter 6, The Trading Edge is a Number, and Here is the Formula.*

The SQN is a regular t-stat with gain expectancy and signal count as input variables. We multiply the square root of trades by the information ratio of the gain expectancy. The execution trader English translation is: we factor in trading frequency to the trading edge.

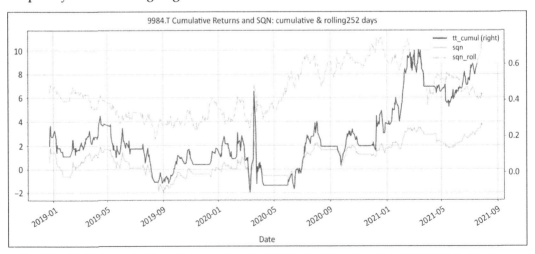

Figure 9.6: Softbank cumulative returns and t-stat (Van Tharp's SQN): cumulative and rolling

Without trading frequency, SQN would be yet another variation on the Sharpe ratio, using gain expectancy instead of average returns. Instead, it's a very useful function, which incorporates both trading frequency and edge. For example, if a strategy makes money but trades on appointments every leap year, chances are investors will not stick with you. Conversely, if a strategy maintains the same positive edge at a lower timeframe from daily to 1 hour, it would make more sense to trade the lower time frame to compound profits faster.

Robustness score

"Masala: a varying blend of spices used in Indian cooking."

– Merriam Webster dictionary

The Grit Index, Common Sense Ratio, and Van Tharp's SQN all measure robustness. The Grit Index is probably the most elegant and accessible metric for non-finance people. The CSR is a good canary in the coal mine to ferret out dodgy mean reversion strategies. SQN is a solid staple measure of quality. They all do the job. They measure a specific aspect of robustness:

1. The Grit Index integrates losses throughout the period. It gives an accurate vision of performance of all aspects of downside: magnitude, frequency, and duration.

2. The CSR combines risks endemic to the two types of strategies in a single measure. It shows how risk is balanced for each metric.

3. The t-stat SQN incorporates trading frequency into the trading edge formula to show the most efficient use of capital.

Yet, after publicly railing against the proliferation of risk metrics, coming out with three robustness measures may come across as a bit hypocritical. The easiest solution is to throw all of them in the pot and stir using the transitivity of multiplication:

```
def robustness_score(grit,csr,sqn):
    start_date = max(grit[pd.notnull(grit)].index[0],
            csr[pd.notnull(csr)].index[0],
            sqn[pd.notnull(sqn)].index[0])
    score = grit * csr * sqn / (grit[start_date] * csr[start_date] *
    sqn[start_date])
    return score
```

```
df['score_roll'] = robustness_score(grit = df['grit_roll'], csr =
df['csr_roll'],sqn= df['sqn_roll'])
df['score'] = robustness_score(grit = df['grit'],csr = df['csr'],sqn =
df['sqn'])

df[window:][['tt_cumul','score','score_roll']].plot(
    secondary_y= ['score'],figsize=(20,6),style = ['b','k','k-.'],
title= str(ticker)+' Cumulative Returns and Robustness Score:
cumulative & rolling '+ str(window)+' days')
```

The robustness score function rebases all variables to the first date where all variables are not null. This puts all variables on the same starting value. We produce the following chart:

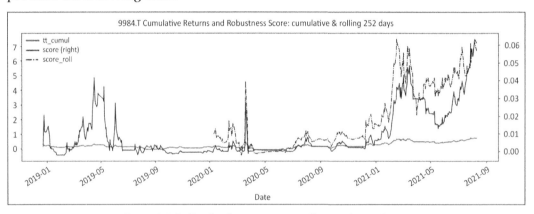

Figure 9.7: Softbank robustness score: rolling and cumulative

The robustness score metric is aimed at participants who want one final score to rule them all, or more likely one sorting key to rank several strategies. This score is as recomposed as Frankenstein, so it is difficult to read. Each risk metric brings its own value to the table. This is why the metric rebases all values to the beginning of the series. Combining them into a single metric is not going to produce a super risk metric, but one tangible benefit would be as a unified sorting key. This metric will privilege strategies that:

1. Trade frequently thanks to SQN

2. Have acceptable drawdowns thanks to the Grit Index

3. Generate decent returns

Conversely, it will penalize strategies that:

1. Have no positive trading edge thanks to all the metrics
2. Have nasty tail ratios thanks to the CSR index
3. Trade infrequently thanks to the SQN

As long as the moving average metric remains above 1 and the value appears to be rising, the strategy can be considered reasonably robust. One of the use cases for this robustness score may be as a sorting key for ranking or asset allocation purposes. When there are several metrics to choose from, combine them into one unified rebased indicator and sort. Proceed with caution, however. Familiarize yourself with it before deploying it in production.

Summary

In this chapter, we did not have a polite conversation about risk. We explored risk metrics that will unapologetically assess your ability to live to trade another day. We considered the Grit Index, which integrates drawdowns (magnitude, frequency, and duration). Then, we introduced the common sense ratio, which recaptures risk specific to both trend-following and mean reversion strategies. Finally, we looked at the system quality number ratio, before combining all three into a combined robustness score, which helps assess risk by combining trading frequency and trading edge.

In *Part II, The Outer Game: Developing a Robust Trading Edge*, we looked at how to generate ideas on the short side. We then looked at what the trading edge exactly is and how to boost it. We came up with an innovative equity trading algorithm. Finally, we looked at risk metrics that really measure robustness.

Now that we have plenty of ideas on both sides, and know how to size and prioritize them, it is time to organize them. *Part III, The Long/Short Game: Building a Long/Short Product*, is about long/short portfolio construction.

10

Refining the Investment Universe

Market participants usually find the vastness of the market quite intimidating. Thus, before we start putting the ideas we've covered in previous chapters into a combined investment strategy, we will dedicate a short chapter to reducing the market to a manageable investment universe.

In this chapter, we will start with some conceptual blind spots of the long/short business in an attempt to provide some valuable context to the real world you will be trading in. Next, we will follow the money to uncover what investors really want, by considering some major incidents and topics that have shaped the way that traders and markets operate.

We will cover the following topics:

- Avoiding short selling pitfalls
- What do investors really want?

Avoiding short selling pitfalls

This section is all about applying smart filters to avoid classic short selling pitfalls. Practitioners may hopefully revisit some of those points as they become more familiar with short selling. Most of the points here come from painful experiences.

Liquidity and market impact

Liquidity is the currency of bear markets. If you cannot get out of a position without significant market impact, you do not own anything. It owns you. The way to approach liquidity on the short side is radically different. On the long side, liquidity increases as more investors are drawn to rising prices. Early birds end up selling to a much larger pool of market participants.

On the short side, when investors liquidate their positions, it is a one-way street. After a beating, they don't come back for round two. Nothing captures the emotional journey of long market participants more faithfully than the Kübler-Ross model. Market participants grieve their losses. Each phase even has a distinctive signature on the markets. Interest wanes, and as the pool of market participants shrinks, so does liquidity. Early bear markets are a lot more liquid than later-stage ones. Short sellers exit into thinner liquidity than they entered.

Add short squeezes to the mix, and you've got a recipe for an explosive cocktail. The last thing you want is to be caught in a short squeeze with a large position that you cannot cover without serious market impact. On the short side, the way to approach liquidity and market impact is not about how long it takes to build a position, but about how easy it is to get out.

This limits the investment universe to issues where liquidity is not a problem. The resolution of the 2008 great financial crisis got the markets addicted to quantitative easing, otherwise known as free money. In layman's terms, monetary authorities flooded the world with painkillers to ease the pain of an economic crisis. As soon as monetary authorities hint at tapering off, markets spiral down in withdrawal, and traders flock to safer, more defensive stocks, which is known as "risk-off." This forces monetary cavalry to keep pumping more painkillers into the system, which sends all kinds of speculative assets deep into bubble territory. When risk is 'on' and traders are looking for riskier stocks with more profit potential, small-mid caps are where the action is happening. Meanwhile, on the short side, boring blue chips are out of style. Whenever there is no accountability for failure, there is no incentive to play safe. When risk is 'off', and market participants are investing more defensively, they gravitate toward larger capitalizations, where liquidity remains abundant. Reverting the long-small/short-large caps trade is not easy. Shorting small caps is a bloody sport. Liquidity evaporates, and you can dock a supertanker in the bid/ask spread. So, gains can be wiped out at the first squeeze.

Bottom line: match your net market exposure with the general market regime and level of liquidity. No matter how seductive some ideas might look, only keep those where liquidity is not a problem.

Crowded shorts

"Elvis has left the building."

Back in 2007, I developed a **Weapon of Mass Short Destruction (WMSD)** named "**squeeze box**." The mechanics might have been counterintuitive, but it had a surreal accuracy rate to predict potential short squeezes. All it took was a long-only manager to take a minuscule speculative long position. Since the buy/sell equilibrium was already out of balance, this would push the price up and flush the tourists out. They would frantically cover, which would rapidly morph into a short squeeze. At this point, the long-only manager would leisurely exit their long position with a comfortable profit. When I realised that this program directly hurt my friends back in the hedge fund world, this WMSD was permanently dismantled.

Moral of the story: eliminate all crowded shorts, issues where borrow utilization exceeds 50%, from your investment universe. They should not even be on your radar. Think of all the people who routinely go through red traffic lights. It all works fine until they wake up in a hospital.

The way to make money on the short side is to find what institutional investors are liquidating and ride their tails. Good short stories usually make up for bad short trades. Every bit of information has a tick price tag attached to it. Do not wait for all the pieces of the puzzle to fit. By the time a story has deteriorated enough to become an obvious short candidate, institutional investors will have liquidated their long positions. The only people left will be short sellers fighting over a dry bone. This leads us to a simple and powerful supply-and-demand indicator called **borrow utilization**.

Borrow utilization is the ratio of borrow taken out for short selling divided by the supply of shares available for borrow. Large institutions have lending programs wherein they lend a portion of their long holdings for a fee. When they trim those positions, supply dries up.

$$Borrow\ utilization = \frac{Borrow\ taken\ out\ for\ short\ selling}{Total\ supply\ of\ shares\ available\ for\ borrow}$$

Meanwhile, as shorts gain popularity, demand for borrow increases. Demand on the numerator and supply on the denominator is what makes borrow utilization the most effective measure of both institutional ownership and popularity. For example, borrow utilization north of 50% simply means that the shorting appetite exceeds institutional ownership. Since institutions are the major players in the markets, the risk/reward ratio evidently deteriorates.

Borrow utilization can vary significantly based on a company's ownership structure. Some shareholders do not participate in lending programs. For example, tightly held companies have few shareholders, who, for inscrutable reasons, often fail to appreciate their babies being the targets of vicious bear raids.

Short selling is an expensive sport. Short sellers are charged borrowing fees. These range from **general collateral** (GC) on easy-to-borrow issues to prohibitive rates on hard-to-borrow or crowded shorts. As borrow gradually gets taken out, the quality of the remaining pool deteriorates. Adding to this, hard-to-borrow issues do not only fetch usury rates that would make Shakespeare's Shylock blush; they are sometimes callable. This means the lenders have the option of withdrawing their lending back on short notice. This is referred to as "**recall**." When recalls happen, short sellers are left to either locate borrow elsewhere or close their positions. Recalls sometimes cause short squeezes.

The last tourist short sellers to get on board are often too excited to think twice about borrowing callable stocks. When a recall happens, they cannot locate borrow and are forced to close. Since selling pressure has already reached a climax, the new buying pressure creates an imbalance in supply/demand. Share price rises effortlessly. This triggers other short sellers to stop losses, and they proceed to cover. This rapidly snowballs into a full-blown short squeeze that flushes out not only tourists but also the more seasoned short sellers as well. Bottom line: stay away from issues where other short sellers tap into low-quality borrow.

Crowded shorts tend to have lower sensitivity to the market than the more popular issues. When the market hits a periodic air pocket, crowded shorts barely move. Meanwhile, high-flying stocks on the long side nosedive. In relative terms, this means that crowded shorts outperform and longs underperform. One possible explanation for this phenomenon is the lack of participation from institutional and retail investors. There is no institutional long money in crowded shorts, so when a periodic pullback happens, there is no one to sell and drive the stock price down. Bottom line: crowded shorts do not edge long positions when they drop precipitously. If the only thing that crowded shorts ever bring to the table is feeding the expensive need to be right, then it's not an approach you should be taking.

Conclusion: just like dieters need to remove ice cream and potato chips from reach, weed out crowded shorts from your investment universe altogether.

The fertile ground of high dividend yield

"They say the best weapon is one you never have to fire. I respectfully disagree. I prefer the weapon you only need to fire once."

– Tony Stark, Iron Man

Companies sometimes increase their dividend yield to bring dividend support to their share price. High dividend yield attracts value investors and retailers who look for more stable cash flow. This effectively deters short sellers from engaging in bear campaigns. However, while a high dividend yield might stem immediate short selling pressure, it does not prevent the share price from falling in the long term. A high dividend yield is usually synonymous with ex-growth companies. They have stopped growing, so they redistribute cash back to shareholders. This is what makes the high-yielding stock universe fertile ground for profitable, peaceful short selling.

The good news about dividends is that they are predictable corporate events. There are a few events that short sellers need to be mindful of. The first two are record and payment dates. Short sellers need to curb their enthusiasm in these moments. Companies sometimes decide to raise dividends around the time they make earnings announcements. Time your trading around those dates, and you will have a surprisingly pleasant time. For example, investors tend to reduce immediately past the ex-date, the moment when dividends are declared. This accentuates the drop into dividend payment date.

Another way to reframe high-yield stocks as viable short candidates is to focus on the underlying reason for the dividend being so high in the first place. Growth stocks usually have miserable dividend yields. They need their cash to reinvest in their businesses. On the other hand, stable, mature companies have excess cash but unattractive long-term prospects. A little bit of dividend goes a long way to court investors.

Bottom line: value traps hide behind high dividends. Look for high yield underperformers and navigate around dividend dates and you will have a surprisingly easy time.

Share buybacks

> *"A man generally has two reasons for doing one thing. One that sounds good and the real one."*
>
> *– J.P. Morgan*

Conventional wisdom has it that corporates will buy back their shares on the open market when they are undervalued. In practice, they are just as clueless as sell-side analysts when it comes to timing undervaluation. Share buy-backs peaked in late 2007 and bottomed out in March 2009.

Proponents for share buy-backs argue that there is no better use of their cash and cheap credit than buying back their shares. This creates a trickle-down effect and benefits the economy at large.

This shareholder supremacy dates back to a school of thought pioneered by Milton Friedman in the 80s. Corporations have become increasingly big players on the markets through share buy-back programs. The rally that followed former President Trump's tax cut was primarily driven by corporations buying back their own stock.

Adversaries argue that cash is siphoned from stakeholders (employees, customers, R&D, and suppliers) and then channeled toward shareholders. Simply said, the coach skimps on the players but spreads largesse onto the fans. The majority of top executives' compensation comes from stock options. They therefore have a direct incentive to prop up share prices to pad their stock option plans. The most powerful way is to buy back stock. This reduces liquidity, inflates earnings per share, and drives share prices up.

The coronavirus pandemic of 2020 shed a crude light on this hypocrisy and settled the debate once and for all. Share buybacks siphon the life out of companies. This obsessive focus on short-term market impact is not aligned with the long-term interests of companies. When the world went into lockdown, companies found themselves almost immediately insolvent. Their share prices collapsed but they still had to face loan obligations contracted for the buybacks. In the history of capitalism, never had the emperor been so aimlessly wandering around haggard and naked.

This is, however, beside the point for short sellers. Corporations have pockets deep enough to artificially levitate share prices. Short sellers should therefore refrain from shorting companies that engage in share buyback programs. The good news is that share buybacks are highly correlated to market gyrations. Share buybacks evaporate when most needed, during corrections. This means the shorting season is open and in full swing.

Bottom line: do not short companies outright that roll out share buybacks. Allow them to hollow themselves out and wait for the inevitable vulnerability.

Fundamental analysis

> *"Time is on my side."*

> *– Mick Jagger*

Fundamental analysis gives its letters of nobility to the stock market analysis. Few endeavors are as intellectually stimulating as stock analysis. Regime definition can greatly simplify the work of fundamental analysts.

When fundamental analysts consider market regime, they essentially try to answer a theoretical question. They try to figure out why a stock should go down and why it should happen now. There are multitudes of reasons.

They may eventually be vindicated. Yet they take on massive timing, reputational, and ultimately business risks. They hope markets will agree with their thesis before investors lose patience. There are too many random variables to expect consistent results.

On the other hand, subjecting fundamental analysis to market regimes tries to answer a practical question: why is this stock going down? The good news is the answer generally falls in to one of three buckets:

- First, it can be a temporary mispricing. The regime may have switched from bull to sideways. After a vigorous bull phase, stocks tend to pause and digest the advance. This phase is known as consolidation. Stocks may be dead money for a while. If so, the solution is simple. Dead money walking looks a lot better with a vigorous haircut. Trim your positions. Re-allocate capital to fresh ideas. If stocks start to perform again, there will be ample time to restock.

- Second, if a few stocks within a sector start to underperform in unison, this suggests sector rotation. This cuts out the work for analysts: pick almost any stock in an underperforming sector.

- Third, if one stock does not behave in line with its sector, it might indicate some stock-specific problems. This is the time to shine for fundamental analysts. This is the time to spot the real profitable structural shorts out there. Value traps often go unnoticed because they have all the exterior signs of value stocks. They often have generous dividend policies. Valuations are at a discount relative to their peers, which makes them look superficially attractive. Yet, they stubbornly underperform. They are cheap and stay cheap for a reason. The job of a fundamental analyst is to find out why.

On the short side, conventional fundamental analysis is difficult to do. Asymmetry of information is something short sellers must contend with. Companies rarely volunteer bad news. Analysts keep their "buy" ratings until the fateful day when they happen to read in the press that companies have filed for bankruptcy the night before.

Sell-side cheerleaders may, however, have some involuntary marginal utility. In the permafrost tundra of misleading "buy" ratings, the code word for underperformance is "Buy for the long-term investors." Look for stocks where ratings are not refreshed, earnings models gather dust, and where even maintenance research is not properly maintained. One phone call to confirm that "those are stocks for long-term investors" and you are in business.

What do investors really want?

The long/short industry seems to go through a severe existential crisis every time the market "hits a soft patch." Investors are rudely reminded that downside protection only means limited downside with virtually no upside. The industry has operated from a "build it and they will come" product supply model. If the objective is to build sustainable businesses, it is high time we paused and looked at the world from an investor's perspective. This will provide crucial context to build a long/short product that meets investors' demands step by step.

Lessons from the 2007 quants debacle

"And so castles made of sand,

melt into the sea,

eventually."

– Jimi Hendrix

In August 2007, cross-sectional volatility took markets around the world by surprise. Although indices did not move much, constituents jumped across the board for a few days. Soon, rumors of unwinding from various quantitative market-neutral funds began to spread. This was the beginning of the end for Quants 1.0.

Those smart market-neutral funds were all like Venetian pizzas: 37 different names on the menu but the same crust for everyone. They had fairly similar models. Since they were market-neutral, cash proceeds from short selling could be used to leverage up almost infinitely. Some funds levered up seven times to magnify otherwise underwhelming returns. For a time, everything was working well. All fund managers had to do was keep selling short more shares to match the ever-expanding long side. This all worked nicely until summer 2007, when the real estate bubble started to fester.

Every avalanche starts with a snowball. At that time, in a different corner of the market, a few large multi-strategy shops were asked to post more collateral for their **Credit Default Obligations** (CDO) and **Credit Default Swap** (CDS) portfolios. When they could not raise cash for their credit books, they were forced to liquidate their most liquid asset class. They turned to their quantitative market-neutral books. This was the original snowball. In mid-summer, liquidity usually dries up. Their short books were illiquid. When the first shops started to cover their positions, they pushed prices up. This triggered the stop losses of their neighbors. They proceeded to close their own positions. This triggered a contagious chain reaction that culminated in a messy cross-sectional market. That was the definition of contagion.

People sometimes argue about what constitutes good quality, but they rarely disagree on the bad stuff. Everyone found themselves in the same shorts. Since there is a finite supply of shares available for short selling, trades got really crowded. Liquidation by multi-strategy funds exacerbated the problem. Managers eventually realized it would take them weeks to unwind their short positions, and they proceeded to pare them down to manageable levels. Liquidity was the dominant risk. Everyone with roughly the same models came to the same realization at the same time. The elite quants scrambling to cover their shorts was the financial equivalent of an elephant stampede through a china shop.

Back in those days, market-neutral funds were advertised as safe investment vehicles: equity returns with low volatility. In the minds of many, market-neutral meant capital protection. So, when some of these funds started posting -3-4% monthly returns during what seemed like quiet markets, two things happened. Prime brokers raised margin requirements as **Value at Risk** (**VAR**) increased, forcing funds to reduce leverage. Secondly, investors turned Bob Marley on fund managers: "redemption song."

Those redemptions forced managers to close positions, adding more volatility to the funds. With reduced leverage, increased volatility, and piling redemptions, it would take months, if not years, to recover losses. Plus, the reputational damage was irreparable. It was game over for quantitative market-neutral funds 1.0.

This meltdown began with one simple mistake: the architects of those funds made the fatal assumption that the short side would mirror the long. For a while, it did. But as the funds grew bigger, the unique dynamics of the short side came back to haunt them. Liquidity dried up. Shorts became crowded. By the time managers realized risk had gone up exponentially on the short side, it was too late.

Moral of the story: If you want to run a sustainable long/short business, you need to build your portfolio from the short side up.

 For more on this subject, see *Turbulent Times in Quant Land*, by Matthew S. Rothman, Ph.D. at Lehman Brothers, August 9, 2007.

The next two parts will focus further on what investors really want. They do not park money with a sophisticated long/short to buy the same AAPL stock that a low-tech **exchange traded fund** (**ETF**) can do at a fraction of the cost. Investors want low-volatility returns uncorrelated with market gyrations.

The Green Hornet complex of the long/short industry

"What IS, is more important than what SHOULD BE. Too many people look at what is from a position of what should be."

– Bruce Lee, Great Chinese American Philosopher

The 1966 television series *The Green Hornet* featured Brett Reid, an ambitious publisher at the Daily Sentinel by day and crime-fighting Green Hornet by night, and Kato, his loyal valet. If it wasn't for the sidekick butler played by an unknown actor named Bruce Lee, that highly forgettable show would never have entered the pantheon of cult series.

The long/short industry suffers from an unresolved Green Hornet complex. Many long/short participants are sheep dressed in wolves' clothing. Sharp agile hedge fund managers love to boast their superior analytical ability to pick stocks on the long side. Who cares? No one needs the onerous "sophistication" of a hedge fund manager to buy AAPL. Any "boring" long-only fund manager will provide the exact same service at a fraction of the cost. Better still, any low-tech, low-cost, plain vanilla ETF will do better than any active manager over time.

What really gets long/short market participants into the pantheon of cult fund managers is their ability to make money when no one else does. That comes from the sidekick called the short book.

The long/short industry is a highly competitive arena. Market participants know they must hit the ground running to attract investors. So, they default to trading within their comfort zone. They spend most of their time picking stocks on the long side. Meanwhile, endless frustration with their shorts discourages them from learning the intricacies of the "dark arts." Despite the best initial intentions, the short book gradually gets relegated to a sideshow.

This goes on as long as markets move up. As soon as markets hit a "soft patch," the neglected short side fails to compensate for the losses on the long side. When performance goes through an air pocket, investors suffocate. They had to swallow exorbitant fees and stomach "alpha-challenged" returns. No wonder they choke when they realize that downside protection really meant losing less than the market. It is therefore no surprise that the long/short industry is now met with growing cynicism.

Lessons from Bernie Madoff

"You will be amused when you see that I have more than once deceived without the slightest qualm of conscience, both knaves and fools."

– Giacomo Casanova

Every market participant has some alpha-generating "secret sauce." They accordingly launch a product that suits their investment style. They operate on the "build it and they will come" model, a belief that alpha generation alone will suffice to attract investors. Soon enough, they're left wondering why other participants with placid returns outpace market wizards with solid performance in the cut-throat race for **assets under management (AUM)**.

As an asset class, systematic **commodity trading advisors (CTAs)** have dominated the performance game for decades. Yet, according to friend and best-selling author Michael Covel, their aggregate AUM represents 0.4% of global assets under management. Despite outstanding long-term collective track records, their aggregate AUM remains a rounding error. This is where it gets confusing for fund managers. On the one hand, investors openly say they are looking for returns. On the other hand, when it is time to put the money where their mouth is, they opt for something else. The good news is money leaves a trail.

Before praising the marketing acumen of Mr. Madoff, let's get one thing straight. Any white-collar criminal who defrauds investors deserves decades behind bars. Bernard L. Madoff is a good contender for the greatest con artist of all time in the private sector minor league. He spent decades defrauding thousands of investors of billions of dollars. His tale offers a valuable insight into the mind of investors.

What Madoff offered was so powerful that it muted the professional skepticism of some of the most sophisticated players in the finance industry. In a rare interview from prison, Mr. Madoff confessed that investors "should have known better." Below is a table of Madoff's alleged returns:

	S&P 500	Fairfield Sentry (Madoff)
Annual average return	7.7%	11.0%
Compounded return	201.0%	504.0%
Months positive	63.0%	92.0%
Max. drawdown	-46.3%	-1.6%
Drawdown duration (month)	80	2
Semi-correlation		0.03

At an average of 11.04% per annum, performance was decent, but hardly jaw-dropping. As previously mentioned, investors say they want returns, but they react to drawdowns. What set Madoff apart were four things:

- First, the duration of drawdowns: Never test the patience of investors. One of the questions lingering on the back of the mind of every investor from retailer to institutional asset allocator is: "Is it too late to invest?" Only when greed, or the fear of missing out, is stronger than the fear of losing money will they put their hard-earned savings to work. In practice, peak inflows often coincide with the top of bull runs. Patsies who subscribed to the "Dow at 36,000" charlatanism and took the plunge in August 2000 had to endure 80 consecutive months of drawdown before they could make their money back in May 2007. That was just in time for the next dive. In contrast, Mr. Madoff was always open for business. He had only 2 consecutive down months. Every month was a good month to get in. Such a small drawdown duration is statistically improbable. The only market participant who has ever come close is the legendary Edward Thorp, who ironically blew the whistle on Madoff 14 years before the scandal erupted.

- Second, the magnitude of drawdowns: Never test the stomach of investors. Once in a drawdown, investors worry about how bad this could get. The markets might go up by 7% long-term average return, conveniently omitting the abysmal -40-50% drawdowns in between. Even though positive returns were not spectacular, the maximum drawdown of -1.56% made it look like a risk-free investment. Kahneman-Tversky formulated their prospect theory in a much more brilliant way: loss aversion is more powerful than profit-seeking. It illustrates a powerful concept: "It does not matter how much you make, as long as you don't lose." Investors could set and forget.

- Third is the frequency of drawdowns: Never test the nerves of investors. Madoff was supposedly up 92% of the time as opposed to 63% for the S&P. S&P had 6 years of annual returns above 20%. It also had 4 years of negative double-digit returns. In comparison, Madoff's fraudulent average return was 11.04%. Yet, the compounded return of S&P was 200% versus 500% for Madoff.

- Fourth is semi-correlation (correlation to down months of the S&P Index), or the ability to make money in down markets. At 3%, Madoff was allegedly up whenever the market was down. That one sealed the deal. Managers who still stand up when everyone else is down stand out. Their phones ring off the hook with interested investors.

In the real world, generating returns like Madoff is statistically improbable. However, the closer you get, the more attractive your proposition becomes. If you manage to build a product somewhere between Madoff's Holy Grail and a passive investment in the index, you will get a serious edge over your competitors.

Summary

This short chapter is not meant to test the braincells of the reader. It is simply a collection of practical tips on how to avoid classic expensive pitfalls and meet investors' expectations. Investors do not buy into long/short products for long ideas. They want low-volatility uncorrelated returns. This chapter considered investors' expectations, while avoiding the trap of thinking of the short book as an afterthought of the more fun long book. If those problem stocks are removed from your field of vision, they will not be on your mind and this will eliminate temptation.

Once you have distilled your investment universe and understood what is expected of you by investors, it is time to pull the trigger. In the next chapters, we will put everything together, and see how this can be done in practice.

11

The Long/Short Toolbox

Long-only portfolios are by definition correlated to the market. Introducing a short component enables managers to engineer the type of performance they want to deliver. We will make long/short portfolio management accessible to all dedicated market participants in this chapter.

Creating a long/short portfolio requires the consolidation of two relative portfolios: a long and a short book. The transition from a long-only or absolute long/short into a relative strength-long/short portfolio can be quite disconcerting at first. There are lots of moving parts. An effective way to manage this transition is to begin with the objectives in mind: liquidity, correlation, volatility, and performance. Then, concentrate on a handful of variables that have the highest impact on these objectives: gross and net exposure, net beta, and concentration, which make up your investment toolbox when constructing your strategy.

The following table indicates which of our objectives are affected by each of these variables.

	Liquidity	Correlation	Volatility	Performance
Gross Exposure	✓		✓	✓
Net Exposure		✓	✓	✓
Net Beta		✓	✓	✓
Concentration	✓		✓	✓

Finally, we live up to what we write down. Time for some disciplined creativity, with a step-by-step guide on constructing your own investment strategy. Along the way, we will cover the following topics:

- Importing libraries
- Gross exposure: a tactical approach to leverage
- Net exposure: the headline bullish/bearish directionality
- Net beta: residual sensitivity to the markets
- Concentration: the number of stocks on either side
- Other exposures
- Design your own mandate

Let's start with gross exposure. This is the amount of leverage you are willing to take on. Leverage is a powerful double-edged sword. It will make and then break a business when not wielded properly.

 You can access color versions of all images in this chapter via the following link: `https://static.packt-cdn.com/downloads/9781801815192_ColorImages.pdf`. You can also access source code for this chapter via the book's GitHub repository: `https://github.com/PacktPublishing/Algorithmic-Short-Selling-with-Python-Published-by-Packt`.

Importing libraries

For this chapter and the rest of the book, we will be working with the pandas, numpy, yfinance, and matplotlib libraries. So, please remember to import them first:

```
# Import Libraries
import pandas as pd
import numpy as np
import yfinance as yf
%matplotlib inline
import matplotlib.pyplot as plt
```

Gross exposure

Gross exposure is the absolute sum of long and short books. Selling stocks short generates cash, which can be used to enter additional long positions. In theory, leverage could be increased ad infinitum. In practice, prime brokers limit leverage to 3 or 4 times to limit their counterparty risk. Nobody wants to deal with margin calls at the first sign of a market hiccup.

Gross exposure has a direct impact on:

- **Liquidity**: The higher the leverage, the bigger the positions. This has a direct effect on market impact. This is especially felt on the short side, as the 2007 quants attest.
- **Volatility**: Leverage magnifies the volatility of returns.
- **Performance**: Leverage magnifies returns: A paltry 0.1% at low leverage can be juiced up to 0.5% and so on.
- **Concentration**: If the objective is to keep volatility low, the number of names should move in tandem with leverage: higher gross means more names and vice versa.

Gross exposure is ultimately a reflection of market participants' confidence in the markets. The more confident they are, the more they tend to increase leverage to capture opportunities. Nothing looks more like a kid in a candy store than a growth manager in a tech bubble. Conversely, market participants tend to reduce their gross and increase their cash exposures to protect capital in periods of turbulence or uncertainty. Strategically managing gross exposure can be a powerful tool to boost performance in good times and protect capital in rough markets.

Market participants tend to manage gross exposure in one of two ways. Either they stick to a fixed level of exposure, or they take an unstructured approach. Fixed exposure participants stick to the same level of gross exposure throughout the cycle. The rationale for a constant level of gross exposure is simplicity. Participants like to keep the number of names to a level they can safely manage. They may leave money on the table in good times, yet they keep drawdowns to a manageable level during losing streaks. On the other hand, unstructured participants get bulled up in good times, load up the truck, and hoard cash in bad times.

If your objective is to deliver attractive returns with reasonably low volatility, there may be a more scientific approach. In the following sections, we will consider a simple, effective, step-by-step method to manage gross exposure. The idea is to allow gross exposure to follow the cycle of your performance. This is referred to as managing portfolio heat.

Portfolio heat

In *Part II, The Outer Game: Developing a Robust Trading Edge*, we discussed position sizing and risk management before entering a trade. What happens when we are already invested and the market takes an unexpected unpleasant turn? Markets are a good reflection of life. This is what happens to us when we have other plans.

We can neither predict nor control what happens in the world. Those of us who still believe they can predict anything should definitely not be in charge of managing pension funds anyways. We can, however, control what happens in the portfolio in two ways:

- Firstly, we can control how much risk goes into the portfolio through position sizing. We have complete control over how much risk we will allocate to the next trades. This happens before entering positions.

- Secondly, we can control how much risk we tolerate in the portfolio. These are the existing positions. Some work, some don't. Some are vulnerable. Some are still at risk. Some are risk-free.

This leads us to the concept of open risk, portfolio heat, and correlation:

- Open risk is the potential detraction at the stock level. Should the stop loss be triggered, will the position be closed at a loss or at a profit? If profitable, open risk is null. In financial creole, the position is known as a free carry. No matter what happens next, the trade will not lose money.

- Portfolio heat is the sum total of open risk on all positions. Open risk is aggregated by side and strategy. For example, assume you trade two long/short strategies: a mean reversion and a trend following one. Aggregate those four open risk and equity curves separately. In this context, open risk and maximum potential drawdown are two different things. Portfolio heat on open risk only deals with vulnerable positions. Free carry positions are governed by a different set of rules.

- Correlation is how the long book moves versus the short book in aggregate. When markets tank, short books do not always lead the way. Speculative issues on the long side drop faster and farther than low beta stocks, for instance. The point is to assume that "correlation goes to 1," meaning everything drops like a stone across the board. Long and short portfolio heats do not cancel one another. In theory, one would assume that the short side compensates the drop on the long side. In practice, shorts sometimes outperform longs during market pullbacks. Panicked momentum buyers dump their long holdings, thereby precipitating prices down. So, do not offset long and short portfolio heats.

Portfolio heat needs to be range-bound. Next, let's look at a few general principles to set the heat bands.

Portfolio heat bands

If you take too many risks, one day you won't have a business. If you do not take enough risks, you won't have a business to begin with. So, the secret is to keep risk range-bound.

The maximum heat band should be defined as follows. The goal is not to reduce gross exposure across the board. The objective is to reduce the open risk at the position level, which will result in a contraction of the gross exposure. Stocks have different volatility signatures. Low-volatility stocks warrant bigger positions. For example, cutting the risk on defensive stocks has a vastly different impact on gross exposure than on highly volatile stocks. This system is more effective than actual gross exposure bands. One thing market participants should bear in mind is the upper bound of the portfolio heat.

There is a rational maximum risk number that ensures an optimal geometric growth rate of the equity curve. Excellent, yet it is completely irrelevant. What matters is how much risk your clientele can stomach. For example, if clients say they can live with a 10% drawdown, then your acceptable maximum portfolio heat should be around 5%. Humans in general, and clients in particular, vastly overestimate their tolerance for pain. Besides, it will take time and effort to redress the situation. The upper bound is literally a business decision. Volatility is a by-product of risk—the more risk you tolerate at the portfolio level, the more volatility you invite in the portfolio. This will in turn limit the type of clientele you will be able to target. Pension funds are volatility-adverse, for instance. It will define everything from the number of names to the performance and information ratio.

When in doubt, err on the side of caution. A classic solution is to increase the number of names, for instance. Furthermore, as we will see in the *Tactical deployment* section, investors think in calendar years. Consequently, your upper tolerance varies according to whether it's closer to the beginning or end of the year. All things being equal, risk should start small, progressively increase, peak in the third quarter, and wind down by the end of the calendar year. Keep surprises for Christmas presents, not your investors' money.

The minimum can be defined thus. Long/short managers are ultimately judged on their ability to protect capital. Your system must be able to trade its way out of a drawdown. A simple rule of thumb is to set the minimum at half the maximum. If you expect investors to redeem on you at 10%, your maximum should be around 5% and your minimum at 2.5%.

Worst-case scenario, you would incur a 7.5% drawdown before clawing your way back to par. Besides, as soon as performance turns around, the convex oscillator introduced in *Chapter 8, Position Sizing: Money is Made in the Money Management Module*, will re-accelerate.

Even though the difference in portfolio heat looks minimal, the impact on gross exposure may look a lot more dramatic. A +/-0.1% difference in portfolio heat could easily sway the gross exposure by 5-10%. This will have a direct impact on volatility, performance, and liquidity as in market impact. In practice, there is some magic in this skill. Investors will pick up on disciplined risk management, which is ultimately the skill they are willing to pay good money for.

Tactical deployment

Bull markets may go on for years, yet investors tend to think in quarterly and annual time segments. If investors think in calendar years, then so should you. Leverage should therefore be strategically deployed throughout the year. If you start the year all leveraged up, and performance tanks right out of the gate, you will spend the rest of the year trading yourself out of a hole, with investors breathing down your neck. Stress is bad for good decision-making. On the other hand, once you build performance, it will give a cushion to play with leverage. So, start every year at the minimum leverage. The year may start off slowly. Investors will forget a slow start, but they will not forgive a rough one.

Conversely, as the year winds down, gradually reduce leverage to start the next period at the minimum leverage. This seasonal management of portfolio heat does not make mathematical sense. Investors rarely compete for Nobel prizes in abstract maths. They are humans. They react with their guts.

Step-by-step portfolio heat and exposure management

In *Chapter 8, Position Sizing: Money is Made in the Money Management Module*, we used the equity curve to calculate how much risk should be allocated to trades going into the portfolio. This is risk per trade at the individual level. Now, we will revisit the convex oscillator for the positions already in the portfolio. The relationship at the micro level (risk per trade) before entry remains true at the portfolio macro level (portfolio heat). The market is constantly moving, so risk should be adjusted accordingly. Risk per trade oscillates within a maximum and minimum band at the stock level. Similarly, portfolio heat oscillates from a maximum and minimum. The beauty of this approach lies in its elegant simplicity. We do not concentrate on the size of positions, only on their open risk. This rapidly reduces leverage, while leaving successful risk-free positions unaffected.

Implementing the convex oscillator on the maximum portfolio heat has a direct impact on all the exposures. Let's illustrate this with some step-by-step numerical examples.

Step 1: Convexity configuration

What works at the stock/micro level also works at the portfolio/macro level. The overall portfolio risk is called **open risk** or **portfolio heat**. The objective is to run at maximum heat for as long as possible. As drawdown worsens, portfolio heat is reduced until a minimum floor. This risk can be reduced using the `risk_appetite()` function we saw in *Chapter 8, Position Sizing: Money is Made in the Money Management Module*:

```python
def risk_appetite(eqty, tolerance, mn, mx, span, shape):
    '''
    eqty: equity curve series
    tolerance: tolerance for drawdown (<0)
    mn: min risk
    mx: max risk
    span: exponential moving average to smoothe the risk_appetite
    shape: convex (>45 deg diagonal) = 1, concave (<diagonal) = -1,
else: simple risk_appetite
    '''
    # drawdown rebased
    eqty = pd.Series(eqty)
    watermark = eqty.expanding().max() # all-time-high peak equity
    drawdown = eqty / watermark - 1 # drawdown from peak
    ddr = 1 - np.minimum(drawdown / tolerance,1) # drawdown rebased to
tolerance from 0 to 1
    avg_ddr = ddr.ewm(span = span).mean() # span rebased drawdown

    # Shape of the curve
    if shape == 1: #
        _power = mx/mn # convex
    elif shape == -1 :
        _power = mn/mx # concave
    else:
        _power = 1 # raw, straight line
    ddr_power = avg_ddr ** _power # ddr

    # mn + adjusted delta
    risk_appetite = mn + (mx - mn) * ddr_power

    return risk_appetite
```

In the following example, we will build a fictitious portfolio composed of 10 stocks — 5 longs, 5 shorts. We will demonstrate how portfolio heat reduction is carried out at the individual stock level.

Step 2: Drawdown rebased

Our hypothetical portfolio is benchmarked to the S&P 500 index. Initial capital (K) is set at USD 1 million. Beta (sensitivity to the market) has been extracted from the Yahoo Finance website. The number of shares and relative stop losses are calibrated to -0.50% relative risk adjusted to the portfolio. The portfolio is run from December 31, 2020, through June 30, 2021. First, we'll generate the dataset:

```python
port = np.nan
K = 1000000
lot = 100
port_tickers = ['QCOM','TSLA','NFLX','DIS','PG', 'MMM','IBM','BRK-B','UPS','F']
bm_ticker= '^GSPC'
tickers_list = [bm_ticker] + port_tickers
df_data= {
'Beta':[1.34,2,0.75,1.2,0.41,0.95,1.23,0.9,1.05,1.15],
'Shares':[-1900,-100,-400,-800,-5500,1600,1800,2800,1100,20800],
'rSL':[42.75,231,156,54.2,37.5,42.75,29.97,59.97,39.97,2.10]
}
port = pd.DataFrame(df_data,index=port_tickers)
port['Side'] = np.sign(port['Shares'])

start_dt = '2021-01-01'
end_dt = '2021-07-01'
price_df = round( yf.download(tickers= tickers_list,start= '2021-01-01'
, end = '2021-07-01', interval = "1d",group_by = 'column',auto_adjust =
True, prepost = True, treads = True, proxy = None)['Close'],2)

bm_cost = price_df[bm_ticker][0]
bm_price = price_df[bm_ticker][-1]

port['rCost'] = round(price_df.iloc[0,:].div(bm_cost) *1000,2)
port['rPrice'] = round(price_df.iloc[-1,:].div(bm_price) *1000,2)
port['Cost'] = price_df.iloc[0,:]
port['Price'] = price_df.iloc[-1,:]

print(port)
```

There is no big mystery here. We create a dataframe using dictionaries and lists. We then download prices from Yahoo Finance. Cost is set at December 31, 2020 and the current price is the end of June. At the time of writing, this gives the following dataframe.

	Beta	Shares	rSL	Side	rCost	rPrice	Cost	Price
QCOM	1.34	-1900	42.75	-1	40.16	33.26	150.85	142.93
TSLA	2.00	-100	231.00	-1	187.87	158.16	705.67	679.70
NFLX	0.75	-400	156.00	-1	143.96	122.91	540.73	528.21
DIS	1.20	-800	54.20	-1	48.24	40.90	181.18	175.77
PG	0.41	-5500	37.50	-1	36.59	31.40	137.43	134.93
MMM	0.95	1600	42.75	1	45.82	46.22	172.10	198.63
IBM	1.23	1800	29.97	1	32.71	34.11	122.85	146.59
BRK-B	0.90	2800	59.97	1	61.73	64.67	231.87	277.92
UPS	1.05	1100	39.97	1	44.34	48.39	166.54	207.97
F	1.15	20800	2.10	1	2.34	3.46	8.79	14.86

There is one small difference with the `relative()` function introduced in *Chapter 4, Long/Short Methodologies: Absolute and Relative*, which had the option to rebase to the beginning of the series. We have chosen to use continuous series instead. Market participants trade around positions all the time. Rebasing rapidly becomes an unnecessary computational headache. It therefore makes sense to use the same day closing price multiplied by a constant — 1000 in this case. Stop loss and all calculations are based on the relative series.

Next, let's calculate a few important measures:

- BV stands for book value. This is the cost in fund currency (USD) multiplied by the number of shares for all open positions.

- MV stands for Market Value. This is the number of shares adjusted for currency (USD) multiplied by the current close price.

- rMV stands for relative market value.

- Gross exposure is the absolute sum of all market values in the fund currency divided by the assets under management — K in this case.

- Net exposure is the arithmetic net sum of all market values divided by the absolute sum total of market values.

- Net beta is the sum product of market values times beta divided by the absolute sum total of market values.

Now let's look at the code:

```python
BV = port['Shares'] * port['Cost']
MV = port['Shares'] * port['Price']
rMV = port['Shares'] * port['rPrice']

port['rR'] = (port['rCost'] - port['rSL'])
port['Weight'] = round(MV.div(abs(MV).sum()),3)
port['rRisk'] = -round(np.maximum(0,(port['rR'] * port['Shares'])/K),4)
port['rRAR'] = round( (port['rPrice'] - port['rCost'])/port['rR'],1)
port['rCTR'] = round(port['Shares'] * (port['rPrice']-port['rCost'])/
K,4)
port['CTR'] = round(port['Shares'] * (port['Price']-port['Cost'])/ K,4)
port_long = port[port['Side']>0]
port_short = port[port['Side']<0]

concentration = (port_long['Side'].count()-port_short['Side'].count())/
port['Side'].count()
gross = round(abs(MV).sum() / K,3)
net = round(MV.sum()/abs(MV).sum(),3)
net_Beta = round((MV* port['Beta']).sum()/abs(MV).sum(),2)
print('Gross Exposure',gross,'Net Exposure',net,'Net Beta',net_Beta,'co
ncentration',concentration)
rnet = round(rMV.sum()/abs(rMV).sum(),3)
rnet_Beta = round((rMV* port['Beta']).sum()/abs(rMV).sum(),2)
print('rGross Exposure',gross,'rNet Exposure',rnet,'rNet Beta',rnet_
Beta)
```

The output will be similar to the following:

```
Gross Exposure 3.327 Net Exposure 0.141 Net Beta 0.24 concentration 0.0
rGross Exposure 3.327 rNet Exposure 0.141 rNet Beta 0.24
```

Gross exposure at 3.327 is medium to high leverage. A gross exposure of 2 means the **Assets Under Management (AUM)** are leveraged one time on the long and 1 time on the short side. 3.327 means AUM is leveraged about 1.6 times. Net and rNet exposure at 0.141 means the portfolio is evenly balanced and mildly bullish. Net and rNet Beta at 0.24 means the portfolio is residually bullish. It is not susceptible to major shocks either way.

Overall, apart from the high concentration and elevated open risk, the portfolio looks well balanced. Next, we calculate risks:

- R is a measure popularised by Dr Van Tharp in his book *Trade Your Way to Financial Freedom*. It is simply the difference between cost and stop loss. Here, we will be using the relative version of R, or rR.

- Weight is the market value in fund currency (USD) divided by the absolute sum total of market values.

- rRisk is the weighted relative risk to the equity. The formula contains a mysterious `np.maximum(0, (port['rR'] * port['Shares']))` sequence. As soon as the stop loss is reset beyond the current stop loss, this turns negative. This ensures that the open risk remains negative.

- rRAR is the relative returns expressed in units of initial relative risks. This is the truest and simplest risk-adjusted returns measure. This will be our workhorse.

- rCTR and CTR are relative and absolute contributions, or P&L divided by equity.

Next, let's print the portfolio sorted by side and relative risk-adjusted returns.

```
port[['Side', 'Weight', 'rRisk', 'rRAR', 'rCTR', 'CTR']].sort_
values(by=['Side','rRAR'] )
```

	Side	Weight	rRisk	rRAR	rCTR	CTR
TSLA	-1	-0.020	-0.0043	0.7	0.0030	0.0026
DIS	-1	-0.042	-0.0048	1.2	0.0059	0.0043
NFLX	-1	-0.063	-0.0048	1.7	0.0084	0.0050
QCOM	-1	-0.082	-0.0049	2.7	0.0131	0.0150
PG	-1	-0.223	-0.0050	5.7	0.0285	0.0138
MMM	1	0.095	-0.0049	0.1	0.0006	0.0424
IBM	1	0.079	-0.0049	0.5	0.0025	0.0427
UPS	1	0.069	-0.0048	0.9	0.0045	0.0456
BRK-B	1	0.234	-0.0049	1.7	0.0082	0.1289
F	1	0.093	-0.0050	4.7	0.0233	0.1263

Positions are sorted neatly by side and relative risk-adjusted returns. Let's look at the aggregates using the groupby() method applied to the long and short books.

```
port[['Side', 'Weight', 'rRisk', 'rRAR', 'rCTR', 'CTR']].
groupby('Side').sum()
```

This will produce the following table:

	Weight	rRisk	rRAR	rCTR	CTR
Side					
-1	-0.43	-0.0238	12.0	0.0589	0.0407
1	0.57	-0.0245	7.9	0.0391	0.3859

This gives us the big aggregates by side. Both sides have been performing well. As expected, the net exposure has widened. The short side has shrunk. This dislocation is the mark of a healthy short side. The long side has increased as well. The total relative risk is roughly -4.8% spread across 10 names. Next, let's cut exposure to the slowest performing stocks.

Step 3: Pro-rate open risk

Gross exposure is 333% and open risk is +13.9% with a net beta of 0.24. Let's take a classic case. Someone up there in the rarefied atmosphere of management hits pause on a Solitaire game and decides to reduce exposure across the board. In execution trader English, this means cutting leverage. There is no cookie-cutter formula to shave position size across a portfolio. There are several methods available to market participants. They range from axing all positions across the board to surgically excising marginal risk out of the most vulnerable positions. Since anyone can do the former, let's explore how the latter can be done with minimal effort.

Hypothetically, we will aim to reduce open risk from -4.8% to -2.8%. Since open risk is evenly distributed, we will shave -1% off risk on each side. The code works for dissociated risk reduction, but this will keep it simple. The logic is to reduce the size, starting by using relative risk (rRisk) as a sorting key: port_long['rRisk'] / (port_long['rRisk'].sum(). The higher the risk, the bigger the reduction, and so on.

```
adjust_long = adjust_short  =  -0.01

pro_rata_long = port_long['rRisk'] / (port_long['rRisk'].sum() *
port_long['rRAR'])
risk_adj_long = (abs(adjust_long) * pro_rata_long * K /
port_long['rR'] // lot) * lot
```

```
shares_adj_long =  np.minimum(risk_adj_long,
port_long['Shares'])*np.sign(adjust_long)

pro_rata_short = port_short['rRisk'] / (port_short['rRisk'].sum() *
port_short['rRAR'])
risk_adj_short = (abs(adjust_short) * pro_rata_short * K /
port_short['rR'] // lot)*lot
shares_adj_short =
np.maximum(risk_adj_short,port_short['Shares'])*np.sign(adjust_short)

port['Qty_adj'] = shares_adj_short.append(shares_adj_long)
port['Shares_adj']  = port['Shares'] + port['Qty_adj']
port['rRisk_adj'] = -round(np.maximum(0,(port['rR'] *
port['Shares_adj'])/K),4)
MV_adj= port['Shares_adj'] * port['Price']
rMV_adj = port['Shares_adj'] * port['rPrice']
port['Weight_adj'] = round(MV_adj.div(abs(MV_adj).sum()),3)

print(port[['Side','rRAR','rRisk','rRisk_adj','Shares','Qty_adj',
'Shares_adj', 'Weight','Weight_adj']].groupby('Side').sum())
```

The logical thing to do is to reduce positions at risk first. Those are the most vulnerable ones. Positions with stop losses beyond cost can be spared until the proverbial ventilation system faces a manure storm. When stop loss is beyond cost, open risk is zero. np.maximum(0, (port['rR'] * port['Shares'])) is rustic but it works. In our example, stop losses have not been reset and all positions miraculously contribute. As Groucho Marx once said: "No man goes before his time, unless the boss leaves early." So, we will still have to cut exposure.

We will pro-rate open risk by side and divide by risk-adjusted returns. This will rank positions by side and open risk-adjusted returns. Those that have contributed the least are by definition the riskiest ones.

Let's consider how this code works:

1. We factor the risk reduction of -1% into the pro rata to calculate the number of shares. We multiply by the capital and divide by the relative distance between cost and stop loss, rR, to obtain the exact number of shares. We find the modulo (//) with the lot size and multiply back to reach a round number.

2. The risk reduction cannot be larger than the existing number of shares. On the long side, we take the minimum of the number of shares or the adjustment. On the short side, we take the maximum of the number of shares or the adjustment.

3. We add a new column, Qty_adj, where we append the shares to be adjusted. We calculate the new shares with ['Shares_adj'] = port['Shares'] + port['Qty_adj'].

4. We run the same calculations as before to see how the reduction affected the portfolio. We print the dataframe.

This gives an aggregate table that should be similar to the following (depending on how the stocks are performing when you run the code):

	rRAR	rRisk	rRisk_adj	Shares	Qty_adj	Shares_adj	Weight	Weight_adj
Side								
-1	10.8	-0.0251	-0.0164	-8700	1300.0	-7400.0	-0.430	-0.511
1	7.9	-0.0245	-0.0127	28100	-5800.0	22300.0	0.571	0.490

The returns on the long side have been uniform, thereby warranting a big cut in risk.

Note that the adjusted risk on the short side has not reached the target. As we will see further down, there was a wide disparity in performance leaving some positions barely untouched and others drastically reduced. Now, this example has a small number of positions. These uneven reductions can happen.

```
print(port[['Side','rRAR','rRisk','rRisk_adj','Shares','Qty_adj',
'Shares_adj', 'Weight','Weight_adj']].sort_values(by=
['Side','rRisk_adj' ], ascending=[True,False]))
```

The expanded view gives something like this.

	Side	rRAR	rRisk	rRisk_adj	Shares	Qty_adj	Shares_adj	Weight	Weight_adj
TSLA	-1	0.7	-0.0043	-0.0000	-100	100.0	0.0	-0.020	0.000
DIS	-1	1.2	-0.0048	-0.0030	-800	300.0	-500.0	-0.042	-0.039
NFLX	-1	1.7	-0.0048	-0.0036	-400	100.0	-300.0	-0.064	-0.071
QCOM	-1	2.7	-0.0049	-0.0041	-1900	300.0	-1600.0	-0.082	-0.102
PG	-1	4.5	-0.0063	-0.0057	-5500	500.0	-5000.0	-0.222	-0.299
MMM	1	0.1	-0.0049	-0.0000	1600	-1600.0	0.0	0.096	0.000
IBM	1	0.5	-0.0049	-0.0011	1800	-1400.0	400.0	0.079	0.026
UPS	1	0.9	-0.0048	-0.0031	1100	-400.0	700.0	0.069	0.065
BRK-B	1	1.7	-0.0049	-0.0039	2800	-600.0	2200.0	0.234	0.273
F	1	4.7	-0.0050	-0.0046	20800	-1800.0	19000.0	0.093	0.126

This is the exact same order as before despite using two different sorting keys. We initially sorted by rRAR risk-adjusted returns. Now, we've sorted by rRisk_adj instead. Positions that did not contribute but still had open risk were reduced. At this juncture, there are two big takeaways from this exercise.

- Weight was reduced in this exercise. It can also be increased. It can be increased on one side and reduced on the other.

- This was admittedly a tedious exercise with no particular objective in sight. It has, however, a far sexier nickname. Once you are done yawning, go back through it with the knowledge that you have seen an **embryonic asset allocation** method.

Next, let's see how this -2% risk reduction affected all the major variables:

```
print('Gross Exposure',gross,'Net Exposure',net,'Net Beta',net_Beta,'co
ncentration',concentration)
gross_adj = round(abs(MV_adj).sum() / K,3)
net_adj = round(MV_adj.sum()/abs(MV_adj).sum(),3)
net_Beta_adj = round((MV_adj* port['Beta']).sum()/abs(MV_adj).sum(),2)
net_pos_adj = port.loc[port['Shares_adj'] >0,'Shares_adj'].count()-
port.loc[port['Shares_adj'] <0,'Shares_adj'].count()
print('Gross Exposure_adj',gross_adj,'Net Exposure_adj',net_adj,
        'Net Beta_adj',net_Beta_adj,'concentration adj',net_pos_adj)
rnet_adj = round(rMV_adj.sum()/abs(rMV_adj).sum(),3)
rnet_Beta_adj = round((rMV_adj* port['Beta']).sum()/abs(rMV_adj).
sum(),2)
print('Gross Exposure_adj',gross_adj,'rNet Exposure_adj',rnet_adj,'rNet
Beta_adj',rnet_Beta_adj)
```

Our output is as follows, with the addition of some helpful comments:

```
# Before risk reduction
Gross Exposure 3.327 Net Exposure 0.141 Net Beta 0.24 concentration 0.0
# After risk reduction: absolute
Gross Exposure_adj 2.243 Net Exposure_adj -0.021 Net Beta_adj 0.13
concentration adj 0
# After risk reduction: relative
Gross Exposure_adj 2.243 rNet Exposure_adj -0.021 rNet Beta_adj 0.13
```

A reduction of a mere 2% of the open risk brings gross exposure down from 3.327 to 2.243. Net exposure moves from +0.141 to -0.021. Net beta goes from 0.24 to 0.13. The adjusted portfolio remains residually bullish despite a net exposure that's virtually neutral.

In this instance, the absolute and relative totals coincidentally have the same value. As you can see, it does not take much to drastically reduce gross exposure, all the while keeping the healthiest positions. This is a powerful exercise to quickly re-allocate resources across a portfolio or strategies.

Net exposure

Net exposure is the percentage difference between long and short exposures. Net exposure is an approximate reflection of the directional view on the markets: bullish when positive, bearish when negative. Net exposure has a direct impact on:

- **Liquidity** is one of the most overlooked and critical components. Long and short positions have opposite dynamics. To keep net exposure low, the short book needs to be constantly replenished. Meanwhile, the supply of borrow is finite. This leads to an increase in borrowing costs. Always keep an eye on borrow utilization. Do not let it go past around 66%.

- **Correlation**: The lower the net exposure, the lower the correlation. Mutual funds have a correlation of 1, for instance, meaning they mirror the market gyrations. Markets go up, so do mutual funds, and vice versa on the way down.

- **Volatility**: Net exposure has the largest impact on volatility. The lower the net, the lower the volatility. Targeting zero net exposure, however, has its own systemic risk. It works well in stable markets but can be extremely painful during major market shifts, as in bull to bear.

- **Performance**: The lower the net exposure, the lower market directionality influences returns.

- **Yield**: Short-sellers are liable for dividends. Low net exposure implies that dividends received on the long side are cancelled out by dividends paid on the short side. This has implications on stock selection on the short side: high-dividend yield stocks are often under-represented on the short side.

Everyone in the long/short business is familiar with the concept of net exposure. People who are serious about their long/short mandates will gravitate toward lower exposures, while opportunists will more freely oscillate. Average net exposure is therefore a quick and dirty way to reclassify long/short market participants. Here are some broad buckets that participants fall into:

- **Above +50%**: Those are special situation long-only funds charging hedge fund fees. They offer something else than downside protection. They are not trying to hedge the downside with the short book. They have views on their short positions as individual stocks.

- **Above +30%:** Those market participants are usually referred to as directional hedge funds. This is the most relatively unsophisticated bunch of the long/short club. They are usually asset aggregators who pretend to know what they are doing on the short side yet they struggle in the idea generation department. Their characteristics are high correlation, limited upside participation, and zero downside protection. They are the sushi conveyor belt of hedge funds. When one fails, the next colorful one rolls around.

- **Net exposure contained between -20% to +20%:** The most serious long/short players operate in that space. They have understood that exposure control and risk management are the business. This low net exposure offers low volatility returns but still benefits from limited market directionality.

- **Sub -10% to +10% net exposure** is the province of market-neutral funds. Alpha strictly comes from stock selection and position sizing. Only a few strategies can accommodate that level of exposure. Bear in mind that low net exposure does not equate to low risk. The risk with those funds is often in the tail. It is difficult to constrain exposures at all times. This often comes at the cost of some factor. Think of it as rewinding a spring. At some point, pent-up energy may spring up and cause damage.

Long/short vehicles are supposed to perform, or at least protect capital, during down markets. During the **Global Financial Crisis (GFC)**, they did not do what it said on the tin. While they were running at +50% and beyond during bull markets, net exposures struggled to go below +20%. As bearish as managers might have claimed to be, the numbers told a different story. Funds were cautious, but not outright bearish. At +20% net exposure, it might have been boxing gloves instead of bare knuckles, but it was still the same punch in the mouth.

Net exposure can be a deceiving metric. Low net exposure does not necessarily mean low correlation. Most market participants resort to several expedients to bring their net exposure down. The most classic technique is to oversize their few short bets. Concentration increases volatility. Another technique to reduce net exposure is to sell futures, which have lower beta than single stocks. Both techniques have a material impact on correlation and volatility. But, net exposure is to portfolio management what price-to-earnings ratio is to valuations. It is a good enough shortcut, but it should not be the sole basis for a decision. It is better to contextualize net exposure along with other variables. It is therefore important to go past the net exposure headline figure and look at the composition of the portfolio through net beta.

Net beta

In early 2005, the Japanese equities market had an epic year. It felt like this time, it was different. The party came to a screeching halt when the Japanese authorities decided to arrest Takafumi Horie, CEO of Livedoor (JT:4753) and symbol of the new Japan. High-flying small caps rediscovered Newtonian physics.

We long high-flying small caps with esoteric business models, and short a few asthmatic "structural shorts" along with index futures. The fund manager quickly responded to the crisis by selling futures. Despite a reasonable +30% net exposure, the ship was taking on water fast. As a self-appointed risk manager, I promptly brought to his attention that we were synthetically exposed on the beta, market cap, exchange, and liquidity sides. With small caps at 1.7 and beyond on the long side, agonizing shorts at 0.8, and futures at 1 on the short side, our net beta was hovering around 0.7. As one investor later pointed out, we had a "beta of 1.5 on the way up, and 3 on the way down."

Beta is a central concept of the relative long/short business. Beta is the sensitivity to the markets. If the market returns $1, a beta of 1.5 would return $1.5. In mathematical terms, this is the slope of the return of a stock versus the benchmark. Net beta is the difference between the beta adjusted long and short exposures expressed as a decimal value. It goes past the net exposure headline to reflect a portfolio's underlying directional sensitivity. When risk is on and Mr. Market is in a good mood, high beta stocks tend to do well. The market rewards risk takers who go for riskier issues. Liquidity is the primary risk of any market. As a result, small caps have higher beta than large caps. High beta stocks are also industries where there are significant failure risks such as tech or biotech, or balance sheet risks such as financials. Critics of the hedge fund industry often describe hedge funds as beta merchants, or beta disguised as alpha. Critics are right. A relative long/short portfolio is by definition an arbitrage on beta. Similarly, a painter is someone who throws pigments at a blank canvas.

In a bull market, a long book would have a beta higher than 1. The short book would be constituted of stocks that return less than the market, or beta below 1. This can result in net exposure hovering around +20% but net beta firmly at +0.5. Headline net exposure may appear low, but residual sensitivity to the markets can be elevated. In a bear market, the long book would be constituted of defensive issues such as foods and utilities with a beta traditionally below 1. The short book would list all the leaders of the previous bull phase disgorging their euphoria. This would result in a positive net exposure of somewhere between +5 to +20% and a negative net beta of -0.1 to -0.5. Bearish portfolios have defensive stocks on the long side and market-sensitive stocks on the short side.

Despite the apparent bullishness of positive net exposure, negative net beta demonstrates a bearish stance. Conflicting net exposures is the sign of a balanced portfolio. Negative net exposures in bear markets will generate alpha, but it will have violent volatility swings. Net beta is an essential component of the toolbox. Market participants intuitively understand how beta works. Adding a bit of discipline goes a long way to deliver smooth performance.

Next, let's see what shorting futures bring to the table.

Three reasons why selling futures is the junk food of short-selling

To reiterate the statement from the previous section, a relative long/short portfolio is an arbitrage on sectorial beta. Unsophisticated market participants who have failed to understand this crucial distinction often sell futures to reduce their net exposure, while ignoring the impact on net beta. Below are three reasons why selling futures is not an effective hedge.

Selling futures is a bet on market cap

Market participants often respond to the scarcity of ideas on the short side by selling index futures.

On the long side, market participants like to flex their stock-picking muscles by fishing for small-mid caps. This is where the fun and gold nuggets are. Small-mid caps rally harder than blue chips in bull markets. They are relatively poorly covered by the sell-side analyst community. It is easier to have access to senior management. Find a few 3 or 4 baggers (stocks that triple or quadruple their original value), and a new stock-picking legend is born.

Meanwhile, futures reflect the top market capitalizations of the index. This makes the long small-mid caps/short futures trade an implicit bet on market capitalization. Small-mid caps outperform large caps in bull markets, but gravity is less than kind to small speculative stocks in bear markets.

Selling futures is a bet on beta

Futures have a beta of 1. Small-mid caps have higher sensitivity to the market. They are bull market racehorses that fail miserably in bear markets. When markets tank, small-mid caps nosedive faster than big, boring blue chips. Long small-mid caps/ short futures markets put a drag on performance during bull markets but offer no downside protection during turbulent markets.

The only way to hedge beta would be to take a deep net short approach.

Since market participants who "hedge" via futures are unlikely to be comfortable short selling in the first place, they are likely to remain net beta positive, or residually bullish through bull and bear markets alike. Ironically, selling futures against stocks synthetically captures outperformance over the benchmark. This works well only when that asset class is supposed to outperform the market. A less flattering description of this type of strategy is called **beta jockey**.

Selling futures is an expensive form of laziness

Many institutional investors already hedge their exposures in mutual funds with options and futures. They already have the sophistication to hedge their long bets. They do not need to pay a bunch of tourists an additional 2 and 20 for something they can do themselves. At the end of the day, selling futures indicates irresponsible amateurism, something which investors have become keenly aware of since the GFC.

If you ever wondered why your performance still suffers during bear phases, despite low net exposure, net beta is probably the culprit. If the objective is to deliver low correlation returns, then a lower net beta is the place to start.

Concentration

Concentration refers to the number of stocks in a portfolio. Net concentration is the difference between the number of stocks on the long minus the short side, expressed either as a percentage of the total number of positions or in absolute.

Concentration has a direct impact on:

- **Liquidity**: Building and liquidating positions has a market impact
- **Volatility**: If the objective is to deliver low-volatility returns, concentration is the place to start. The higher the number of names, the lower the volatility.
- **Performance**: Big concentrated bets hit home runs. Small bets compound singles.

Concentration is often perceived as an attribute of an investment style and as such, does not receive the attention it deserves. It is a bit like garlic—a tasty seasoning not recommended on a first date, but also a cancer-fighting super-food and vampire repellent.

Some market participants believe the key to superior performance is hitting home runs with a few high-conviction big bets. This may be a winning strategy, but it is beside the point. The best-performing products are not the best-selling ones. Sports cars attract a limited clientele.

When it comes to asset allocation, investors will allocate the bulk of their assets to lower-volatility investment strategies. They trade returns for stability for a simple reason. Institutions need to match defined liabilities, such as pension cash outlays, with reasonably predictable assets. They will then juice up returns with small allocations on higher-volatility products. So, the real question for any manager is: Which pool of money are you targeting? Do you want to swim in the Olympic-size pool of low-volatility products or the paddling pool of disposable gambling money?

Next, we will challenge a few clichés about concentration.

Human limitation

Market participants often believe there is a natural human limitation to the number of stocks they can manage. Past a certain number of positions, everything blurs. They cannot keep up with the information flow and make timely decisions.

This is a portfolio management system issue. Data is not structured and visualized in a way that helps managers make trading decisions. We will discuss this in *Chapter 13*, *Portfolio Management System*.

Hedges are not tokens

Some market participants take a few large bets and keep a long tail of exploratory small positions, referred to as **hedges**. Some exotic hedges include sensitivity to commodities: China, gold, interest rates, etc. Those positions are often too small to materially hedge risk on an individual basis, but heavy in aggregate. As such, they are examples of tokenism that allow market participants to say they have hedged their portfolios against exogenous risks.

The long tail strategy is a classic in the small mid cap long/short arena. Again, this is a portfolio management system issue more than a risk management strategy.

The paradox of low-volatility returns: structural negative net concentration

The way to sustainably attract and retain investors is to have structurally more names on the short than the long side, or net negative concentration. Portfolios often have more names on the long side than the short. When confronted with the scarcity of ideas on the short side, market participants resort to oversizing their short bets to bring net exposure down. They end up rationalizing these decisions by calling their outsized positions "high-conviction shorts," "structural shorts," or "tactical shorts."

The problem is that big concentrated bets increase volatility. Since the short side is notoriously volatile, this results in the short book driving the volatility of the overall portfolio. Now, investors want low volatility. The only way to lower volatility is to reduce the concentration on the short side. This means smaller bets and more diversified names. As we saw in *Chapter 5, Regime Definition*, this is feasible in a relative long/short portfolio but much harder to accomplish in an absolute long/short. The short book needs to have structurally more names than the long side to compensate for the volatility.

Practical tips about concentration

Concentration is a function of three variables: the average number of names, the ratio of big bets to small, and transaction costs.

Average number of names

A healthy portfolio should have somewhere between 30 and 60 names on each side. No single position is too large to torpedo performance but big enough to materially contribute. Besides, the number of positions is still manageable.

Ratio of big to small bets

The second factor is the ratio of big to small bets. An internal study by Fidelity Boston measured the ratio of biggest to smallest bets in managers' portfolios, outperformance, and ultimately, the retention of assets under management. The results were unequivocal:

- The higher the ratio of large to small bets, the higher the volatility. Big concentrated bets drive performance but the downside is elevated volatility of returns. This is a big deterrent for investors. They like the returns but cannot justify volatility to their bosses.

- Managers with ratios lower than 2.5 had substantially lower tracking errors than managers with big bet disparities. Their biggest bets were not so big as to drive the volatility of their entire portfolios. Low tracking errors are correlated with the stability of AUM. In execution trader English, this means that you will be heralded as a "stock picker" when things work but branded as a high tracking error risk when your style falls out of favor. This is the institutional investor equivalent of "no-one ever got fired for buying AAPL."

Big winners will expand on the long side and contract on the short side. On the long side, winners should not dwarf the rest of the portfolio. Conversely, on the short side, they should not be allowed to melt away.

A simple way to maintain a healthy, dynamic portfolio is to track the ratio of the aggregate weight of the top 10 to the bottom 10 bets. The higher ratio, the higher the concentration and, consequently, the higher the volatility. Keeping this ratio below 3 ensures that neither oversized bets nor token positions are floating around the portfolio.

Keep your powder dry

Finally, here is a simple and powerful tip from the short side: reject small positions. This is endemic on the short side. On the long side, even bets as small as 0.50% can expand into formidable positions. Back in August 1997, Bill Gates bought a $2 million stake in a moribund penny stock at $12 named AAPL. However, on the short side, successful trades shrink. Even if a stock went down 10%, a -0.50% initial bet would only return +0.05%. Add transaction costs and slippage and there is barely enough money left for coffee and croissants. On the short side, keep powder until the fat pitch shows up. Market participants are all too often scared to sell short. They respond by taking positions too small to hurt but also too tiny to contribute. So, work on your risk management first, then execute your strategy. Here is some advice that is as old as the Jedi master who said it: "Do, or do not, there is no try."

Other exposures

Some market participants like to keep track of other hedges, such as industry or sector risk, or exchanges and factor risk.

Sector exposure

Keeping diversified sector exposure is good practice. Typically, you do not want your entire long/short sector exposures to look like *technology long in 1999, short in 2000*. Some market participants like to fully hedge their sector exposure to mitigate industry risk. This introduces another unnecessary layer of complexity. In practice, entire sectors dominate or trail the markets. A case in point: In 2008, one would have been hard-pressed to find any stock in the financial sector on the long side.

Sector neutrality works with only pairs trading or arbitrage strategies. Not all the stocks within the same sector travel at the same speed. Sector neutrality introduces an interesting capital allocation problem: Should sector allocation reflect the market capitalization of the underlying sectors or the disparity among constituents? The former allocation will move passively along with the broad market. Sector capitalizations and exposures will be matched. It will give the appearance of being low-risk, but not the promise of attractive returns. Conversely, high intra-sector disparity offers more opportunities to capture alpha but deviates from sector capitalization.

Sector neutrality generates alpha only when intra-sector disparities between winners and losers are clearly defined. The tech sector is a good example with, for instance, long Facebook/short Twitter.

Exchange exposure

Whoever came up with the concept of "rational investors" has obviously never set foot on a trading floor during a raging bull market. The winner effect is in full swing. Testosterone is wildly pumping through the systems of cold, calculating, rational, self-serving economic agents otherwise referred to as "stock punters." Yesterday's highly speculative issues are knighted as "new investment paradigms." The backward rationalization sings the same old routine: "This time it's different!"

Such *nouveaux riches* issues are rarely found on the venerable main exchange. They list on NASDAQ in the United States, JASDAQ in Japan, KOSDAQ in Korea, and so on.

During bull markets, a classic strategy is to go long on speculative stocks and short on blue chips. This is, however, a one-way street. The reverse does not work that well. Going long blue chips and short speculation is a difficult strategy to execute in practice. Past the biggest capitalization, borrow is hard to locate, liquidity evaporates, and the bid-ask spread is cavernously wide.

Liquidity is the currency of bear markets. When turbulence hits, stick to the liquid issues on the main exchanges.

Factor exposures

The 2007 quantitative funds debacle clearly proved that the short side has its own dynamics and deserves its endemic factors. We would all greatly benefit from the brilliance of academics to further the research on short selling. But, since the discussion on optimal portfolio construction seems to have reached a "permanently high plateau" during the pre-Beatles era of **Modern Portfolio Theory (MPT)** 70 years ago, academics have little incentive to come up with factors indigenous to the short side.

In theory, factors make sense. In the clinical environment of backtesting, factors also perform well. In practice, however, the short side is not an exercise in molecular cuisine. AMZN is not a series of factors. It is a company, a stock, and a story.

Managing a long/short portfolio gives a lot more latitude for creativity than a traditional long-only portfolio. It also invites complexity. It is therefore wise and fun to sit down and design portfolio management guidelines from the ground up. We'll cover this in the remainder of the chapter.

Design your own mandate

"People live up to what they write down,"

– Robert Cialdini

Finance is the only segment of the fashion industry where last year's collection sells well. Money flows effortlessly to last year's best performers. Everybody does more or less the same things: fundamental analysis, company visits, earnings models, technical analysis. It is difficult to come up with a differentiated pitch. If you want to leave a durable impression on your potential clients, show them something they rarely get to see: a documented process. They may choose not to invest today, but they will remember you.

Investors love to put managers in boxes. They already have a set number of them. If you don't fit in any box, they probably will not make a new one for you, unless performance compels them to. So, make their job easy: tell them which box best suits you. To the outside world, your mandate is your identity. The more you refine it, the more credible you appear to investors. You will no longer be "the next [insert latest lucky stock jockey name...]" bragging about your superior stock picking ability. You will become someone with a vision and a process to follow through. Nothing is as attractive as a prudent steward of other people's money, someone who understands risks and takes calculated bets.

Very few market participants take the time to explicitly formalize their process. The most effective way to stick to a plan is to put it down in writing and hold yourself accountable. If your objectives are not formalized, everything will remain wishful thinking. Below is a step-by-step method that will help you clarify your process. First, we will start with the signal module. Second, we will go through position sizing. Third, we will add exposures and risk management. Finally, we will consider your objectives. We will explore each topic with a set of questions.

Please pick up something to take notes and your trading journal.

Step 1: Strategy formalization

"Persona is the Latin name for the mask worn by an actor."

– Joseph Campbell

Start with a synopsis of your strategy. Write down your elevator pitch in 2-3 sentences max. This is the box you are asking your investors to put you in. Don't worry if you do not have a precise idea now. By the time you are done with the process, the box will reveal itself.

Two-thirds of the people hospitalized after a car accident would still describe themselves as above-average drivers. Who we think we are, what our deep inner critic screams we are, who we publicly claim to be, and what we do all live in a synchronous parallel multiverse.

We are not going the traditional route of growth versus value, fundamental versus quantitative, and so on. This is not a marketing exercise. You are not trying to raise capital. We are trying to restore inner alignment between all the facets of your persona. We are going to formalize your strategy to the point it could be computer coded.

The signal module

Compare your performance with the benchmark you operate in. What markets are you good at? More importantly, what markets are you not good at? Are they trending up, down, or sideways? Are they volatile? Do you peak before or after the market? Do you recover before or after the market? Does your performance tank and recover faster or slower than the market?

Calculate a short-dated rolling Sharpe, or Grit Index. Focus on the times when it tanks and recovers. Our objective is to make you resilient during losing streaks. For the following set of questions, please refer to your trading journal or track record. Refrain from labeling non-standard behaviors as good or bad.

List all entry types by strategy, including opportunistic trades:

- What is your rolling trading edge on a quarterly and annual basis on each side of the portfolio? Next time someone asks about your trading edge, those numbers should roll off your tongue. Besides, it will sound far more impressive than some nebulous dissertation on your unique powers of analysis.

- What is your classic entry signal on each side? Go one step beyond the general idea. Go through your trading journal. What made you pull the trigger at that particular time for each position over the last 50 trades on both sides? If you do not have a specific reason, write that down too.

- How often do you take opportunistic trades? Sometimes we switch from autopilot to manual. We all come across opportunistic trades that do not abide by our standard rules. For example, it could be some bad news that throws a stock into a tailspin. Opportunistic trades have a place in a portfolio. However, when they are either frequent or heavyweight, then there becomes a legitimate concern for structure and discipline. The consecrated industry vernacular is "style drift," which should be a major red flag.

- When your strategy is not working, what happens to your trading frequency? Do you trade more or less? Do you go through false positives before halting trading altogether, for instance? Compare the number of entries at the onset of a losing streak versus the end. There could be some trading fatigue there. You would pass up signals because of the belief they will be false positives again.

- Do you scale in? On both sides? How many entries do you take? Go back to your trading journal and be specific about the rules that lead you to pull the trigger. Are there special cases? Are there trades where you choose not to scale in?

- What trades that otherwise met your entry criteria did you pass up? Not trading is also an investment decision. Looking at our trading choices from the decision not to enter provides a valuable perspective on the trust in your system. What was the context that led you to reject those signals?

- If you routinely pass up trades, start journaling those rejected trades. Also note the reasons why you rejected them.

Next, focus on your exits, and take a long hard look in the mirror:

- What is your stop loss rule? How many times have you breached your stop loss rule over the last 50 trades? Do you close trades before a stop loss is triggered? What are the rules? How often did you override the rules in percentage points?

- Do you use trailing stop loss? What is the rule? Does your trailing stop rule change depending on a winning/losing streak.

- How do you reset stop loss?

- Do you scale out (reduce position)?

- Do you have a time exit strategy? How many periods? Does it also apply to older positions with embedded P&L? Do you procrastinate on time exits?

- What is your profitable exit strategy? How many times did you deviate over the last 50 trades?

- What are your rolling false positive rates on both sides? If in doubt, use your batting averages. Focus on drawdowns. Do you widen or tighten your stop losses in losing streaks?

- Do you reverse trades: switch from long to short and vice versa?

- Where is the mode of trades: loss or profit side? Are you a trend follower or do you use mean reversion tactics?

Have you honestly done the homework or simply intellectually answered the questions? Fine, answer this then: name three areas where your actions do not match your beliefs. What is the maximum number of consecutive stop losses over the last 50 trades? What is the correlation with the benchmark? What would happen if the market stayed sideways, turned bearish, or turned bullish over the next 6 months? How many months of the year would you be under water?

Remember, criticism is a healthy practice when it comes to testing the robustness of your system. The thing that stands between you and your system's success is your ego. You will probably come to the conclusion that your bulletproof trading system has the structural integrity of Swiss cheese. There is no need to beat yourself up. No one was born with a black belt. It is neither good nor bad. We all had to push through that phase. It is only an invitation to tune up your engine.

Next, use the answers to the above questions to draw a flowchart of your strategy. There are quite a few free websites available on the internet.

- Start with the classic entry/exit case
- Add scale-in/scale-out

- Add stop loss
- Add final exit
- Repeat the above process with special case entries

Flowcharts are powerful tools to build strategies. They force us to think logically. Build a template of your strategy with the sequence of entries and exits. Then fill in the conditions that trigger such events. In reality, all strategies boil down to a few templates. They start from the simplest Warren Buffett template: buy and do nothing thereafter, and go all the way to long/short reversal scale-out/scale-in. Strategies are like building blocks. As you work on optimizing your trading edge, you may add or subtract bricks.

Remember that you compete against rigorous people who take this process seriously. Every step that you take in clarifying your process will set you apart from those who don't. The flowchart of your strategy is a beacon of light in times of despair and the voice of reason in times of giddy euphoria. Do not neglect this part. How many market participants do you think take the time to clarify their strategy? Investors can probably count on one hand the number of managers who can produce a flowchart of their signal engine. They may not invest with you today, but they will remember your professionalism.

Now that we have pulled the engine apart, let's look at the transmission.

The money management module

This module comprises position size management, which should be considered in the context of the market variables we've looked at in this chapter:

- What is your position sizing algorithm?
- How does it change whether you are on a winning or losing streak? What does it look like at the end of a winning or a losing streak?
- What other position sizing algorithm would be better suited to your style?
- How many names do you have on each side? How does it evolve through your performance cycle?
- What is your ratio of big/small positions?
- Map your exposures versus the market: gross, net, net beta, portfolio heat, concentration, net trading (buys versus sells in percentage of the gross), and performance.
- What were your exposures like during losing streaks? Be specific.

This is the transmission part of your presence on the markets. Your engine generates signals through the thick and thin. The markets throw stuff at you. Your position sizing, concentration, and exposure management define how you choose to respond. Plot that data. The "who are you?" chart is the most important visual tool you will ever build. Plot the following elements on a single chart: cumulative benchmark and strategy returns, gross exposure, net exposure, net beta, and net trading (buys minus sells as a percentage of the gross exposure). That chart will show what the market throws at you and how you respond both in terms of trading net buy/sell, confidence through gross, and directionality through net and net beta. Very few data visualization exercises have this "wow" effect.

Step 2: Investment objectives

Rookie hedge fund managers always say they want to make as much money as possible. Veterans want to make money as consistently as possible. There are old traders and there are bold traders. There are no old bold traders. Managing for returns or consistency is mutually exclusive. Veterans simply have survived the initial bravado and come to accept themselves as they are and what they can accomplish.

Many trading coaches will encourage you to define your objectives before you start trading. They will force you into something you are not. Either you conquer yourself and morph into those objectives, or you rebel and end up trading something else entirely. Humans have an awful track record with manifesting idealistic visions. Every other long/short player says they aim for low correlated 15-20% annual returns. The reality is only an elite minority consistently delivers double-digit % returns. Everyone wants a six-pack on January 1st but gyms are empty from March onward. This process is designed to generate integrity from your beliefs to your actions. Making money is simply bringing inner alignment from your subconscious belief to your consciousness all the way up to your unconscious habits. Market wizards are not smarter, they have smarter trading routines.

Now, you know where you are. You also know where you want to go. For this to happen, you know what changes need to take place. You also have a realistic view of what can and cannot be done. Objectives are not esoteric aspirations. Your goals may be lofty. They are still rooted in reality. The next step is to articulate your objectives into a portfolio management process. Go back to the transmission part and focus on the variables. What is your position sizing algorithm? Define your portfolio using the four main exposures in your toolbox: gross, net, net beta, concentration. Those will determine correlation, volatility, drawdowns, and ultimately performance.

Given the multi-dimensional array of data and conditional paths, this exercise is difficult to simulate. For example, some strategies have only a few trades a year. If you missed a trade because you did not have enough cash on hand to buy a security that went on to outperform by 20%, your entire results would be skewed. There is no easy way around this issue. These back-testing issues are beyond the immediate scope of this book.

Step 4: Design your own mandate: product, market, fit

Long/shorts are subject to the law of supply and demand like any other product. A long/short portfolio is just like any other commodity product like toothpaste or soap. Nothing happens until a sale happens. Your job is to make that soap bar irresistible.

Once you have formalized your investment objectives, then it is time for a reality check. Are your objectives attainable? By now, you should have a reasonable idea of the box you could fit in. For example, you probably understand that +30% returns with net exposure at +/-5% and gross at 200% are highly improbable. You also know that by reducing volatility in half, you would jump the queue.

Would there be an appetite for your product? Remember that investors would rather park their money with something that returns 0.5% month after month than something that posts +20% returns but spends 9 months of the year under water.

This is the step where you consider the "product, market, fit" process. Your style may not be exactly what the market wants, but as long as you are willing to make adjustments, you may still have an attractive product. The good news is that you will be competing with people whose mindset is "build it and they will come."

Step 5: Record keeping

Every market participant suffers from trading selective amnesia. Unfortunately, most market participants spend considerable time developing trading systems only to trade something else... Every time we pass up a trade, override a stop loss, supersize a bet, we trade something else than our original system.

Unless we incorporate our trading history in our current trading decision, we are condemned to repeat the same mistakes. Like Sisyphus, we will lift the boulders of our performance only to watch them roll down at the next hiccup.

The two main ways we can prevent further damage are through position sizing and trade rejection. For example, we all have our nemesis stock that we have tried and failed multiple times. Rather than risking the same amount for a second time, risk less. The Turtle traders had a rule: they stopped trying after 3 failures.

Keep a record of all trades by strategy, side, and security. For example, it could be ABC stock, long trend following. This way, you will be able to calculate statistics such as gain expectancy and hit rate by strategy, side, and stock.

Those statistics are useful to grade your system. Your trading journal gives an incomplete view of your adherence to your trading system. There are four areas beyond your trading history where adherence can be directly measured: entry, exit, position-sizing, and journaling. All of them relate to trading psychology.

Entry

As well as trades you entered, keep track of the trades you passed up. As Claude Debussy said: "music is also the silence in between the notes." The trades you did not take define you as much as those you took. Passing up an otherwise valid trade is also a trading decision. It sheds a different light on your investment style. There are broadly four reasons why market participants pass entries:

1. **Insufficient cash balance**: That remains the number one cause of watching signals go by.
2. **Distrust of the system**: That is a deep-rooted fear of failure and inadequacy. The remedy is good stats and more work.
3. **The system is incomplete**: Some systems are not designed for tail events. Taking a trade in an unstable environment may jeopardize performance.
4. **Not in the right mental state**: This is the classic beaten-down trader who passes up free money in the middle of a deep losing streak. This one has a simple solution: trade small.

As a final warning on when not to enter a position, a hedge fund manager once confessed under Cabernet Sauvignon-induced enhanced interrogation that one of his contrarian shorts was a revenge trade. He had passed the trade as a long some time ago and now was punishing himself (and his investors) by revenge trading on the short side.

Exits

You will exit your trades one way or another. This will show in your trading journal. What may not be immediately visible is whether you followed your system when you closed a position.

Pay particular attention to stop losses. Count +=1 for every stop-loss override and premature profit-taking. It may sometimes be the right decision, but this is a departure from your system. Grade your mental state whenever you override your system.

Position sizing

A trading journal that does not log emotions is like a movie without sound. We trade our emotions. This manifests both in over/under trading as well as position sizing. Euphoric traders overtrade and oversize their positions. Traders in a slump pass up "free money" trades and bet too timidly. You must strive to trade like a psychopath, with as little emotional interference as possible.

Tracking your emotions is simple. Grade your subjective emotional stability from downtrodden (-3), the holy space of equanimity for every trade upon entry and exit (0), to the statistically challenged 200% (over)confident (+3). After a few entries, there will be a baseline. This is a fun game I discovered reading Dr Van Tharp. I personally found boredom to be positively correlated with adherence to the system. Boring is good apparently!

Journaling

Debriefing and journaling are effective techniques to bring a critical eye to your process. This will bring creativity and impartiality to your work. Journaling is not an exercise in free-flow self-flagellation. Market participants are quite verbose when emotions are at an extreme but silent when things are fine. Structure your journal in four parts:

- **Context**: Highlight what you see in the markets. This gives context to your trading decisions. Maybe you did not buy because at that time the world looked like it was about to end.

- **Your positioning**: This needs to be specific. Make a habit of attaching numbers to your views. For example, my gross is at 180% versus 200% average and my net beta stands at +0.1 higher than a month ago. I am cautiously optimistic. Risk management is a language.

- **Strategy improvements**: What works and what does not. This is the fun part.

- **Investment ideas**: *Evernote* is good journaling software. Use tags and notebooks to categorize your journal.

That record-keeping discipline alone will set you apart from the faceless magma of stock punters. Not every investor will invest with you, but everyone will remember your record-keeping discipline.

Step 5: Refine your mandate

"Discipline is doing what you hate like you love it."

– Mike Tyson

This is an iterative process. It will take time to come up with something that you will feel comfortable trading and that will appeal to investors. The process outlined above is "deliberate practice" applied to the stock market. Fleshing out your process will force you to focus on specific points of your strategy. Your record will provide immediate feedback. This will boost confidence and will set you apart from the competition.

Summary

Managing a long/short portfolio feels like upgrading from a family SUV to a sports car. Without proper training, people tend to take their shiny new toy for an off-road spin. In this chapter, we looked at the major levers to engineer the returns you need to attract the clientele you want. Those are gross exposure or leverage, portfolio heat or open risk, net exposure or directionality, net beta or residual sensitivity to the market, and concentration or the net number of names in the portfolio. Those variables give access to volatility, performance, correlation, and liquidity as in market impact.

Over the next chapters, we will take you through a step-by-step method to build an equities long/short product. We will use a powerful technique to reclassify stocks in a bullish, bearish, sideways regime. From there, we will discuss execution: entries, exits, order prioritization. We will conclude with a portfolio management system, the most underrated tool. But first, let's start with one of the major stumbling blocks: a scarcity of ideas. This method will enable you to position yourself ahead of the broader market and make you look like a short-selling guru.

12
Signals and Execution

"We have two ears and one mouth, so that we can listen twice as much as we speak,"

– Epictetus

This chapter will tell you exactly how you should prioritize orders and the reasons behind this. We will look at managing portfolios with relative series, but executing in absolute series. We will deep dive into exits, starting with unprofitable and profitable ones. We will consider the mental hygiene of exits. Then, we will move on to a popular topic: entries and re-entries. We will come up with counterintuitive yet effective low-risk high-reward entry techniques. The entire book has led up to this and the following chapter, so we will be revisiting parts of the book, putting out some code that synthesizes everything we have seen so far, and visualizing the results.

Along the way, we will discuss the following topics:

- Importing libraries
- Timing is money: the importance of timing orders
- Order prioritization
- Exits
- Entries

Importing libraries

For this chapter and the rest of the book, we will be working with the pandas, numpy, yfinance, and matplotlib libraries. We will also be working with find_peaks from the ScientificPython library. So, please remember to import them first:

```
# Import Libraries
import pandas as pd
import numpy as np
import yfinance as yf
%matplotlib inline
import matplotlib.pyplot as plt
from scipy.signal import find_peaks
```

Timing is money: the importance of timing orders

In 2005, the Japanese market experienced an exponential rise. Zombie stocks were alive again! In late January 2006, the police raided the party, literally. They arrested the poster child of this new-Japan paradigm. And suddenly, it felt like a nightclub closing. Crude neon lights were suddenly switched on. Haggard drunk people were staring at each other on the dance floor, confused and disoriented. Reality was back with a vengeance. The levitating zombies had rediscovered Newtonian physics. Unfortunately, the availability and cost of borrow on any single issue was dissuasive, so with my buddies on the Merrill Lynch stock lending desk, we came up with a **Credit Rating Asset Price (CRAP)** basket-swap idea. We dumped in all the zombies we could find. The cost of borrow was an affordable 2%. The price would be end of day closing price. Capacity was virtually unlimited. At a composite beta of 2.3, it had far more torque than index futures. We were in business.

But when it was time to pull the trigger, the principal balked. He complained that it was too volatile, too risky, too unorthodox. So, we ended up "monitoring" it, a fancy word for minting Monopoly money: -2%, -4%, -5%, day in, day out. Still, he was not comfortable with the trade. After three weeks, I concluded that exotic is a holiday destination, not a short position in a three-quarter of a billion-dollar portfolio. Then, one day, the swap got in. It had my name on it too. I couldn't sleep that night. The next day, it tanked an additional -2%. The day after that, it fell another -0.5%, but then, it started to stabilise. It went up +0.5%, +3%, +6%. We had perfectly timed the bottom. But now, the mother of all short squeezes was bringing democracy to short-sellers. Eventually, we closed the position with a large loss on a short instrument that had come down -63% in less than 2 months.

The moral of the story: timing is money. Having the right idea is one thing. Executing it well is another. Bear market rallies happen with metronomic regularity. There are three certainties in life: taxes, death, and somewhere in between, bear market rallies. Some market participants claim that markets cannot be timed. On the long side, markets are more forgiving. Idea generation and execution can be blended. The same upward drift that bails long participants penalises short sellers. Many fundamental short sellers often lament they were too early, or sometimes too late.

Order prioritization

Entry is a choice and exit a necessity. You may enter as you see fit, but you rarely have the luxury to exit on your own terms. In execution trader English, entries are limit orders while exits are stop or market orders. Long-only managers often struggle with cash balances. They need to know how much they can buy on a daily basis. A long/short portfolio has a few more moving parts than a classic long-only book. Things can get messy quite quickly. It is therefore prudent to set "right of way" for entries and exits. In execution trader English, exits always come first. Cash-depleting orders have the "right of way." This can be summed up as follows:

1. Buy-to-cover is the highest priority. It functions like a buy order. It depletes cash. Short-cover has an impact on long buying power and gross exposure. Buy-to-cover may in rare cases trigger margin calls.

2. Sell long is the second-highest priority. It frees up immobilized cash.

3. Sell short: short entries generate cash. This excess cash can be used to buy more stocks. Some jurisdictions compel short sellers to secure stock borrow before placing short orders. Failure to do so results in **naked short selling**. This practice refers to selling short without locating the borrow beforehand. This is not illegal per se, but severely frowned upon. Trades are usually reclassified as "failure to deliver" and closed. If you want to be taken seriously, just don't…

4. Buy long: once again, the most prestigious trade comes last. Only when all trades have been lined up should buy long orders take place. If shorts are not covered but longs are entered, this will reduce the cash balance. This may present some risk if short positions need to be covered hastily.

Let's recap. Trades that reduce risk come first. Those are buy-to-cover and sell long. Then, trades that aim to increase the cash balance come next: sell short and buy long.

Re-entry signals are one case where repeat offenders should be given a front-row seat. Any re-entry signal is a confirmation that the longer trend is still valid. Besides, there is already embedded P&L from prior positions. Consolidated open risk is therefore lower than any new entry. This has limitations, however. Adding to an existing position is called **pyramiding**. Like everything in life, trends mature. Every new position is taken closer to the maturity—and eventually the exhaustion—of a trend. This increases concentration risk and volatility. It is therefore prudent to depreciate risk, for example by taking smaller positions for each re-entry. Position sizes will eventually be too small and rejected.

Next, we will look in more detail at what happens when we run a system on relative series.

Relative prices and absolute execution

While your system runs on currency-adjusted and benchmark-relative prices, sending an order for Japanese stocks in U.S. dollars relative to MSCI World is guaranteed to elicit some comical facial expressions on the trading desk. This may be as clear as day to you, but for the record, traders suck at mind-reading. When communicating in the real world, orders must be placed in local currency.

Since the system runs on currency-adjusted and benchmark-relative prices, stop loss does not need to be translated. In fact, stop loss has no relationship to the local absolute price. In the preceding chapters, stop losses were based on relative price instead of absolute. This is because your system should run on relative series. This means stop-loss orders do not need to rest on your broker's server. One benefit of not having resting stop-loss orders is that they cannot be gamed by the predatory smart money: **High-Frequency Trading (HFT)** players.

Order types

The advent of HFT has seriously embellished the repertoire of trading orders. Market participants who want to refine their execution beyond beating volume-weighted average price are more than welcome to explore the ordering landscape.

For the purpose of this book, let's stick to a simple principle: entry is a choice, exit a necessity. This means exit trades are either at market, stop, or stop limit orders. Entries are either fill or kill, limit or stop limit orders. When we pull the trigger, we want to be filled. Our inner idiot loves the chase, but our track record hates poor execution. A lack of discipline in your entries and exits will affect your track record, so stick to the plan. A little restraint pays off. There will be minor slippage in the conversion from relative to absolute series with what the system suggests, but this all rounds up in the end.

Next, let's go over exits and entries—we discuss them in that order since, as we already noted, exits should be prioritized over entries.

Exits

Exits are split between unprofitable and profitable exits. The former aims at survival while the latter builds prosperity. We copiously discussed exits in *Part II, The Outer Game: Developing a Robust Trading Edge*. Below is a step-by-step short encapsulation that covers both the practical aspect and the mental hygiene of exits.

Stop loss

Stop loss has a direct measurable impact on three out of the four variables in the trading edge formula: win rate, loss rate, and average loss. For this reason only, it always sits at the top of the priority list. Remember that what separates pro short sellers from tourists is the ability to set stop losses and honor them. Think of what follows as an essential checklist. We covered all those topics throughout the book, with particular emphasis in *Chapter 7, Improve Your Trading Edge*.

1. Set the stop loss at a logical articulation where the thesis is invalidated
2. Set a loss mitigation trailing stop: This has two positive impacts:
    - It mitigates losses and tilts gain expectancy toward break-even
    - It will psychologically be easier to deal with and stop a smaller position
3. Position size: Run your risk management to calculate your exposures before sending trades
    - Conservative at a fixed stop loss
    - Aggressive at a trailing stop

Up next is mental preparation. Taking small losses takes its toll on your emotional capital. Do not neglect your mental hygiene. As a reminder, all great traders focus on the mental capital, while the mediocre ones worry about moving average duration or other meaningless trivia.

Pre-mortem

Visualize yourself closing the trade at a loss and take in the associated negative emotions. Repeat the process and resize until you feel comfortable taking a loss. That pre-packages your grief. Hit send and say goodbye to your money, taking the following into consideration:

1. **Time stop**: Cut or reduce position size. Time stops are psychologically difficult to execute: "If I give it just one more day, week, month..." One trick is to think of a real-life time waster and anchor the image to the position.

2. **Mitigation loss**: Meditate, be mindful. This prevents eagerness or fear. Losses are part of the game.

3. **Stop loss**: This is the worst-case scenario. If you did your homework on the pre-mortem, this should be a formality. First and foremost, forgive yourself.

Pre-mortem dates back to Stoic philosopher and Roman emperor Marcus Aurelius. It is one of the most powerful visualization exercises for remaining stoic under pressure.

The Zeigarnik effect

Remind yourself of the following:

1. Once the position is out of sight, you will barely remember that position in 2 weeks. Your capital is more important than the brain fog caused by a single bad trade.

2. Taking small losses will ensure you live to trade another day. Bring the ruler (prefrontal cortex) and the warrior mentality to execute the trade.

When you periodically go through your trading journal, pay particular attention to stop losses. Be mindful of your feelings. This is not as emotionally charged as it once was. You see, it was not that hard after all. If you smile, great. Store that feeling. You are building new neural pathways of a wise trading warrior.

Profitable exits

Below is a step-by-step method for profitable exits:

- Decide on the risk reduction method in advance: target price, trailing exit, options. Do not deviate.

- Do not wait for the bear market rally. Cover your shorts as people continue to sell to avoid market impact.

- This is the minimum quantity to close to break even on the trade:

$$Quantity\ to\ exit = \#Shares \times \frac{(Cost - Stop\ Loss)}{(Price - Stop\ Loss)}$$

- Roll with the bear market rally. Let it wash over. If you have reduced risk in advance, this should not affect your mental state. When the bear rally rolls over, reset your stop loss.

- If the peak of the rally is lower than the previous one, then reload; else, do nothing.

Let's wrap this up with some Python code. First, we will set up a target exit price using three variables: price, stop_loss, and r_multiplier. We calculate r as the distance from price to stop_loss. We then apply a multiplier, aptly named r_multiplier. This number is added back to cost to calculate a target price. Then, we will calculate the quantity to exit using the same r_multiplier. In *Chapter 7, Improve Your Trading Edge*, we saw the inverse relationship between target price and quantity to exit.

```python
def target_price(price, stop_loss, r_multiplier):
    r = price - stop_loss
    return price + r * r_multiplier

def partial_exit(qty, r_multiplier):
    if (qty * r_multiplier)!= 0:
        fraction = qty / r_multiplier
    else:
        fraction = 0
    return fraction

price = 100
stop_loss = 110
qty = 2000
```

```
r_multiplier = 2

pt = target_price(price, stop_loss, r_multiplier)
exit_qty = partial_exit(qty, r_multiplier)
print('target price', pt,'exit_quantity',exit_qty)
```

The output will be as follows:

```
target price 80 exit_quantity 1000.0
```

Half of the position will be exited at 80. This reduces risk by 100%. Next, let's consider how to time your entries.

Entry

> *"Look at market fluctuations as your friend rather than your enemy; profit from folly rather than participate in it."*
>
> *– Warren Buffett*

Great poker players do not play their hand. They play other players' hands. To be successful, you need to systematically tilt probabilities in your favor. Markets happen to be a probabilistic game. The way to achieve greatness is not only to play your hand but the market's invisible hand as well.

The first way to play the market's hand is something we saw in *Chapter 5, Regime Definition*. Let the market decide on which side stocks should go. Let's be honest for one second. Market participants who short bubbly stocks are repressed revenge traders. Deep down, they are angry at their shadow selves for not participating on the long side. Maybe they closed out too early. Maybe they dismissed that boat altogether. Either way, they vent their frustration by putting other people's precious money in immediate harm's way on the short side. Behind the adult call for a return to "fair" valuation lies the shadow "need to be right" of a a 6 year old child's wounded ego.

There is no better illustration of that phenomenon than TSLA. This is a car manufacturer, in a notoriously difficult fragile sector, valued as a tech stock, whose bonds are priced as junk. Something has to give. This gives short sellers ample reason to ferociously raid the stock. In the wake of the Coronavirus pandemic, the share price dropped to $400. That gave short sellers the ammunition to double their efforts, only to face a steep triple bagger rally in the following six months.

Had short sellers seized the drop as an opportunistic buying opportunity, would they still have laid siege? Of course not, they would laugh and dance their way to the bank. Everyone on the planet, from Nauru to Bobo-Dioulasso, would know how smart they were for picking that stock. Now, they are miserably reduced to demanding justice for that rude price. Either way, other people's money is not a valid IQ test. Yet again, they allowed their ego to step on their toes in the everlasting dance of the markets. Beware of the Cassandras who play God with Icarus stocks, for they might drag you down to the underperforming world. When heeding their advice, save the last coin for the Styx ferryman. If the short selling game is about playing the invisible hand of the markets, then let the markets do the heavy lifting for you. Short sell issues that the markets denigrate and enter long on the ones in demand.

The second way to play the market's hand is to time the entry. For years, I used to whine about short squeezes. I would enter a position, feel good, and then be unceremoniously stopped out at the next bear market rally. The financial capital suffers injury and the emotional capital suffers yet another insult. More importantly, it seemed like the lesson was lost. Then one day, the energy of a short squeeze dawned upon the density of my intellect. Since price seemed to rally beyond my "line in the sand" stop loss anyways, all I had to do was to wait for the next bear market rally to see the new shoreline and get a better execution.

I began to see bear market rallies as gifts. They brought their treasure trove to shore for the picking. Once a bear market rally starts to recede, price wobbles like a career politician. Short sellers are stranded ashore. Optimistic long holders have yet to be dragged out to new depths. The line of demarcation is clear. In execution trader English, this is a low-risk high-reward entry price with a clear stop loss around the top and a probable drop ahead. Wait for the market to roll over, then print a new lower swing high along a bearish trend to enter short. By the way, this is the mirror entry of the "buy the dips" technique on the long side.

The third way to play the market's hand is execution. Short sellers are dealt disproportionately unfavorable probabilities. If you short on breakdowns, just remember that 90%+ of market participants will only enter long, and that someone somewhere sees the current weakness as an opportunity to buy at a discount. If you short bearish stocks as they rally, you might be carried out by a short squeeze or the beginning of a bull phase. As a short-seller, there is only a narrow window of time when probabilities are in your favor. For this, you need to pay close attention to price action.

A good analogy is the leopard, the smallest of the African big four. Despite outsmarting, outrunning, and outgunning their prey, leopards never chase. They hide in trees and wait for the kill to come to them. Short sellers need to behave in the same way. This is a three-step process.

1. First, your regime analysis (from *Chapter 5, Regime Definition*) should have determined that stocks may be in either sideways or bearish mode. Agreeing with the market generally tilts probabilities in your favor.

2. Second, the universe has been narrowed down into a short list of investable candidates.

3. Third, the bear market rally rollover sends a clear signal that bulls are not in charge.

Two steps are dictated by the market: setup and execution. One step comes out of analysis: the short list of investable candidates. We have already discussed how to tilt your trading edge in *Part II, The Outer Game: Developing a Robust Trading Edge*, but we will revisit some of the key ideas:

- First, use relative series.

- Second, triage underperformers and outperformers with the regime.

- Third, enter short after a swing high or long after a swing low.

- Fourth, set a stop loss at a logical articulation.

- Fifth, plan a partial exit to reduce risk.

Let's go back to the leopard. Once it pounces, it does not pause mid-air to reflect upon the meaning of life, animal cruelty, or the comparative benefits of a vegetarian diet at a cellular level. The time for introspection is over. Now, it is execution time. Tourists will jump and swim after the boat as soon as they conclude it is the right one. Pros will patiently wait for the market to rally and flush out tourists. They will stand by as the rally docks in and rolls over, and only then will they take a seat on the ferry. The best news about short selling is the metronomic regularity of bear market rallies.

Rollover: the aikido of bear market rallies

Every short seller who has been practicing the craft long enough has been hurt in a bear market rally. A simple change in perspective can turn this energy from devastation into power to harness.

The objective is to enter as early as possible with a reasonable probability of success. Short squeezes can be tricky. They always go further and last longer than expected.

The hallmark of short sellers on their way to mastery is to be right on the next big down move, but still underestimate the energy of the bear market rally. Respect the markets, for they most certainly have no respect for you. The market does not know your name, nor should it care. Accept that you will have to pay for confirmation. Wait for the local peak to pass and the rollover to start. We will illustrate this with a few charts later, but for now, let's look at the pros of this method.

This rollover or rolling of the tide method has a few advantages:

- **Risk management**: the current high is below the peak. Bulls are not in charge anymore. Should the peak rise above, it is an early indication that the regime may have changed. The trend is your friend.

- **Entry is close to the top**. Bears are in disarray. Bulls are optimistic. You are opportunistic. Probabilities are in your corner of the ring for now.

- **Availability of borrow**: bear markets usually flush out tourists. Borrow is available again. Even the most vocal short sellers are too scared to dip their feet in the water.

- **Bigger position size**: the proximity of the top warrants a bigger size than at breakdown level. You are closer to a logical stop loss. Should price rally beyond the current top, you have your exit plan drawn out for you

- **Clear demarcation line**: the top is where bulls and bears settle. There is information available on supply, demand, and volatility.

As follows are some other classic entry methods, which we discussed previously.

Moving averages

Moving averages are simple, valid, and sufficiently robust signals. Although there's no perfect strategy, it's generally best to use a short duration moving average, something like closing below the 5-day moving average. Please refer to *Chapter 5, Regime Definition*, for further information on the moving average crossover.

Retracements

Retracements signal the distance from the highest point. This can be either the distance from the highest high or the highest low, expressed in the average true range. Think of it as a form of trailing stop loss. As a reminder, please have a look at the retracement swing function we outlined in *Chapter 5, Regime Definition*:

```
def retracement_swing(df, _sign, _swg, _c, hh_ll_dt, hh_ll, vlty,
retrace_vol, retrace_pct):
    if _sign == 1: # swing high
```

```
        retracement = df.loc[hh_ll_dt:, _c].min() - hh_ll

        if (vlty > 0) & (retrace_vol > 0) & ((abs(retracement / vlty) -
retrace_vol) > 0):
            df.at[hh_ll_dt, _swg] = hh_ll
        elif (retrace_pct > 0) & ((abs(retracement / hh_ll) -
retrace_pct) > 0):
            df.at[hh_ll_dt, _swg] = hh_ll

    elif _sign == -1: # swing Low
        retracement = df.loc[hh_ll_dt:, _c].max() - hh_ll
        if (vlty > 0) & (retrace_vol > 0) & ((round(retracement /
vlty ,1) - retrace_vol) > 0):
            df.at[hh_ll_dt, _swg] = hh_ll
        elif (retrace_pct > 0) & ((round(retracement / hh_ll , 4) -
retrace_pct) > 0):
            df.at[hh_ll_dt, _swg] = hh_ll
    else:
        retracement = 0
    return df
```

Next, let's remind ourselves about the `retest_swing` function.

Retest

The swing detection code provided in *Chapter 5, Regime Definition* is based on retest.
Price prints a high, followed by a low. Price tries to climb to new highs, but fails
and drops below the previous low. The farther the distance from the previous swing,
the less noisy retests tend to be. As a reminder, please see the source code:

```
def retest_swing(df, _sign, _rt, hh_ll_dt, hh_ll, _c, _swg):
    rt_sgmt = df.loc[hh_ll_dt:, _rt]

    if (rt_sgmt.count() > 0) & (_sign != 0): # Retests exist and
distance test met
        if _sign == 1: # swing high
            rt_list = [rt_sgmt.idxmax(), rt_sgmt.max(),
df.loc[rt_sgmt.idxmax():, _c].cummin()]

        elif _sign == -1: # swing Low
            rt_list = [rt_sgmt.idxmin(), rt_sgmt.min(),
df.loc[rt_sgmt.idxmin():, _c].cummax()]
```

```
        rt_dt,rt_hurdle, rt_px = [rt_list[h] for h in
range(len(rt_list))]

        if str(_c)[0] == 'r':
            df.loc[rt_dt,'rrt'] = rt_hurdle
        elif str(_c)[0] != 'r':
            df.loc[rt_dt,'rt'] = rt_hurdle

        if (np.sign(rt_px - rt_hurdle) == - np.sign(_sign)).any():
            df.at[hh_ll_dt, _swg] = hh_ll
    return df
```

Next, we will consider a Wells Fargo example, where both the retest and retracement swing are active. If one method fails, the other can compensate.

Putting it all together

It is now time to bring the ideas together, and synthesize the approach in one block of code. In *Chapter 5*, *Regime Definition*, we put out a chart of Wells Fargo versus the S&P 500 in absolute and relative series:

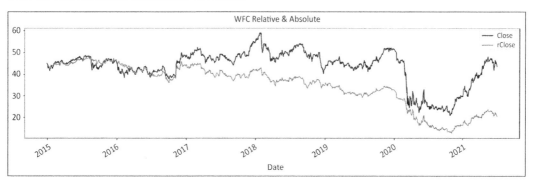

Figure 12.1: Wells Fargo price in absolute and relative to S&P500 from Sept 2015

We have covered pretty much everything already, so there is no real need to comment on the code except for two things:

1. We start with the initialization of the benchmark and download data for the stock below. If you want to repeat the process for a list of tickers, insert a loop above the df download line.

2. Secondly, we re-initialized the _o, _h, _l, and _c attributes via a list comprehension. This will make sense in the next part of the code.

Next, we use the swing detection functions to calculate swings and the regime across the absolute and relative series. It is more efficient to run the same functions twice but assign either the absolute or relative series. This is why we re-initialized _o, _h, _l, and_c before and the swing values below.

```
### STEP 1: ### Graph Regimes Combo ###
def graph_regime_combo(ticker,df,_c,rg,lo,hi,slo,shi,clg,flr,rg_ch,
                    ma_st,ma_mt,ma_lt,lt_lo,lt_hi,st_lo,st_hi):


#### removed for brevity: check GitHub repo for full code ####


### Graph Regimes Combo ###


### STEP 2: ### RELATIVE
def relative(df,_o,_h,_l,_c, bm_df, bm_col, ccy_df, ccy_col, dgt,
start, end,rebase=True):


#### removed for brevity: check GitHub repo for full code ####


### RELATIVE ###


### STEP 3: import library
from scipy.signal import *


### STEP 4: #### hilo_alternation(hilo, dist= None, hurdle= None) ####
def hilo_alternation(hilo, dist= None, hurdle= None):


#### removed for brevity: check GitHub repo for full code ####


#### hilo_alternation(hilo, dist= None, hurdle= None) ####


#### historical_swings(df,_o,_h,_l,_c, dist= None, hurdle= None) ####
def historical_swings(df,_o,_h,_l,_c, dist= None, hurdle= None):


#### removed for brevity: check GitHub repo for full code ####


#### historical_swings(df,_o,_h,_l,_c, dist= None, hurdle= None) ####


### STEP 5: #### cleanup_latest_swing(df, shi, slo, rt_hi, rt_lo) ####
def cleanup_latest_swing(df, shi, slo, rt_hi, rt_lo):
```

```
#### removed for brevity: check GitHub repo for full code ####

#### cleanup_latest_swing(df, shi, slo, rt_hi, rt_lo) ####

### STEP 6: #### latest_swings(df, shi, slo, rt_hi, rt_lo, _h, _l, _c,
_vol) ####
def latest_swing_variables(df, shi, slo, rt_hi, rt_lo, _h, _l, _c):

#### removed for brevity: check GitHub repo for full code ####

#### latest_swings(df, shi, slo, rt_hi, rt_lo, _h, _l, _c, _vol) ####

### STEP 7: #### test_distance(ud, bs, hh_ll, vlty, dist_vol, dist_pct)
####
def test_distance(ud,bs, hh_ll, dist_vol, dist_pct):

#### removed for brevity: check GitHub repo for full code ####

#### test_distance(ud, bs, hh_ll, vlty, dist_vol, dist_pct) ####

#### ATR ####
def average_true_range(df, _h, _l, _c, n):

#### removed for brevity: check GitHub repo for full code ####

#### ATR ####

### STEP 8: #### retest_swing(df, _sign, _rt, hh_ll_dt, hh_ll, _c, _
swg) ####
def retest_swing(df, _sign, _rt, hh_ll_dt, hh_ll, _c, _swg):
    rt_sgmt = df.loc[hh_ll_dt:, _rt]

#### removed for brevity: check GitHub repo for full code ####

#### retest_swing(df, _sign, _rt, hh_ll_dt, hh_ll, _c, _swg) ####

### STEP 9: #### retracement_swing(df, _sign, _swg, _c, hh_ll_dt, hh_
ll, vlty, retrace_vol, retrace_pct) ####
def retracement_swing(df, _sign, _swg, _c, hh_ll_dt, hh_ll, vlty,
retrace_vol, retrace_pct):

#### removed for brevity: check GitHub repo for full code ####
```

```
#### retracement_swing(df, _sign, _swg, _c, hh_ll_dt, hh_ll, vlty,
retrace_vol, retrace_pct) ####


### STEP 10: #### regime_floor_ceiling(df, hi,lo,cl, slo,
shi,flr,clg,rg,rg_ch,stdev,threshold) ####
def regime_floor_ceiling(df, _h,_l,_c,slo, shi,flr,clg,rg,rg_
ch,stdev,threshold):


#### removed for brevity: check GitHub repo for full code ####


#### regime_floor_ceiling(df, hi,lo,cl, slo, shi,flr,clg,rg,rg_
ch,stdev,threshold) ####
```

Below is the actual important code, which will print the graph shown in *Figure 12.1*:

```
params = ['2014-12-31', None, 63, 0.05, 0.05, 1.5, 2]
start, end, vlty_n,dist_pct,retrace_pct,threshold,dgt= [params[h] for h
in range(len(params))]


rel_var = ['^GSPC','SP500', 'USD']
bm_ticker, bm_col, ccy_col = [rel_var[h] for h in range(len(rel_var))]
bm_df = pd.DataFrame()
bm_df[bm_col] = round(yf.download(tickers= bm_ticker,start= start,
end = end,interval = "1d",
                group_by = 'column',auto_adjust = True, prepost =
True,
                treads = True, proxy = None)['Close'],dgt)
bm_df[ccy_col] = 1


ticker = 'WFC'
df = round(yf.download(tickers= ticker,start= start, end =
end,interval = "1d",
                group_by = 'column',auto_adjust = True, prepost =
True,
                treads = True, proxy = None),2)


#### removed for brevity: check GitHub repo for full code ####


    rohlc = ['rOpen','rHigh','rLow','rClose']
    _o,_h,_l,_c = [rohlc[h] for h in range(len(rohlc)) ]
    rswing_val = ['rrg','rL1','rH1','rL3','rH3','rclg','rflr','rrg_ch']
    rg,rt_lo,rt_hi,slo,shi,clg,flr,rg_ch = [rswing_val[s] for s in
range(len(rswing_val))]
```

We run a loop over the absolute series first. We calculate swings and regime using the floor ceiling method. At the end of the first loop, we re-initialize _o, _h, _1, _c and swing variables using the relative series. We have now calculated swings and regime for Wells Fargo in absolute and relative to S&P 500. Let's visualize the results:

```
plot_abs_cols = ['Close','Hi3', 'Lo3','clg','flr','rg_ch','rg']
plot_abs_style = ['k', 'ro', 'go', 'kv', 'k^','b:','b--']
y2_abs = ['rg']
plot_rel_cols = ['rClose','rH3', 'rL3','rclg','rflr','rrg_ch','rrg']
plot_rel_style = ['grey', 'ro', 'go', 'yv', 'y^','m:','m--']
y2_rel = ['rrg']

df[plot_abs_cols].plot(secondary_y= y2_abs,figsize=(20,8),
          title = str.upper(ticker)+ ' Absolute',# grid=True,
          style=plot_abs_style)

df[plot_rel_cols].plot(secondary_y=y2_rel,figsize=(20,8),
          title = str.upper(ticker)+ ' Relative',# grid=True,
          style=plot_rel_style)

df[plot_rel_cols + plot_abs_cols].plot(secondary_y=y2_rel + y2_
abs,figsize=(20,8),
          title = str.upper(ticker)+ ' Relative & Absolute',#
grid=True,
          style=plot_rel_style + plot_abs_style)
```

We will plot three distinctive charts: absolute, relative, and combined. We will therefore store absolute and relative parameters in lists. Without further ado, here are the three charts:

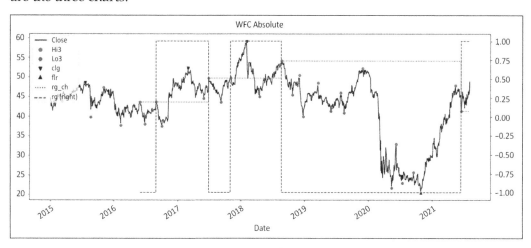

Figure 12.2: Wells Fargo swings and floor/ceiling regime in absolute

Regime has been a fair predictor of behavior, especially in the latter part of the period. The 2020 rally did not lead to a change in regime until a swing low was registered in 2021. Next, we will plot the relative series:

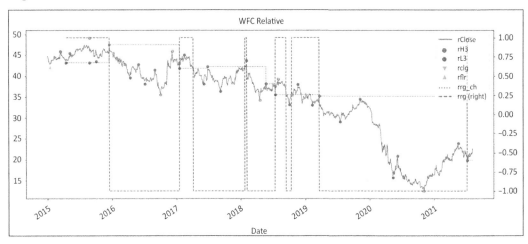

Figure 12.3: Wells Fargo swings and floor/ceiling regime relative to S&P 500

As we saw in an earlier chapter, Wells Fargo took it hard when the scandal erupted and didn't recover until 2021. The regime looks superficially more nervous. There were quite a few bullish false positives along the way. They were short in scope and duration. Note how the red dots above the price line constitute good entry and/or mobile stop levels. There is of course a small lag between printing a swing high and their discovery. Finally, we combine both in one chart:

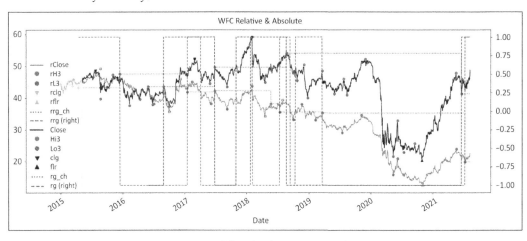

Figure 12.4: Wells Fargo swings and floor/ceiling regime absolute and relative to S&P 500

This final chart looks a lot noisier than the previous two. Note how the floor/ceiling method nailed the September 2016 scandal. The relative series consistently leads the regime throughout the entire duration.

Let's visualise the absolute and relative charts one more time using the graph regime function:

```
ma_st = ma_mt = ma_lt = lt_lo = lt_hi = st_lo = st_hi = 0

rg_combo = ['Close','rg','Lo3','Hi3','Lo3','Hi3','clg','flr','rg_ch']
_c,rg,lo,hi,slo,shi,clg,flr,rg_ch=[rg_combo[r] for r in
range(len(rg_combo))]
graph_regime_combo(ticker,df,_c,rg,lo,hi,slo,shi,clg,flr,rg_ch,
ma_st,ma_mt,ma_lt,lt_lo,lt_hi,st_lo,st_hi)


rrg_combo = ['rClose','rrg','rL3','rH3','rL3','rH3','rclg','rflr',
'rrg_ch']
_c,rg,lo,hi,slo,shi,clg,flr,rg_ch=[rrg_combo[r] for r in
range(len(rrg_combo))]
graph_regime_combo(ticker,df,_c,rg,lo,hi,slo,shi,clg,flr,rg_ch,
ma_st,ma_mt,ma_lt,lt_lo,lt_hi,st_lo,st_hi)
```

The following is the regime plotted in absolute: the darker colors are loss-making periods:

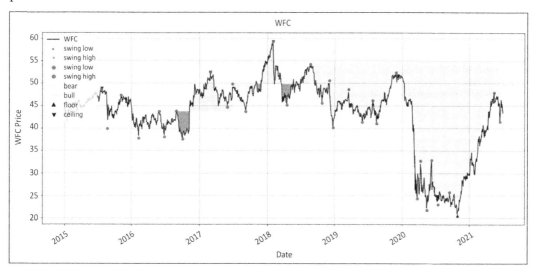

Figure 12.5: Wells Fargo colored floor/ceiling regime in absolute

Next, let's look at the relative series:

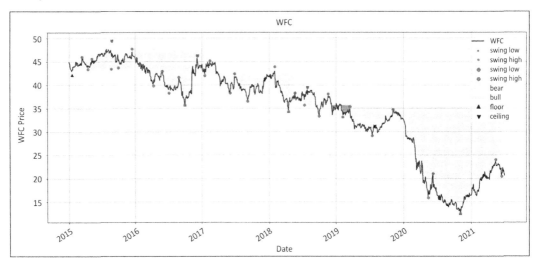

Figure 12.6: Wells Fargo colored floor/ceiling regime relative to S&P 500

This last chart really shows the extent of the underperformance over the last few years. There are numerous methods that identify trend exhaustion, such as stochastics, RSI, MACD, DeMark indicators, and the latter's ancestor, Fibonacci retracements. Most of those techniques boil down to bringing order to chaos. Unfortunately, popularity does not necessarily indicate statistical robustness. If you still believe in using predictive technical analysis, you could split your order in two, where the first tranche uses predictive analysis and the second tranche is added upon confirmation that the prediction was accurate. You will have marginally better average execution when it works and will not be bankrupted when it does not.

Above all, remember that one person's breakdown is someone else's "buy-on-weakness." This is the short side; the market does not cooperate. Use bear market rallies and short squeezes to time your entry. Cover when everyone else pukes. Reduce risk when you can by trimming your positions and/or resetting your stop losses.

Summary

This entire book has led to this and the next chapter. In summary, to put together all we have covered in the preceding chapters, switch to relative series and triage with the market regime. Enter short after a swing high or long after a swing low. Set a stop loss above or below the swing and a target price to reduce risk. Calculate your position size using your cost, stop loss, and risk budget.

Keep a separate risk budget for each long/short side of each strategy. Honor your stop losses and respect your strategy. Keep a clean trading journal. Refine your mandate along the way.

In the next chapter, we will be looking at one of the most underrated tools in your arsenal: your portfolio management system. Being a stock picker and a portfolio manager are two distinct jobs that require different skill sets. The moment you chose to manage a portfolio, you are no longer a stock jockey. You have become a stable master. Your job is not to cross the finish line on horseback. Your job is to nurture (or discard) horses that will cross (or fail to cross) finish lines for the foreseeable future.

A relative long/short portfolio is a different beast from a classic long-only or even an absolute long/short. Whatever tools you have been using so far are in dire need of a radical upgrade. If you want a fighting chance in the markets, you need an Iron Man suit.

13

Portfolio Management System

"Toto, I have a feeling we are not in Kansas anymore."

– Dorothy, The Wizard of Oz

My first job in the hedge fund world was to build and maintain a **Portfolio Management System (PMS)** for a start-up hedge fund with less than $5 million under management. The principals believed that risk management was not some ornament of the business, but the business itself. Fast forward to now, and they are the dominant player in the Japanese alternative space. In this chapter, we will continue with our work from the last two chapters, and introduce a customized PMS which shows risk visualization across the portfolio.

To illustrate the importance of a robust PMS, let's connect a few concepts we explored throughout this book. In *Chapter 1, The Stock Market Game*, we set the context that the market is an infinite, complex random game. In *Chapter 6, The Trading Edge is a Number, and Here is the Formula*, we unveiled the magical, mysterious, and mythical trading edge formula. In *Chapter 8, Position Sizing: Money is Made in the Money Management Module*, we demonstrated that position sizing determines performance. And we learned in *Chapter 11, The Long/Short Toolbox*, about the tools in our toolbox. So, we know that position sizing is the key determinant, but we don't know which positions will work out, yet we must maintain a positive expectancy while managing exposures. Rinse and repeat every day for years to attract and keep investors.

Over the course of my career, friends and colleagues have been generous enough to unveil their PMSes. Survival is directly correlated to the quality of their PMSes. Not everyone who had a proper system made it. Yet every single manager who did not have a system eventually crashed.

A PMS is like flight instruments. Any rookie can fly a plane in clear skies. Instruments are there to prevent crashes during takeoff and when landing at night, through fog and turbulence. Without instruments, not everyone will be coming home. The market is not fair weather and smooth sailing all the time. Things do get ugly unexpectedly. Emotions do steer us off course. In execution trader English, how can you claim to be a portfolio manager if you don't have a solid PMS? Building a customized PMS using Python deserves its own book, if not its own dedicated literary genre, and therefore exceeds the scope of this book. However, in this chapter we will briefly touch on a few fundamental concepts and guiding principles that will hopefully guide you:

- Symptoms of poor portfolio management systems
- Your portfolio management system is your Iron Man suit
- Automating the boring stuff
- Building a robust portfolio management system

 You can access color versions of all images in this chapter via the following link: `https://static.packt-cdn.com/downloads/9781801815192_ColorImages.pdf`. You can also access the source code for this chapter via the book's GitHub repository: `https://github.com/PacktPublishing/Algorithmic-Short-Selling-with-Python-Published-by-Packt`.

Importing libraries

For this chapter and the rest of the book, we will be working with the `pandas`, `numpy`, `yfinance`, and `matplotlib` libraries. So, please remember to import them first:

```
# Import Libraries
import pandas as pd
import numpy as np
import yfinance as yf
%matplotlib inline
import matplotlib.pyplot as plt
```

Symptoms of poor portfolio management systems

When it comes to turning performance around, a good PMS is the lowest hanging fruit. In 2005, I joined a hedge fund whose PMS was so ugly, looking at it could have caused brain damage. I promptly tooled it up, at least to get rid of the health hazard. Suddenly, problem children lit up like garlands on a Christmas tree. Volatile penny stocks on the short side, lazy dogs, and unappreciated racing hounds were all swiftly dealt with. Volatility came down. Performance was more consistent. The Sharpe ratio jumped. Investors noticed. **Assets Under Management (AUM)** grew. It was that simple.

Everyone wants to know the "secret sauce" of the winners, but this is one area where the lessons of the "alpha-challenged" ones might help us from inadvertently repeating the same mistakes. Here is a simple exercise that will help you figure out if your system is in need of an upgrade. Deficient PMSes share one or more of the following symptoms.

Ineffective capital allocation

As much as portfolio managers like to project an Olympian demi-god image to the public, they can be reeled back to earth with a few sentences:

- "Nice guys finish last": some stocks post impressive returns that go unnoticed because positions are small. Those are often exploratory tiny positions. They post high returns but contribute poorly because they are not adequately sized.

- "Fat cats don't catch the mice": some big positions contribute only because of their massive weight. This is a classic problem with PMS. It is directly related to the above point. Those are often high-conviction ideas that occupy far too much real estate for their paltry returns.

- "Once we were warriors": those are veteran contributors who are now mooching rent-free. Those are ideas that have been stale for a while. They have a lot of embedded historical contribution but do not pay rent anymore. We have addressed the situation in the game of two thirds in *Chapter 7, Improve Your Trading Edge*.

Undermonitored risk detection

A key metric to keep an eye on is liquidity, to avoid "Hotel California Syndrome." In other words, you do not own what you cannot liquidate, it owns you. Liquidity is the currency of bear markets. Are there positions that cannot be liquidated without severe market impact? Below is a function that restates position size in days to exit at a fraction of the average volume. Sheer terror for a short seller is when you see a bear market rally gain momentum and realize your position is too big to get out unscathed. There are few worse feelings than being squeezed out of a position only to see it resume its downward descent post bear market tsunami.

A simple risk measure is to restate a position size as the number of days necessary to liquidate at a fraction of the average volume. The code below simply calculates a fraction of the average volume. The position quantity is divided by this fraction:

```
ticker = 'UNG' #ETF natural gas
volume = yf.download(tickers= ticker,start= '2021-01-01', end = None,
                     interval = "1d",group_by = 'column',
                     auto_adjust = True, prepost = True,treads = True,
                     proxy = None)['Volume']

def days_liquidation(quantity,volume,window,fraction):
    avg_vol_fraction = volume.rolling(window).mean()* fraction
    return round(quantity/avg_vol_fraction,2)
quantity = 100000
window = 63
fraction =0.01
days_liquidation(quantity,volume,window,fraction)[-1]
```

This produces an output something like the following:

```
3.52
```

We can produce the chart shown in *Figure 13.1*:

```
plt.plot(days_liquidation(quantity,volume,window,fraction))
```

We downloaded `volume` data since the beginning of 2021. The function multiplies a fixed percentage by a moving average of the volume. This number of shares is divided by a fraction of volume: `0.01`, or 1%. This value is arbitrary and deliberately low to show the principle. In practice, 5-10% are reasonable thresholds. At the end of June 2021, it would take roughly 5 days to liquidate the entire position if the order size did not exceed 1% of the average volume. We printed the last number in the series and plotted the moving average:

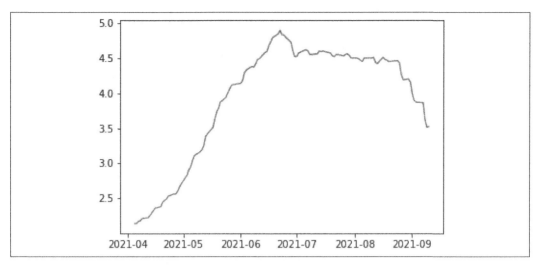

Figure 13.1: Days to liquidate at 1% of 3 months average volume

The above chart shows liquidity is not static. It would originally take about 2 days to liquidate the position trading at 1% of the average daily volume. As liquidity thins out, the number of days necessary to liquidate increases to 5 days, then comes back down to around 3.5 days. A week is an eternity when price moves against you. Liquidity should therefore be monitored.

Market impact is the adverse change in price caused by trading large quantities. Market impact starts when positions are bigger than 5% of the daily volume. If a position takes more than 5 days at 10% of the volume, then expect some serious market impact. Besides, the violence of bear market rallies cannot be understated enough. You will mentally be on your back foot trading yourself out of a hole. So, always monitor liquidity and trim positions when volume thins out.

High volatility

Crowded shorts have high average borrow utilization. Liquidity will thin out, volatility will increase, and returns will deteriorate. Heatmaps of utilization or borrowing fees are very valuable tools. At the date of publication, there are unfortunately no free sources for borrow utilization. As a shortcut, when the lending fee is largely above the average, assume popularity. The simplest way to deal with crowded shorts is to reduce position size as popularity rises. Again, make simple rules, like (for example) cut exposure in half if utilization rises above 40% and by an additional half for every 10% increase. By the time utilization reaches 60%, exposure would be 25% of the original size. This is just food for thought.

Blow-ups do not stand out: people want to feel good about themselves. In the markets, doing what feels good is rarely the most lucrative course of action. Stocks at risk must visually nag managers into taking action. Stocks rarely blow up unexpectedly. They often give subtle signals that things are not going the way they should.

High correlation

The goal of diversification is to reduce correlation. Correlation is difficult to avoid. In *Chapter 4*, *Long/Short Methodologies: Absolute and Relative*, we introduced the relative series to reduce correlation with the benchmark. However, the focus shifts from timing the absolute top or bottom to catching sector rotation, and allocating assets accordingly. Correlation within a portfolio is hard to eliminate. Frankly speaking, I do not know how to accomplish this in practice. Neither have I encountered successful methods so far.

Poor exposure management

There are a few different types of exposures, which can indicate a poorly managed portfolio in the following ways:

- Net exposure: when portfolio net exposure does not match the current bullish/bearish view. This is particularly true in bear phases, when net exposure still points to residual bullishness despite ambient gloom. Portfolio cognitive dissonance is when exposures do not reflect the claims of managers.

- Net beta exposure: true market sensitivity is absent in most deficient systems. When managers focus solely on net exposure, they conflate low directionality with net market sensitivity. Net beta goes one step beyond net exposure to reflect the sensitivity to the market.

- Market cap exposure: shorting futures is the junk food of hedging. As we saw in *Chapter 11*, *The Long/Short Tooolbox*, small and large caps have different risk profiles. Small caps perform well when the general mood of the market is optimistic, while large caps are safer bets. The net market cap exposure reflects the overall optimism of the portfolio

- Gross exposure: too much leverage in good times and too much cash in bad times. Gross exposure is the easiest lever to reduce or add risk. When in doubt, collapse leverage is the simplest risk policy to live by.

- Exchange exposure: exposure by market cap and exchange explains a lot of good/bad performance. As we saw in *Chapter 4, Long/Short Methodologies: Absolute and Relative*, Nasdaq has outperformed S&P 500 for years. Years of easy money have rewarded speculative issues and those who bet on them. When money is easy, it is easy to make money. No bull market has ever boosted anyone's IQ.

All in all, the highest return on investment in the asset management industry is a bespoke PMS. As the information gap closes, market participants scramble to find an edge. If you can spot and address problems earlier than your peers, you gain a sustainable competitive edge.

Your portfolio management system is your Iron Man suit

"You know, the question I get asked most often is, "Tony, how do you go to the bathroom in your suit?" [Long pause] Just like that."

– Tony Stark, Iron Man

Tony Stark may be a genius, a billionaire, a playboy, and a philanthropist. What truly gives him his superpower is his custom-made Iron Man suit. He did not buy his suit off the rack at Macy's. He torpedoed a few Lamborghinis in his garage building something that uniquely enhanced his fighting style. In the same way, your PMS is your Iron Man suit. It is an extension of your trading strategy. Its sole purpose is to help you make trading decisions under uncertainty. Since no one trades like you, it requires a high degree of customization.

A classic mistake is to buy an expensive off-the-shelf software package, thinking that more information will lead to better trading decisions. Software solutions are primarily reporting tools designed by middle office personnel for front office professionals. Your PMS is a trading tool, not a reporting one. A Barra factor decomposition or the Street consensus earnings per share will not tell you how many shares of whichever company you should be buying or selling short today. Information turns into knowledge, which does not readily translate into skill. The key to building skill is to focus exclusively on information that directly leads to action.

In practice, a few months after system integration, portfolio managers often end up managing their portfolio with a low-tech Excel spreadsheet feeding from those shiny toys. They bought a Lamborghini to fetch the milk. Therefore, before you rush to buy the most expensive toy out there, here are a few principles that will help you clarify your needs. Information must be organized under four principles: clarity, relevance, simplicity, and flexibility.

Clarity: bypass the left brain

Under stress, your amygdala releases chemicals that reduce the activity of your prefrontal cortex, or "thinking brain." Your ability to think clearly gets impaired. Your PMS needs clarity: the information must be organized so that problems jump out at you. Secondly, the left brain cannot process rows and columns of numbers. It is slow, 5 to 7 bits per second. It does not make associations. Everything blurs into a sterile number soup. Meanwhile, the right brain processes information one hundred times faster, seeks patterns, and makes associations. Fortunately, data visualization is the new trend in data science. Visual cues bypass the slower-thinking brain. When decisions involve multiple factors, painting by numbers facilitates associations. For example, visualizing your positions within your investment universe as a heatmap will immediately tell you whether you are on the right track and riding the best horse within each sector. We will look at a portfolio heatmap at the end of the chapter.

Another topic is alerts. Did you ever wonder why disaster sirens are so annoying? People might not get the same sense of urgency if the "Ode to Joy" were to announce an imminent earthquake, tsunami, or volcanic eruption. We are hardwired to move away from pain and toward pleasure. Alarms are there to compel the most reluctant people into action. When a position needs to be dealt with, make the alert as nagging as possible. The more annoying the alert, the more likely it will be swiftly dealt with. The best alerts are those you must manually acknowledge first before doing your daily routine. Example: let's say that a stock has reached a stop loss. If an alert is set such that you must click on it to be able to continue to your portfolio, two things can happen. Either you will swiftly deal with the problem, or you will end up avoiding your tool altogether. When the need to be right supersedes the imperative to make money, our inner idiot works extra hard to self-sabotage.

A classic mistake is to have multiple pages, one for each risk factor. This means users must juggle between pages and take notes. Every degree of friction increases information leakage. A pilot should not have to run up and down the plane to see if the hydraulics and the fuel gauge are all in order. If you want to make associations between different risks, you need to bring all relevant information into a one-page summary that allows drill-down in later pages. Think of it like the dashboard of a car or a plane. All the information you need is on display before you.

Put things in context. The left brain does not process numbers effectively. Gross exposure of 295% is just a number. When plotted on a chart that displays benchmark, gross, and net exposures and performance, that number is in context. It is a visual representation of what the market did, how you were positioned, and the resulting performance over time. A picture is worth a thousand words. Let's recycle the example we saw in *Chapter 11, The Long/Short Toolbox*. We simulated a portfolio from the following tickers. We ran the numbers assuming no trading from December 31st 2020 through to June 2021:

```python
# Chapter 13: Portfolio Management System
K = 1000000
lot = 100
port_tickers = ['QCOM','TSLA','NFLX','DIS','PG', 'MMM','IBM','BRK-
B','UPS','F']
bm_ticker= '^GSPC'
tickers_list = [bm_ticker] + port_tickers
df_data= {
'Beta':[1.34,2,0.75,1.2,0.41,0.95,1.23,0.9,1.05,1.15],
'Shares':[-1900,-100,-400,-800,-5500,1600,1800,2800,1100,20800],
'rSL':[42.75,231,156,54.2,37.5,42.75,29.97,59.97,39.97,2.10]
}
port = pd.DataFrame(df_data,index=port_tickers)
port['Side'] = np.sign(port['Shares'])

start_dt = '2021-01-01'
end_dt = '2021-07-01'
price_df = round( yf.download(tickers= tickers_list,start= '2021-01-01',
                            end = '2021-07-01', interval = "1d",
                            group_by = 'column',auto_adjust = True,
                            prepost = True, treads = True,
                            proxy = None)['Close'],2)

bm_cost = price_df[bm_ticker][0]
bm_price = price_df[bm_ticker][-1]

port['rCost'] = round(price_df.iloc[0,:].div(bm_cost) *1000,2)
port['rPrice'] = round(price_df.iloc[-1,:].div(bm_price) *1000,2)
port['Cost'] = price_df.iloc[0,:]
port['Price'] = price_df.iloc[-1,:]
```

In *Chapter 11, The Long/Short Toolbox*, we worked on the port dataframe. This time, we will visualize exposures using price_df. We will first calculate benchmark returns. Then, we will calculate long and short market values in relative and absolute.

We will calculate exposures and returns in absolute and relative.

```python
price_df['bm returns'] = round(np.exp(np.log(price_df[bm_ticker]/price_
df[bm_ticker].shift()).cumsum()) - 1, 3)
rel_price = round(price_df.div(price_df['^GSPC'],axis=0 )*1000,2)


rMV = rel_price.mul(port['Shares'])
rLong_MV = rMV[rMV >0].sum(axis=1)
rShort_MV = rMV[rMV <0].sum(axis=1)
rMV_Beta = rMV.mul(port['Beta'])
rLong_MV_Beta = rMV_Beta[rMV_Beta >0].sum(axis=1) / rLong_MV
rShort_MV_Beta = rMV_Beta[rMV_Beta <0].sum(axis=1)/ rShort_MV


price_df['rNet_Beta'] = rLong_MV_Beta - rShort_MV_Beta
price_df['rNet'] = round((rLong_MV + rShort_MV).div(abs(rMV).
sum(axis=1)),3)


price_df['rReturns_Long'] = round(np.exp(np.log(rLong_MV/rLong_
MV.shift()).cumsum())-1,3)
price_df['rReturns_Short'] = - round(np.exp(np.log(rShort_MV/rShort_
MV.shift()).cumsum())-1,3)
price_df['rReturns'] = price_df['rReturns_Long'] + price_df['rReturns_
Short']


MV = price_df.mul(port['Shares'])
Long_MV = MV[MV >0].sum(axis=1)
Short_MV = MV[MV <0].sum(axis=1)
price_df['Gross'] = round((Long_MV - Short_MV).div(K),3)
price_df['Net'] = round((Long_MV + Short_MV).div(abs(MV).
sum(axis=1)),3)


price_df['Returns_Long'] = round(np.exp(np.log(Long_MV/Long_
MV.shift()).cumsum())-1,3)
price_df['Returns_Short'] = - round(np.exp(np.log(Short_MV/Short_
MV.shift()).cumsum())-1,3)
price_df['Returns'] = price_df['Returns_Long'] + price_df['Returns_
Short']


MV_Beta = MV.mul(port['Beta'])
Long_MV_Beta = MV_Beta[MV_Beta >0].sum(axis=1) / Long_MV
Short_MV_Beta = MV_Beta[MV_Beta <0].sum(axis=1)/ Short_MV
price_df['Net_Beta'] = Long_MV_Beta - Short_MV_Beta
```

The rel_price frame is the price_df dataframe divided by the benchmark close multiplied by 1,000. We use continuous series, not rebased to the beginning of the series. The value of the index at the beginning is 4 decimals long. We therefore multiply the relative price by 1,000 to have easier numbers to work with. We multiply the prices by the number of shares, aggregate by the sign of the positions, and sum up to obtain relative long and short market values. Since there was no trading, there was no change to the market values other than returns. We therefore calculate cumulative returns using the market value daily changes. As we saw in *Chapter 11, The Long/Short Toolbox*, the gross exposure uses the absolute series. This is the actual balance sheet usage.

We plot the main exposures and the returns in a chart. We then plot the relative series:

```
price_df[['bm returns','Returns','Gross','rNet_Beta','rNet' ]].plot(
    figsize=(20,8),grid=True, secondary_y=['Gross'],
    style= ['r.-','k','g--','g-.','g:','b:','c','c:'],
    title = 'bm returns, Returns, Gross, rNet_Beta, rNet')

price_df[['bm returns', 'Returns', 'rReturns', 'rReturns_Long',
        'rReturns_Short']].plot(figsize=(20,8),grid=True,
            style= ['r.-','k','b--o','b--^','b--v','g-.','g:','b:'],
            title= 'bm returns, Returns, rReturns, rReturns_Long,
rReturns_Short')

price_df[['bm returns','Returns','rReturns',
        'rReturns_Long','rReturns_Short','Returns_Long',
        'Returns_Short']].plot(
            figsize=(20,8),grid=True,secondary_y=['Gross'],
            style= ['r.-','k','b--o','b--^','b--v','k:^','k:v',],
    title= 'Returns: benchmark, Long / Short absolute & relative')

price_df[['bm returns',
        'rReturns_Long','rReturns_Short','Returns_Long',
        'Returns_Short']].plot(
            figsize=(20,8),grid=True,secondary_y=['Gross'],
            style= ['r.-','b--^','b--v','k:^','k:v',],
    title= 'Returns: benchmark, Long / Short absolute & relative')
```

We will have four graphs. The first one is the "who are you?" chart:

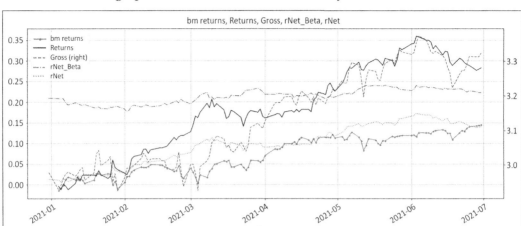

Figure 13.2: The "who are you" chart: market returns and exposures

The above chart is a personal favorite. If there was one chart to sum up the portfolio management skill of a manager, it would be this one. It shows how managers respond to what the market throws at them. The benchmark market returns is the solid red line and all the other lines are the manager's response:

- Gross exposure is the dashed line. Leverage is a direct reflection of confidence. Rising gross exposure displays confidence.

- Net exposure is the dotted line. Net exposure symbolizes optimism. A rising net exposure indicates growing bullishness. As both sides of the portfolio worked out nicely, shorts decreased while longs increased in value. This resulted in a net long drift.

- Net beta is the dashed-dotted stable line. Net beta symbolizes risk appetite. When risk is on, more speculative issues will populate the long book and defensive sectors and names will be on the short side. There was no trading, so the net beta is simply a reflection of the evolution of the market values.

- Finally, the solid black line is the returns. Managing exposures this way resulted in this performance.

- The only missing component in this chart is net trading. Plot net long/short trading in bars and this will display responses. Since there was no trading in this example, there are no bars.

Next, let's look at how the long and short books contributed to performance. Our original premise is that a long/short portfolio is the sum of two relative books. The long book must outperform the index while the short one has to trail the benchmark. Here is how it came about:

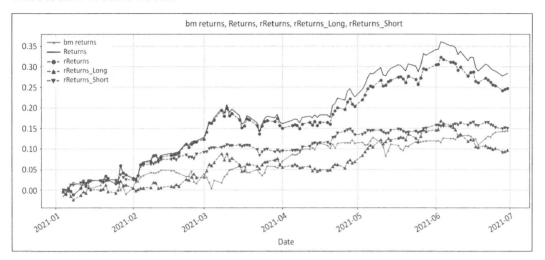

Figure 13.3: Returns: benchmark, absolute, relative, long and short

In practice, it is exceedingly rare to consistently outperform the index over a short period of time. The red solid line is the benchmark. The dotted blue line is the relative performance and the solid black line is the absolute one.

First of all, the performance of the long/short exceeded the index. This is as close to fiction as this book will ever get. The relative long returns are upward triangles. The short relative returns are downward triangles. Secondly, note how close to the index the long and short relative returns are. They are the excess returns over the index. Put this in perspective with the number of stocks in the relative bullish or bearish regime we saw in *Chapter 4, Long/Short Methodologies: Absolute and Relative.* They oscillate around the benchmark.

To fully understand the meaning of excess returns, let's compare the relative long/short returns with the absolute ones:

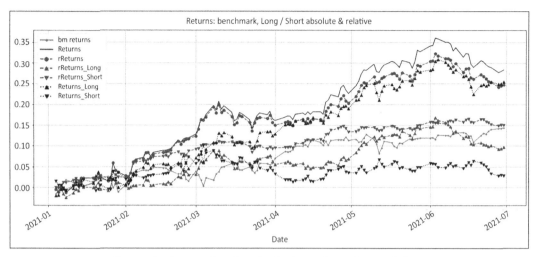

Figure 13.4: Returns: benchmark, absolute, relative, long and short

This noisy chart shows the absolute long and short returns. It shows a principle still foreign to many absolute players. Making money on the short side in a bull market means losing as little as possible. Breaking even is a good thing. Think about it from your long positions in a bear market. You do not expect to make any money, and quite frankly you would be happy if you did not lose your shirt on your longs.

Let's remove both absolute and relative net returns and concentrate on long and short absolute and relative returns to drive the point home:

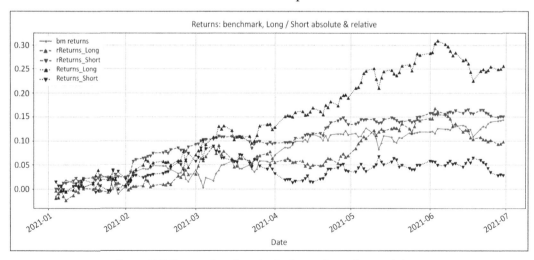

Figure 13.5: Returns: benchmark, absolute, relative, long and short

In execution trader English, expect your shorts to bleed in a bull market. Just make sure you do not let a small scratch turn into an infection and gangrene the entire portfolio. This is where a lot of novice short sellers make the classic mistake of shrinking their short book. Here is how this syllogism usually goes:

1. The long/short arena is a highly competitive sport. Every basis point of performance counts.

2. The short book is leaking alpha, financial creole for losing money.

3. So, let's shrink the short book to jugulate the alpha hemorrhage and focus on the long side.

That line of thinking usually ends up in an atrophied short side. This widens the net exposure and increases the net beta. This directly increases the correlation with the markets and the volatility of returns. Those two are precisely what investors are willing to pay a premium to avoid. Selling short is a muscle that atrophies when not flexed. In conclusion, focus on your mandate, your exposures, and the excess returns over the index.

Relevance: the Iron Man auto radio effect

Despite all the gadgets in his suit, have you ever wondered why Tony Stark does not have a low-tech auto radio in his Iron Man suit? He is also the CEO of Stark Industries and maybe he would like to know what market experts think about his share price. However, listening to the chrematocoulrophony on CNBC is simply a distraction Tony Stark cannot afford when he fights some bad guy.

The Iron Man auto radio effect is the reason why market participants sometimes invoke a human limitation to the number of stocks they can manage. Your PMS is not here to provide information. It is an extension of your trading strategy, here to tell you what to do. It will spit out orders that will either come from signals in your strategy or your risk management. You do not need to know your Sharpe ratio or consensus EPS 2 years out to execute a stop loss. You need to know your main exposures and how many shares you need to trade to hedge your portfolio according to the mandate you designed in *Chapter 11, The Long/Short Toolbox*.

Everyone has a monitoring screen that shows what goes on in their portfolio. Very few market participants have taken the extra step to build a trading screen that embeds their trading rules and processes information into trading decisions.

Build a separate trading sheet with a column for each trading decision: stop loss, profit taking, time exit, re-entry, and so on. Have your trading rules or investment process run in the background. When a decision needs to be made, display the number of shares in the corresponding cell, else leave it blank.

For example, when a stock has reached a profit-taking target, just print the number of shares that need to be closed.

In *Chapter 11, The Long/Short Toolbox*, we performed a pro rata risk adjustment. First, we will republish the code. We will show the aggregates before and after adjustment. We will then print out orders:

```python
# Chapter 13: Portfolio Management System
adjust_long = adjust_short  =  -0.01

MV = port['Shares'] * port['Price']
port['Weight'] = round(MV.div(abs(MV).sum()), 3)
port['rR'] = (port['rCost'] - port['rSL'])
port['rRisk'] = -round(np.maximum(0,(port['rR'] * port['Shares'])/K),
4)
port['rRAR'] = round( (port['rPrice'] - port['rCost'])/port['rR'], 1)
port['rCTR'] = round(port['Shares'] * (port['rPrice']-port['rCost'])/
K,4)
port['CTR'] = round(port['Shares'] * (port['Price']-port['Cost'])/ K,4)

port_long = port[port['Side'] > 0]
port_short = port[port['Side'] < 0]
pro_rata_long = port_long['rRisk'] / (port_long['rRisk'].sum() * port_
long['rRAR'])
risk_adj_long = (abs(adjust_long) * pro_rata_long * K / port_long['rR']
// lot) * lot
shares_adj_long =  np.minimum(risk_adj_long, port_long['Shares'])*np.
sign(adjust_long)

pro_rata_short = port_short['rRisk'] / (port_short['rRisk'].sum() *
port_short['rRAR'])
risk_adj_short = (abs(adjust_short) * pro_rata_short * K / port_
short['rR'] // lot)*lot
shares_adj_short = np.maximum(risk_adj_short,port_short['Shares'])*np.
sign(adjust_short)

port['Qty_adj'] = shares_adj_short.append(shares_adj_long)
port['Shares_adj'] = port['Shares'] + port['Qty_adj']
port['rRisk_adj'] = -round(np.maximum(0,(port['rR'] * port['Shares_
adj'])/K),4)
MV_adj= port['Shares_adj'] * port['Price']
rMV_adj = port['Shares_adj'] * port['rPrice']
```

```
port['Weight_adj'] = round(MV_adj.div(abs(MV_adj).sum()),3)

port.loc[port['Shares_adj'] != 0,'Shares_adj']
```

We decide to update risk equally on the long and short side by -0.01, which equates to reducing risk by 1%. The sorting key to pro-rate the adjustment was the relative risk-adjusted returns. The lower the relative performance in units of relative risk, the bigger the adjustment. The adjusted stocks and quantities to be traded were:

```
QCOM      -1500
NFLX       -200
DIS        -500
PG        -5100
IBM         500
BRK-B      2100
UPS         800
F         19200
```

You can adjust the value of the `adjust_long` and `adjust_short` variables to whatever risk adjustment you'd like to make (positive or negative). Add a column for prices, another for order type, and that is all the system must spit out. You do not need to know anything about malolactic fermentation and aging in barrels every time you drink a glass of wine.

Simplicity: complexity is a form of laziness

When you are fighting for your life, you do not need a heavy, shiny parade costume. You need Spartan armor—light, effective, battle-tested.

As you start building your PMS, you will be tempted to add more bells and whistles. Complexity is a form of laziness. Build what is necessary, not what is nice. For example, if you trade moving averages, you do not need four columns with price, first and second moving averages, and shares. This is information overload. All you need is a column with the number of shares or the weight to be traded and only when the condition is met.

Your PMS does not need to reinvent the wheel. Prime brokers provide a lot of the information you need through their API. For example, performance calculation is a waste of resources. It involves corporate actions such as stock splits, dividends, and subscriptions/redemptions. This all goes into modified Dietz time series performance calculation, separated by share class. Meanwhile, your prime brokers will provide **net asset value (NAV)** and performance calculations via their API every morning before breakfast.

The rule of thumb is to only display information that will lead to a decision, either directly, such as trades to take, or indirectly, such as levels of open risk. Another example is borrow utilization. Your system spits out a short trade for x thousands of shares. You start to salivate, but then the system also shows that borrow utilization is around 40%. It would probably be wiser to trade smaller sizes.

Flexibility: information does not translate into decision

Tooling up managers with a PMS is like giving glasses to a myopic person. At first, they are happy to see anything at all. Then, they start asking for more. Eyesight gives vision. A classic mistake is to buy expensive software before figuring out what you need. Software solutions are conceived by middle-office personnel for front-office warriors. This often results in front-office personnel using a fraction of the software's capability and building a separate tool on Excel.

Another mistake is to hardcode everything from inception. Your PMS will evolve with you. Every small improvement has a knock-on effect. When people take on an exercise routine, the prospect of a night out drinking is not so attractive. No one trades like you do, so no one else can do it for you. It does not have to be perfect, but it must work first. In the beginning, make it cheap and flexible. Excel, Google Sheets, R, Python, and Jupyter Notebooks are enough to start experimenting. In theory, C++ is faster than Python. In practice, C++ is months, if not years, slower than Python. Python is the new Excel!

Automating the boring stuff

All market participants want to be the next Jim Simmons. No one wants to take care of the plumbing. People want to do the exciting stuff. They want to show up with their billion-dollar idea and trade away. They do not want to take care of risk management. In this section are a few examples of time-consuming and ultimately boring processes that should be automated and the reasons why.

Trade reconciliation is the process of reconciling orders placed with trades executed. It shows what trades went through at what price. This is one of the few tasks that would make reading the tax code look like an exciting endeavor. Yet it is an important task as the data is used to perform trade analysis. Did the price beat the **volume at weighted average price (VWAP)** or not?

Updating the PMS is boring but not as easy as it seems. Companies go through all sorts of corporate actions, such as dividends and stock splits. Those corporate actions have an impact on the consistency of the data. It requires attention to detail.

Automate trading orders routing. The vast majority of algorithmic traders have automated execution. After all, if the system says "Buy this much of this" or "Sell that much of that," then just do it. Execution is on autopilot. Discretionary traders still struggle with fully trusting their system. What if the system spits out a ludicrous number? Or, what if the market does this or that? Well, trust is built. A simple solution is to default to automatic execution unless there is a manual override.

Building a robust portfolio management system

Below is a quick step-by-step guide to building a robust PMS. Remember that each PMS requires a high degree of customization. You are building your own Iron Man suit. As a result, this guide will remain fairly vague.

- Formalize your strategy into simple trading decisions: buy/sell, how much, at what price. A trading sequence is fairly straightforward. Draw a flowchart and fill the sequence.

- Add decisions that come out of risk management: liquidity, weight, borrow utilization, net beta, and gross and net exposure. We saw earlier a risk reduction across the entire portfolio.

- From your monitoring tool, create a separate trading sheet with each trading decision in a separate column. This minimalist monitoring tool is particularly efficient for large portfolios.

- Beyond your field of vision, embed your trading rules. This can be columns in the far right of the sheet, macros on Excel, and scripts on Python. All you need is the sausage on your plate, not a visual of the entire cooking process.

- In your field of vision, index your portfolio with tickers as rows and trading decisions as columns.

- Decision visualization: if a trading decision is triggered, print the number of shares, or the weight, in the corresponding cell, and leave everything else blank. This adds visual impact.

- Start small with rule-based actions: stop loss or profit taking are low-effort high-impact decisions.

- Over time, build an integrated tool. Add your trading history to directly calculate position size. A powerful tool is to integrate your portfolio monitoring tool and watchlist into a market heatmap.

- Throw out the auto radio. As you refine your process, you will be tempted to add cells and columns. Work a little bit harder to keep as much as possible in the background.

In *Chapter 11, The Long/Short Toolbox*, there was an expanded table with shares to be traded. We re-sort the dataframe by side (long or short) and relative risk-adjusted returns (rRAR). We slice the dataframe to display only relevant columns:

```
port = port.sort_values(by=['Side','rRAR'])
port_cols = ['Side','Beta','Shares_adj','Weight',
             'Weight_adj','CTR','rCTR',
             'rRAR','rRisk','rRisk_adj']
port[port_cols]
```

It all looked something like this:

	Side	Beta	Shares_adj	Weight	Weight_adj	CTR	rCTR	rRAR	rRisk	rRisk_adj
DIS	-1	1.20	-500	-0.042	-0.040	0.0015	0.0057	1.1	-0.0050	-0.0031
TSLA	-1	2.00	0	-0.020	0.000	0.0050	0.0039	1.2	-0.0034	-0.0000
NFLX	-1	0.75	-200	-0.064	-0.048	-0.0021	0.0074	1.2	-0.0059	-0.0029
QCOM	-1	1.34	-1500	-0.081	-0.097	0.0078	0.0122	2.0	-0.0061	-0.0048
PG	-1	0.41	-5100	-0.222	-0.311	0.0065	0.0294	5.6	-0.0052	-0.0048
MMM	1	0.95	0	0.095	0.000	0.0467	0.0008	0.2	-0.0042	-0.0000
IBM	1	1.23	500	0.079	0.033	0.0456	0.0025	0.6	-0.0042	-0.0012
UPS	1	1.05	800	0.069	0.075	0.0503	0.0051	1.3	-0.0039	-0.0029
BRK-B	1	0.90	2100	0.234	0.266	0.1385	0.0082	1.7	-0.0049	-0.0037
F	1	1.15	19200	0.093	0.130	0.1319	0.0241	5.8	-0.0042	-0.0038

Let's contextualize the above table in a portfolio management framework.

- Let's visualize the side of the portfolio and the sensitivity to the market first. We want to know on which side the high/low beta sits. Do we have a bullish or a bearish skew?

- Next, we want to have our trading decisions. We do not need to finally come to a conclusion on the last column. We want to know what to do first. Then, we can check that the system works as expected.

- We already know that the adjustment will reduce our gross exposure. Now, we want to know the before/after impact on each position. These are the "weight" and "weight_adj" columns.

- Risk purists would show the impact on risk next to weight. Our asset allocation key was to reduce risk prorated to performance instead of weight. We wanted to trim poorly performing positions first. So, we display contribution, "CTR," "rCTR," and relative risk-adjusted return, "rRAR."

- Finally, we display relative risks before and after "rRISK" and "rRisk_adj." The last column shows the residual risk across the portfolio at the stock level.

This conceptual framework is boiled down to its most essential components. Every number in every column has a *raison d'être*. Even the upper echelon of office Solitaire and Tetris grand masters, otherwise referred to as compliance and risk officers, would concur that this was compiled in accordance with the strictest risk management guidelines in vigor in the industry, vernacular for "I don't know, it doesn't look like it is about to blow up the farm."

The only problem is that the left hemisphere of our brain is not equipped to process this information. This is a sterile number soup that the brain cannot process, let alone relate to. The conscious brain can process 5 +/-2 bits of information per second. In execution trader English, by the time your eyes have gone from one end of the table to the other, your brain has forgotten what it needed to look for in the first place. Second bit of bad news: you are nothing special. It happens to everyone. Besides, Rain Man, if you can memorize the table, you would make a better living counting cards at a Blackjack table.

The real question is, how can we turn this sterile soup into something we can accurately process in a single glance? It turns out our brain comes equipped with a right hemisphere. It processes information at lighting speed, making associations between seemingly random bits of data. The only drawback is that the data needs to be repackaged in a format this brain can process. In execution trader English, let's paint by numbers. We will be using a built-in constructor called Styler. It only takes a few lines of code to return a versatile heatmap. These few lines of code can be recycled to draw quick and efficient heatmaps for market returns.

```
perf_cols= ['rCTR', 'CTR','rRisk', 'rRisk_adj','rRAR']
desc_cols= ['Side','Beta','Weight','Weight_adj',]
sort_cols = ['Side','rRAR']
asc = [True,True]

port[port_cols].sort_values(by = sort_cols,ascending= asc).style.
background_gradient(
    subset = desc_cols, cmap = 'viridis_r').background_gradient(
    subset = perf_cols, cmap = 'RdYlGn').format('{:.5g}')
```

We run a long/short portfolio. Numbers appearing on the short side often carry a negative sign. We do not want our subconscious brain to associate short positions with negative returns. So, we dissociate descriptive fields (`desc_cols`) from the performance-related columns (`perf_cols`). The more color maps you want to display on a single dataframe, the more you simply stack back to back.

The sort_values method is added to enhance even further the versatility of the heatmap. This sterile soup number comes alive when painted properly. The frescoes in the Sistine Chapel may look divine, but behind them is just a wall.

	Side	Beta	Shares_adj	Weight	Weight_adj	CTR	rCTR	rRAR	rRisk	rRisk_adj
DIS	-1	1.2	-500	-0.042	-0.04	0.0015	0.0057	1.1	-0.005	-0.0031
TSLA	-1	2	0	-0.02	0	0.005	0.0039	1.2	-0.0034	-0
NFLX	-1	0.75	-200	-0.064	-0.048	-0.0021	0.0074	1.2	-0.0059	-0.0029
QCOM	-1	1.34	-1500	-0.081	-0.097	0.0078	0.0122	2	-0.0061	-0.0048
PG	-1	0.41	-5100	-0.222	-0.311	0.0065	0.0294	5.6	-0.0052	-0.0048
MMM	1	0.95	0	0.095	0	0.0467	0.0008	0.2	-0.0042	-0
IBM	1	1.23	500	0.079	0.033	0.0456	0.0025	0.6	-0.0042	-0.0012
UPS	1	1.05	800	0.069	0.075	0.0503	0.0051	1.3	-0.0039	-0.0029
BRK-B	1	0.9	2100	0.234	0.266	0.1385	0.0082	1.7	-0.0049	-0.0037
F	1	1.15	19200	0.093	0.13	0.1319	0.0241	5.8	-0.0042	-0.0038

Figure 13.6: Portfolio heatmap

This heatmap is sorted by side (long/short) and relative risk-adjusted returns (rRAR). Numbers come alive when painted. This table could be further simplified. Again, the guiding principle is to display as little distraction as possible. Let's note the improvements to this display:

- First, the quantity, cost, price, and stop loss columns are hidden. They are important information, but not critical. Noncritical information that could otherwise distract is removed. If a stop loss is triggered, you need to know how many shares need to be traded. Until then, they are a distraction.

- In this example, the first five columns are strictly descriptive. The number of shares to be traded has no additional meaning. It therefore does not require a paint job.

- The other descriptive columns operate on a yellow to turquoise to purple color code. Side immediately shows which side of the book we are dealing with. Beta shows how we are axed. It looks like most of the low beta stuff is on the short side. The largest weights before/after are still the stocks where post adjustment risk remains high.

- Everything else is color-coded with a three color pattern ranging from red to orange to green, indicating the health or weight of each cell. The system works.

Here are other visualization ideas. When building a PMS, focus on what resonates for you. It is your Iron Man suit. Some people like tables and work with heatmaps. Some people react to charts. In the next block of code, we will visualize the information in the form of bar charts. We will use different keys to sort the data to illustrate different perspectives.

```
bar_cols= ['Weight', 'Weight_adj','rRisk','rRisk_adj','rCTR',
           'CTR','rRAR','Side']
col_style= ['lightgrey','dimgrey','lightcoral','red',
            'forestgreen','lightseagreen','yellowgreen','whitesmoke']
sort_keys= ['Weight_adj','rCTR']
sec_y=['rRAR','Side']
sort= ['rRAR']

port[bar_cols].sort_values(by=sort).plot(kind='bar',
           grid=True,figsize=(20,5),
           secondary_y=sec_y,color=col_style, title=
'PORT, by '+str(sort))

sort= ['Weight_adj','rRAR']
port[bar_cols].sort_values(by=sort).plot(kind='bar',
           grid=True,figsize=(20,5),
           secondary_y=sec_y,color=col_style, title=
'PORT, by '+str(sort))

sort= ['Side','rRisk_adj']
port[bar_cols].sort_values(by=sort).plot(kind='bar',
           grid=True,figsize=(20,5),
           secondary_y=sec_y,color=col_style, title=
'PORT, by '+str(sort))
```

There is nothing really fancy in the code except the color code. Entrust a Frenchman with color coding his own book and the proverbial pig will have pastel and lavender lipstick reminiscent of a summer Monet garden.

We used three different sorting keys to display the data under three different perspectives:

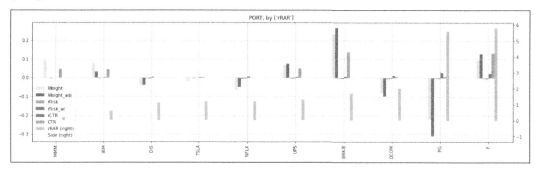

Figure 13.7: Portfolio sorted by "rRAR"

The sorting key is rRAR in ascending order regardless of the side. Overall, the first half of the chart is occupied by long positions. The tide of a bull market lifts all stocks. Even though the short book has not generated massive absolute money, it has clocked massive returns.

Secondly, we sort by "Weight" and "rRAR":

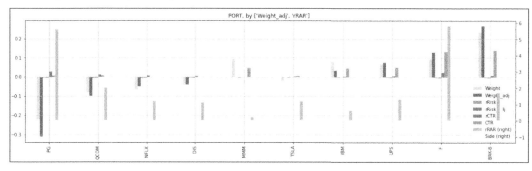

Figure 13.8: Portfolio sorted by "Weight" and "rRAR"

This reclassifies everything into long/short books and puts an "rRAR" perspective on the portfolio. The heaviest positions are the best risk-adjusted contributors, which is in line with this portfolio management strategy.

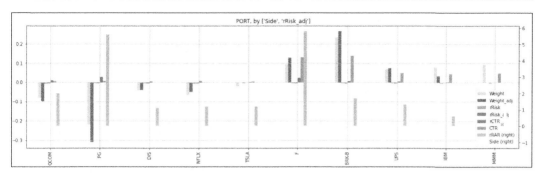

Figure 13.9: Portfolio sorted by "Side" and "rRisk_adj"

This sorts by "Side" and relative risk post-adjustment, "rRisk_adj." This produces a two-sided chart with the short side on the left and the long side on the right. Results are consistent with the strategy. Best performers have bigger weights and higher risk. Next, let's look at a market participant's favorite stalking tool: the watchlist.

A watchlist is inert unless it has some trading decisions embedded. We have all missed a few trades simply because we took our eyes off the ball. Here is a step-by-step method that will ensure you maintain a healthy actionable watchlist:

- Input ticker, target levels, date of entry
- Automate triggers: when the price reaches the target level, print the number of shares to be traded, else blank
- Weed out stale ideas: periodically sort by date. Delete stale ideas after each review
- Sort the list once a day

This semi-automated watchlist will set you apart from the competition. Market participants rarely take the time to formalize their plan. When everyone else tries to improvise while gripped by fear, you will show up with a rational plan.

This process will probably take weeks if not months, depending on your level of formalization. A bespoke PMS will have these positive effects:

- It will force you to formalize your process. If investment is a process, then automation is the logical conclusion. This principle has withstood the test of time since the dawn of the industrial revolution. The evolution of computer processing has reinforced it.

- It will shed a crude light on the flaws in your process. Discretionary and semi-automated market participants have blind spots.

- It will reduce emotional interference: making decisions out of a monitoring screen is 100% discretionary. Running an algorithm is 100% systematic. You will fall somewhere along the spectrum.

- It reduces stress: when all decisions run in the background and only show up when needed, you do not need to worry and preemptively take action.

- It frees up mental bandwidth to either manage more names or spend more time thinking. When your system is aligned with your process, you will spend less time worrying, in other words, consuming mental bandwidth, and more time planning.

When you are an analyst or a hobby retail trader, you are a stock jockey. You champion a few stocks. You have some skin in the game, but you do not go to bed with million-dollar tickets hanging over your sleep like swords of Damocles. When you choose to become a portfolio manager, you are not a jockey anymore. You take on the responsibility of stable master. Your job is to optimize finite resources among all the horses in your stable. This is why you need a PMS.

Summary

Investing in a PMS is the highest return on investment decision you will ever make. Without one, you might get lucky a few times picking the right stocks here and there, but nothing compares to the disciplined consistency of a robust PMS. You will top up winners and deal with flesh wounds before gangrene sets in and limits performance. You will become a more disciplined market participant. Risk management is not part of the business. It is the business. Portfolio managers are not in the business of picking stocks. They are in the business of managing risk with the stocks they either picked or passed. Small benefits compound over time and set you apart from the competition who still run around believing stock picking is the key to success. When your portfolio management becomes your Iron Man suit, you will be competing against people who think they trade a system.

Short selling is risky. The market does not cooperate. Yet choosing not to learn to sell short is riskier. You may well choose never to engage in short selling, but regardless, learning to sell short can only enrich your repertoire. We sincerely hope that this book will spark a conversation about short selling. The field has been demonized and under-researched for too long. We hope to have given its letters of nobility to the discipline.

We began by dispelling myths about short selling and explaining why the long mindset predictably fails on the short side. We continued by looking into idea generation with the relative series and regime definition. It was also about position sizing and risk management. The final part of the book was much more than long/short portfolio construction. It was about designing a product that investors find attractive—uncorrelated low volatility returns—using a long/short vehicle.

You will find an automated stock screening tool in *Appendix, Stock Screening* that we hope you will find useful!

Appendix: Stock Screening

This appendix provides a stock screener tool that will allow you to put everything we have learned in this book into practice. It addresses the most pressing issue for market participants: **idea generation**. We will build a screener across all the constituents of the S&P 500 index.

The sequence of events is as follows:

1. Download all the current constituents of the S&P 500 from its Wikipedia webpage.

2. Batch download OHLCV prices data from Yahoo Finance. We will drop the level to process each stock individually.

3. Calculate the rebased relative series.

4. Calculate regimes—breakout, turtle, moving averages (**Simple Moving Average (SMA)** and **Exponential Moving Average (EMA)**), and floor/ceiling—on both absolute and relative series. There will be an option to save each stock as a CSV file.

5. Create a dictionary with the last row of each stock and append a list, from which we will create a dataframe.

6. Sum up the regime methods and sort the dataframe. You will have an option to save the save this last row dataframe as a CSV file.

7. Join the original dataframe containing the Wikipedia information with the last row dataframe. You will have an option to save this dataframe as a CSV file.

8. Generate heatmaps by sector and sub-industry.

9. If you want to visualize any stock in particular, there will be a single stock download, process, and visualization module at the end of the screening.

 You can access color versions of all images in this chapter via the following link: https://static.packt-cdn.com/ downloads/9781801815192_ColorImages.pdf. You can also access source code for this chapter via the book's GitHub repository: https://github.com/PacktPublishing/Algorithmic-Short-Selling-with-Python-Published-by-Packt.

Import libraries

We start with importing standard libraries. `pathlib` has been commented out. If you wish to save CSV files somewhere on your computer or a server, you can use libraries such as `pathlib` or `os`.

```
# Appendix

# Data manipulation
import pandas as pd
import numpy as np
from scipy.signal import *
# import pathlib

# Data download
import yfinance as yf

# Data visualisation
%matplotlib inline
import matplotlib.pyplot as plt
```

This was, of course, profoundly Earth shattering—we will use the ensuing momentary lapse of reason to swiftly proceed to the next step.

Define functions

As follows are are functions that have been used throughout this book. You can find the full versions on the GitHub. Functions will generally be preceded with their chapter of appearance. The screening will feature both absolute and relative series, so we need the relative function. This will be followed by the classic regime definition functions:

```
# CHAPTER 5: Regime Definition

### RELATIVE
def relative(df,_o,_h,_l,_c, bm_df, bm_col, ccy_df, ccy_col, dgt,
start, end,rebase=True):
    #### removed for brevity: check GitHub repo for full code ####

### RELATIVE ###

def lower_upper_OHLC(df,relative = False):
```

```
        if relative==True:
            rel = 'r'
        else:
            rel= ''
        if 'Open' in df.columns:
            ohlc = [rel+'Open',rel+'High',rel+'Low',rel+'Close']
        elif 'open' in df.columns:
            ohlc = [rel+'open',rel+'high',rel+'low',rel+'close']

        try:
            _o,_h,_l,_c = [ohlc[h] for h in range(len(ohlc))]
        except:
            _o=_h=_l=_c= np.nan
        return _o,_h,_l,_c

def  regime_args(df,lvl,relative= False):
    if ('Low' in df.columns) & (relative == False):
        reg_val =
['Lo1','Hi1','Lo'+str(lvl),'Hi'+str(lvl),'rg','clg','flr','rg_ch']
    elif ('low' in df.columns) & (relative == False):
        reg_val =
['lo1','hi1','lo'+str(lvl),'hi'+str(lvl),'rg','clg','flr','rg_ch']
    elif ('Low' in df.columns) & (relative == True):
        reg_val =
['rL1','rH1','rL'+str(lvl),'rH'+str(lvl),'rrg','rclg','rflr','rrg_ch']
    elif ('low' in df.columns) & (relative == True):
        reg_val =
['rl1','rh1','rl'+str(lvl),'rh'+str(lvl),'rrg','rclg','rflr','rrg_ch']

    try:
        rt_lo,rt_hi,slo,shi,rg,clg,flr,rg_ch = [reg_val[s] for s in
range(len(reg_val))]
    except:
        rt_lo=rt_hi=slo=shi=rg=clg=flr=rg_ch= np.nan
    return rt_lo,rt_hi,slo,shi,rg,clg,flr,rg_ch


# CHAPTER 5: Regime Definition

#### regime_breakout(df,_h,_l,window) ####
```

```
def regime_breakout(df,_h,_l,window):
    #### removed for brevity: check GitHub repo for full code ####


#### turtle_trader(df, _h, _l, slow, fast) ####


#### removed for brevity: check GitHub repo for full code ####


#### regime_sma(df,_c,st,lt) ####


#### removed for brevity: check GitHub repo for full code ####


#### regime_ema(df,_c,st,lt) ####
```

The floor/ceiling methodology is much more computationally intense. It therefore deserves its own sandbox:

```
# CHAPTER 5: Regime Definition


#### hilo_alternation(hilo, dist= None, hurdle= None) ####
def hilo_alternation(hilo, dist= None, hurdle= None):
    i=0
    while (np.sign(hilo.shift(1)) == np.sign(hilo)).any(): # runs until
duplicates are eliminated


        #### removed for brevity: check GitHub repo for full code ####


#### historical_swings(df,_o,_h,_l,_c, dist= None, hurdle= None) ####
def historical_swings(df,_o,_h,_l,_c, dist= None, hurdle= None):

    reduction = df[[_o,_h,_l,_c]].copy()
    reduction['avg_px'] = round(reduction[[_h,_l,_c]].mean(axis=1),2)
    highs = reduction['avg_px'].values
    lows = - reduction['avg_px'].values
    reduction_target =  len(reduction) // 100
#      print(reduction_target )


#### removed for brevity: check GitHub repo for full code ####
#### cleanup_latest_swing(df, shi, slo, rt_hi, rt_lo) ####
def cleanup_latest_swing(df, shi, slo, rt_hi, rt_lo):
    '''

    removes false positives
    '''

    # latest swing
```

```
        shi_dt = df.loc[pd.notnull(df[shi]), shi].index[-1]
        s_hi = df.loc[pd.notnull(df[shi]), shi][-1]
        slo_dt = df.loc[pd.notnull(df[slo]), slo].index[-1]
        s_lo = df.loc[pd.notnull(df[slo]), slo][-1]
        len_shi_dt = len(df[:shi_dt])
        len_slo_dt = len(df[:slo_dt])


#### removed for brevity: check GitHub repo for full code ####


#### latest_swings(df, shi, slo, rt_hi, rt_lo, _h, _l, _c, _vol) ####
def latest_swing_variables(df, shi, slo, rt_hi, rt_lo, _h, _l, _c):
    '''
    Latest swings dates & values
    '''
    shi_dt = df.loc[pd.notnull(df[shi]), shi].index[-1]
    slo_dt = df.loc[pd.notnull(df[slo]), slo].index[-1]
    s_hi = df.loc[pd.notnull(df[shi]), shi][-1]
    s_lo = df.loc[pd.notnull(df[slo]), slo][-1]

    #### removed for brevity: check GitHub repo for full code ####


#### test_distance(ud, bs, hh_ll, vlty, dist_vol, dist_pct) ####
def test_distance(ud,bs, hh_ll, dist_vol, dist_pct):

#### removed for brevity: check GitHub repo for full code ####


#### ATR ####
def average_true_range(df, _h, _l, _c, n):
    atr =  (df[_h].combine(df[_c].shift(), max) - df[_l].
combine(df[_c].shift(), min)).rolling(window=n).mean()
    return atr


#### ATR ####

#### retest_swing(df, _sign, _rt, hh_ll_dt, hh_ll, _c, _swg) ####
def retest_swing(df, _sign, _rt, hh_ll_dt, hh_ll, _c, _swg):
    rt_sgmt = df.loc[hh_ll_dt:, _rt]

    #### removed for brevity: check GitHub repo for full code ####
```

```
#### retracement_swing(df, _sign, _swg, _c, hh_ll_dt, hh_ll, vlty,
retrace_vol, retrace_pct) ####
def retracement_swing(df, _sign, _swg, _c, hh_ll_dt, hh_ll, vlty,
retrace_vol, retrace_pct):
    if _sign == 1: #
        retracement = df.loc[hh_ll_dt:, _c].min() - hh_ll


#### removed for brevity: check GitHub repo for full code ####


# CHAPTER 5: Regime Definition


#### regime_floor_ceiling(df, hi,lo,cl, slo, shi,flr,clg,rg,rg_
ch,stdev,threshold) ####
def regime_floor_ceiling(df, _h,_l,_c,slo, shi,flr,clg,rg,rg_
ch,stdev,threshold):
#### removed for brevity: check GitHub repo for full code ####
```

Let's group this indigestible code into two simple functions, swings() and regime().
All we have to do is pass the relative argument to obtain either the absolute or
relative series.

```
def swings(df,rel = False):
    _o,_h,_l,_c = lower_upper_OHLC(df,relative= False)
    if rel == True:
        df = relative(df=df,_o=_o,_h=_h,_l=_l,_c=_c, bm_df=bm_df,
bm_col= bm_col, ccy_df=bm_df,
                                ccy_col=ccy_col, dgt= dgt, start=start,
end= end,rebase=True)
        _o,_h,_l,_c = lower_upper_OHLC(df,relative= True)
        rt_lo,rt_hi,slo,shi,rg,clg,flr,rg_ch = regime_
args(df,lvl,relative= True)
    else :
        rt_lo,rt_hi,slo,shi,rg,clg,flr,rg_ch = regime_
args(df,lvl,relative= False)
    df= historical_swings(df,_o,_h,_l,_c, dist= None, hurdle= None)
    df= cleanup_latest_swing(df,shi,slo,rt_hi,rt_lo)
    ud, bs, bs_dt, _rt, _swg, hh_ll, hh_ll_dt =
latest_swing_variables(df, shi,slo,rt_hi,rt_lo,_h,_l, _c)
    vlty = round(average_true_range(df,_h,_l,_c, n= vlty_n)
[hh_ll_dt],dgt)
    dist_vol = d_vol * vlty
    _sign = test_distance(ud,bs, hh_ll, dist_vol, dist_pct)
```

```
    df = retest_swing(df, _sign, _rt, hh_ll_dt, hh_ll, _c, _swg)
    retrace_vol = r_vol * vlty
    df = retracement_swing(df, _sign, _swg, _c, hh_ll_dt, hh_ll, vlty,
retrace_vol, retrace_pct)

    return df

def regime(df,lvl,rel=False):
    _o,_h,_l,_c = lower_upper_OHLC(df,relative= rel)
    rt_lo,rt_hi,slo,shi,rg,clg,flr,rg_ch =
regime_args(df,lvl,relative= rel)
    stdev = df[_c].rolling(vlty_n).std(ddof=0)
    df = regime_floor_ceiling(df,_h,_l,_c,slo,
shi,flr,clg,rg,rg_ch,stdev,threshold)

    return df

# df[rg+'_no_fill'] = df[rg]
    return df
```

This screening also allows slick visualization for individual stocks. To achieve that, run the graph_regime_combo() function:

```
# CHAPTER 5: Regime Definition

### Graph Regimes ###
def graph_regime_combo(ticker,df,_c,rg,lo,hi,slo,shi,clg,flr,rg_ch,
                       ma_st,ma_mt,ma_lt,lt_lo,lt_hi,st_lo,st_hi):

    '''

    https://www.color-hex.com/color-names.html
    ticker,df,_c: _c is closing price
    rg: regime -1/0/1 using floor/ceiling method
    lo,hi: small, noisy highs/lows
    slo,shi: swing lows/highs
    clg,flr: ceiling/floor

    rg_ch: regime change base
    ma_st,ma_mt,ma_lt: moving averages ST/MT/LT
    lt_lo,lt_hi: range breakout High/Low LT
    st_lo,st_hi: range breakout High/Low ST
    '''

#### removed for brevity: check GitHub repo for full code ####
```

The next two functions have not been featured in the book yet. Using them, we need to extract single stock data and aggregate it into a dataframe. The yf_droplevel() function gets the OHLC columns for a single ticker out of the multi-index dataframe coming from batch_download, and creates an OHLCV dataframe:

```
def yf_droplevel(batch_download,ticker):
    df = batch_download.iloc[:, batch_download.columns.get_level_
values(1)==ticker]
    df.columns = df.columns.droplevel(1)
    df = df.dropna()
    return df
```

This function is inserted in a loop that will run for the length of the batch_download. The last_row_dictionary(df) function creates a dictionary out of the last row in a dataframe:

```
def last_row_dictionary(df):
    df_cols = list(df.columns)
    col_dict =
{'Symbol':str.upper(ticker),'date':df.index.max().strftime('%Y%m%d')}
    for i, col_name in enumerate(df_cols):
        if pd.isnull(df.iloc[-1,i]):
            try:
                last_index = df[pd.notnull(df.iloc[:,i])].index[-1]
                len_last_index = len(df[:last_index]) - 1
                col_dict.update({col_name + '_dt':
last_index.strftime('%Y%m%d')})
                col_dict.update({col_name : df.iloc[len_last_index,i]})
            except:
                col_dict.update({col_name + '_dt':np.nan})
                col_dict.update({col_name : np.nan})
        else:
            col_dict.update({col_name : df.iloc[-1,i]})
    return col_dict
```

First, we list the columns. Second, we populate them with tickers and dates to make each row uniquely identifiable. Third, we iterate through using enumerate to return both an index and a column name. If the last row contains a missing value, we add _dt to the column name and look for the index of the last occurrence. If the last row contains a value, we simply add the column name as a key and a value.

This dictionary will append a list of last row dictionaries. We will then create a dataframe from this list. An alternative would be to create a dataframe and append it for every stock, which works well but is slightly more time consuming.

Control panel

Having variables disseminated across a notebook is a source of errors. All parameters, variables, websites, lists, and Booleans are centralized in one place before processing the data. This is where you will adjust settings if desired:

```
website = 'https://en.wikipedia.org/wiki/List_of_S%26P_500_companies'


params = ['2014-12-31', None, 63, 0.05, 0.05, 1.5, 2,5,2.5,3]
start,end,vlty_n,dist_pct,retrace_pct,threshold,dgt,d_vol,r_vol,lvl=
[params[h] for h in range(len(params))]

rel_var = ['^GSPC','SP500', 'USD']
bm_ticker, bm_col, ccy_col = [rel_var[h] for h in range(len(rel_var))]

window = 100
st= fast = 50
lt = slow = 200


batch_size = 20
show_batch = True
save_ticker_df = False
save_last_row_df = False
save_regime_df = False

web_df_cols = ['Symbol','Security','GICS Sector','GICS Sub-Industry']
regime_cols = ['rg','rrg',
    'smaC'+str(st)+str(lt),'smar'+str(st)+str(lt), 'boHL'+str(slow),
'borr'+str(slow),'ttH'+str(fast)+'L'+str(slow),'ttr'+str(fast)+'r'+
str(slow)]
swings_cols = ['flr_dt','flr','clg_dt', 'clg', 'rg_ch',
    'Hi'+str(lvl)+'_dt','Hi'+str(lvl),'Lo'+str(lvl)+'_dt','Lo'+str(lvl),
     'rflr_dt', 'rflr', 'rclg_dt', 'rclg', 'rrg_ch',
    'rH'+str(lvl)+'_dt','rH'+str(lvl),'rL'+str(lvl)+'_dt','rL'+str(lvl)
]
symbol_cols = ['Symbol','date','Close']

last_row_df_cols = symbol_cols+['score']+regime_cols+swings_cols
```

The website we're using is the Wikipedia webpage of the S&P500. The parameters are as follows:

- start: yfinance download start date
- end: yfinance download end date
- vlty_n: duration, for average true range and standard deviation calculations
- dist_pct: variable in the test_distance() function
- retrace_pct: variable in the retracement_swing() function
- threshold: units of volatility for floor/ceiling regime definition
- dgt: decimals in the round() function
- d_vol: units of volatility in the test_distance() function
- r_vol: variable in the retracement_swing() function
- lvl: indicates which swing levels should be used to calculate regime definition—Hi2/Lo2 or Hi3/Lo3

rel_var arguments are explained as follows:

- bm_ticker: Yahoo Finance ticker of the benchmark
- bm_col: name of the benchmark column
- ccy_col: name of the currency
- window, st, fast, lt, slow: variables for breakout and moving averages
- batch_size: size of the batch download from yfinance
- show_batch: Boolean, display tickers downloaded
- save_ticker_df: Boolean, providing an option to save individual ticker dataframes post-process
- save_last_row_df: Boolean, providing an option to save last row dataframe
- save_regime_df: Boolean, providing an option to save last row dataframe
- web_df_cols: columns to be displayed from the original Wikipedia dataframe
- regime_cols: regime definition columns re-ordered
- swings_cols: floor/ceiling columns
- symbol_cols: descriptive fields, Symbol, date, Close
- last_row_df_cols: the last row dataframe has 50+ columns. This reduces the number of columns to a minimum.

Data download and processing

We'll start by downloading the ticker lists from Wikipedia. This uses the powerful `pd.read_html` method we saw in *Chapter 4, Long/Short Methodologies: Absolute and Relative*:

```
web_df = pd.read_html(website)[0]
tickers_list =  list(web_df['Symbol'])
tickers_list = tickers_list[:]
print('tickers_list',len(tickers_list))
web_df.head()
```

`tickers_list` can be truncated by filling numbers in the bracket section of `tickers_list[:]`.

Now, this is where the action is happening. There are a few nested loops in the engine room.

1. Batch download: this is the high-level loop. OHLCV is downloaded in a multi-index dataframe in a succession of batches. The number of iterations is a function of the length of the tickers list and the batch size. 505 constituents divided by a batch size of 20 is 26 (the last batch being 6 tickers long).

2. Drop level loop: this breaks the multi-index dataframe into single ticker OHLCV dataframes. The number of iterations equals the batch size. Regimes are processed at this level.

3. Absolute/relative process: There are 2 passes. The first pass processes data in the absolute series. Variables are reset to the relative series at the end and then processed accordingly in the second pass. There is an option to save the ticker information as a CSV file. The last row dictionary is created at the end of the second pass.

Next, let's go through the process step-by-step:

1. Benchmark download closing price and currency adjustment. This needs to be done once, so it is placed at the beginning of the sequence.

2. Dataframes and lists instantiation.

3. Loop size: number of iterations necessary to loop over the `tickers_list`.

4. Outer loop: batch download:

    1. `m,n`: index along the `batch_list`.

    2. `batch_download`: download using `yfinance`.

    3. Print batch tickers, with a Boolean if you want to see the tickers names.

4. Download batch.

5. `try`/`except`: append failed list.

5. Second loop: Single stock drop level loop:

   1. Drop level to ticker level.

   2. Calculate swings and regime: `abs`/`rel`.

6. Third loop: absolute/relative series:

   1. Process regimes in absolute series.

   2. Reset variables to relative series and process regimes a second time.

7. Boolean to provide a `save_ticker_df` option.

8. Create a dictionary with last row values.

9. Append list of dictionary rows.

10. Create a dataframe `last_row_df` from dictionary.

11. `score` column: lateral sum of regime methods in absolute and relative.

12. Join `last_row_df` with `web_df`.

13. Boolean `save_regime_df`.

Let's publish the code and give further explanations afterwards:

```
# Appendix: The Engine Room

bm_df = pd.DataFrame()
bm_df[bm_col] = round(yf.download(tickers= bm_ticker,start= start, end
= end,interval = "1d",
                group_by = 'column',auto_adjust = True, prepost =
True,
                treads = True, proxy = None)['Close'],dgt)
bm_df[ccy_col] = 1
print('benchmark',bm_df.tail(1))

regime_df = pd.DataFrame()
last_row_df = pd.DataFrame()
last_row_list = []
failed = []

loop_size = int(len(tickers_list) // batch_size) + 2
for t in range(1,loop_size):
    m = (t - 1) * batch_size
    n = t * batch_size
```

```
        batch_list = tickers_list[m:n]
        if show_batch:
            print(batch_list,m,n)


        try:
            batch_download = round(yf.download(tickers= batch_list,start=
start, end = end,
                                interval = "1d",group_by =
'column',auto_adjust = True,
                                    prepost = True, treads = True,
proxy = None),dgt)


            for flat, ticker in enumerate(batch_list):
                df = yf_droplevel(batch_download,ticker)
                df = swings(df,rel = False)
                df = regime(df,lvl = 3,rel = False)
                df = swings(df,rel = True)
                df = regime(df,lvl = 3,rel= True)
                _o,_h,_l,_c = lower_upper_OHLC(df,relative = False)


                for a in range(2):
                    df['sma'+str(_c)[:1]+str(st)+str(lt)] =
regime_sma(df,_c,st,lt)
                    df['bo'+str(_h)[:1]+str(_l)[:1]+ str(slow)] =
regime_breakout(df,_h,_l,window)
                    df['tt'+str(_h)[:1]+str(fast)+str(_l)[:1]+ str(slow)] =
turtle_trader(df, _h, _l, slow, fast)
                    _o,_h,_l,_c = lower_upper_OHLC(df,relative = True)
                try:
                    last_row_list.append(last_row_dictionary(df))
                except:
                    failed.append(ticker)
        except:
            failed.append(ticker)
last_row_df = pd.DataFrame.from_dict(last_row_list)


if save_last_row_df:
    last_row_df.to_csv('last_row_df_'+
str(last_row_df['date'].max())+'.csv', date_format='%Y%m%d')
print('failed',failed)


last_row_df['score']= last_row_df[regime_cols].sum(axis=1)
```

```
regime_df = web_df[web_df_cols].set_index('Symbol').join(
    last_row_df[last_row_df_cols].set_index('Symbol'), how='inner').
sort_values(by='score')

if save_regime_df:
    regime_df.to_csv('regime_df_'+ str(last_row_df['date'].max())+'.
csv', date_format='%Y%m%d')
```

`last_row_list.append(last_row_dictionary(df))` happens at the end of the third loop once every individual ticker has been fully processed. This list automatically updates for every ticker and every batch. Once the three loops are finished, we create the `last_row_df` dataframe from this list of dictionaries using `pd.DataFrame.from_dict(last_row_list)`. This process of creating a list of dictionaries and rolling it up into a dataframe is marginally faster than directly appending them to a dataframe. The `score` column is a lateral sum of all the regime methodologies. The last row dataframe is then sorted by `score` in ascending order. There is an option to save a datestamped version. The `regime` dataframe is created by joining the Wikipedia web dataframe and the last row dataframe. Note that the `Symbol` column is set as `index`. Again, there is an option to save a datestamped version.

Next, let's visualize what the market is doing with a few heatmaps.

Heatmaps

The wikipedia page features the **Global Industry Classification Standard** (**GICS**) structure of sectors and sub-industries. We will aggregate the data by:

- Sector, for a top-down view

- Sub-industry, for a bottom-up view

- Finally, sector *and* sub-industry, to pick winners and losers within each sector

We use the `.groupby()` method and sort by `score`. We then use the Styler constructor `.style.background_gradient()` to paint the market by numbers:

```
groupby_cols = ['score'] + regime_cols
sort_key = ['GICS Sector']
regime_df.groupby(sort_key)[groupby_cols].mean().sort_values(
    by= 'score').style.background_gradient(
    subset= groupby_cols,cmap= 'RdYlGn').format('{:.1g}')
```

The heatmap covers all regime methodologies in both absolute and relative:

- **score**: lateral sum of all the methods at the stock level.
- **rg**: floor/ceiling regime in absolute.
- **rrg**: floor/ceiling regime in relative.
- **smaC50200**: moving average crossover ST/LT in absolute.
- **smar50200**: moving average crossover ST/LT relative.
- **bohl200**: range breakout (200 days).
- **ttH50L200**: turtle for dummies 50/200 (fast/slow) in absolute.
- **ttr50r200**: turtle for dummies 50/200 (fast/slow) in relative.

Let's see what it looks like:

GICS Sector	score	rg	rrg	smaC50200	smar50200	boHL200	borr200	ttH50L200	ttr50r200
Consumer Staples	-1	0.5	-0.6	0.2	-0.7	0.03	-0.6	0.3	-0.6
Communication Services	0.04	0.5	-0.2	0.4	-0.5	0	-0.4	0.3	-0.2
Energy	0.2	0.9	0.5	0.4	-0.6	-0.3	-0.6	0.1	-0.1
Materials	0.9	0.5	0.1	0.6	-0.4	0.3	-0.5	0.4	-0.1
Utilities	1	0.7	-0.4	0.9	-0.4	0.7	-0.4	0.5	-0.5
Consumer Discretionary	1	0.6	0.03	0.6	-0.4	0.2	-0.4	0.6	0.02
Industrials	2	0.7	0.04	0.7	-0.2	0.4	-0.1	0.5	-0.06
Health Care	2	0.7	-0.2	0.7	-0.08	0.5	-0.02	0.5	-0.02
Information Technology	2	0.7	0.04	0.7	-0.07	0.5	0.07	0.5	-0.01
Financials	3	0.8	0.3	0.8	-0.1	0.5	-0.2	0.7	0.2
Real Estate	6	0.9	0.6	0.9	0.7	0.9	0.5	0.9	0.4

Figure 1: Industry-level heatmap of regime scores

The sector heatmap gives a bird's eye view of the market. Highly leveraged sectors such as financials, real estate and tech are still at the top of the pyramid. Meanwhile, defensive sectors such as consumer staples trail the pack. At the time of writing, this bull market is alive and well. It is literally that simple.

We then dive into sub-industries:

```
sort_key = ['GICS Sub-Industry']
regime_df.groupby(sort_key)[groupby_cols].mean().sort_values(
    by= 'score').style.background_gradient(
    subset= groupby_cols,cmap= 'RdYlGn').format('{:.1g}')
```

This gives us a pixelized picture of the market, with poorer-performing sub-industries at the top:

GICS Sub-Industry	score	rg	rrg	smaC50200	smar50200	boHL200	borr200	ttH50L200	ttr50r200
Gold	-7	-1	-1	-1	-1	-1	-1	0	-1
Broadcasting	-6	0	-1	-1	-1	-1	-1	-0.5	-1
Gas Utilities	-6	-1	-1	1	-1	-1	-1	-1	-1
Integrated Telecommunication Services	-6	0	-1	-1	-1	-1	-1	0	-1
Household Products	-5	-0.5	-1	0	-1	-0.5	-1	-0.2	-1
Brewers	-5	1	-1	-1	-1	-1	-1	0	-1
Distillers & Vintners	-5	1	-1	-1	-1	-1	-1	0	-1
Drug Retail	-5	1	-1	-1	-1	-1	-1	0	-1
Interactive Home Entertainment	-5	-0.3	-0.3	-0.3	-1	-0.3	-1	-0.3	-1
Airlines	-4	0.6	-0.2	-1	-1	-1	-1	0	-0.8

Figure 2: Sub-industry level of regime scores

The S&P 500 is a broad and deep index. This granular picture of the market shows how each sub-industry is currently faring. Pay particular attention to the absolute/relative dichotomy. Remember that relative performance leads the absolute one. This is how you catch inflections and build or exit positions accordingly, and wait for the rest of the crowd to show up.

This detailed picture is a classic example of information versus decision. This heatmap will make you knowledgeable of what is going on in the market. It is however not formatted efficiently enough to make you act on the information.

This leads us to the final sort, by sector and sub-industry.

```
sort_key = ['GICS Sector','GICS Sub-Industry']
regime_df.groupby(sort_key)[groupby_cols].mean().sort_values(
    by= ['GICS Sector','score']).style.background_gradient(
    subset= groupby_cols,cmap= 'RdYlGn').format('{:.1g}')
```

This produces a heatmap where sub-industries are sorted in ascending order within their industry. Meanwhile, sectors are classified in alphabetical order.

GICS Sector	GICS Sub-Industry	score	rg	rrg	smaC50200	smar50200	boHL200	borr200	ttH50L200	ttr50r200
Communication Services	Broadcasting	-6	0	-1	-1	-1	-1	-1	-0.5	-1
	Integrated Telecommunication Services	-6	0	-1	-1	-1	-1	-1	0	-1
	Interactive Home Entertainment	-5	-0.3	-0.3	-0.3	-1	-0.3	-1	-0.3	-1
	Wireless Telecommunication Services	-3	1	-1	1	-1	-1	-1	0	-1
	Alternative Carriers	-2	1	-1	1	-1	-1	-1	0	0
	Publishing	-1	1	0	1	-1	-1	-1	0	0
	Movies & Entertainment	-0.5	0.3	-0.3	0.3	-1	0.3	-0.7	0.5	0
	Advertising	4	1	1	1	0	0	0	0.5	0.5
	Cable & Satellite	5	1	0.3	1	0.3	1	0.3	0.7	0
	Interactive Media & Services	7	1	0.5	1	1	1	1	0.8	0.8
Consumer Discretionary	Hotels, Resorts & Cruise Lines	-3	-0.2	0.2	-0.6	-1	-0.6	-1	0.4	-0.2
	Casinos & Gaming	-3	0.2	0.2	-0.2	-1	-0.6	-1	0	-0.4
	Household Appliances	-2	-1	-1	1	-1	1	-1	0	0
	Housewares & Specialties	-2	-1	1	1	-1	-1	-1	0	0
	Home Furnishings	-1	0	0	1	-1	0	-1	0.5	-0.5
	Apparel Retail	-0.7	1	-0.3	1	-1	-0.3	-1	0.3	-0.3
	Apparel, Accessories & Luxury Goods	-0.5	0	0	0.5	-0.8	-0.2	-0.8	0.6	0.1
	Internet & Direct Marketing Retail	0.8	1	-1	0.5	-0.5	0.5	-0.5	0.5	0.2
	Auto Parts & Equipment	1	1	-1	1	-1	1	-1	1	0
	Leisure Products	1	1	-1	1	-1	1	-1	1	0
	Homebuilding	1	0.5	-1	1	0	0.5	0	0.8	-0.5
	General Merchandise Stores	2	1	0.3	0.3	-0.3	0.3	0.3	0.3	-0.7

Figure 3: Sector and sub-industry level heatmap

This final heatmap gives actionable information. Sub-industries are ranked in ascending order within their sector. This allows arbitrage between underperformers and outperformers. Repeat the process over sectors and over time and you will smoothly follow the sector rotation. This is the essence of the long/short 2.0 relative method.

Individual process

Once the screening is complete, you may want to have a look at some stocks within that list. So, the remainder of the notebook is about data visualization at the individual stock level. Input a ticker, for example, `ticker = 'FMC'`:

```
bm_ticker= '^GSPC'
bm_df = pd.DataFrame()
bm_df[bm_col] = round(yf.download(tickers= bm_ticker,start= start,
end = end,interval = "1d",
```

```
                  group_by = 'column',auto_adjust = True, prepost =
    True,
                  treads = True, proxy = None)['Close'],dgt)
    bm_df[ccy_col] = 1

    ticker = 'FMC'
    lvl = 2 # Try different levels to see

    df = round(yf.download(tickers= ticker,start= start, end = end,
        interval = "1d", group_by = 'column',auto_adjust = True,
        prepost = True, treads = True, proxy = None),dgt)

    df = swings(df,rel = False)
    df = regime(df,lvl = 2,rel = False) # Try different lvl values (1-3) to
    vary absolute sensitivity
    df = swings(df,rel = True) # Try different lvl values (1-3) to vary
    relative sensitivity
    df = regime(df,lvl = 2,rel= True)
    _o,_h,_l,_c = lower_upper_OHLC(df,relative = False)

    for a in range(2):
        df['sma'+str(_c)[:1]+str(st)+str(lt)] = regime_sma(df,_c,st,lt)
        df['bo'+str(_h)[:1]+str(_l)[:1]+ str(slow)] =
    regime_breakout(df,_h,_l,window)
        df['tt'+str(_h)[:1]+str(fast)+str(_l)[:1]+ str(slow)] =
    turtle_trader(df, _h, _l, slow, fast)
        _o,_h,_l,_c = lower_upper_OHLC(df,relative = True)

    df[['Close','rClose']].plot(figsize=(20,5),style=['k','grey'],
                            title = str.upper(ticker)+ ' Relative &
                            Absolute')
```

This will print something similar to the following chart:

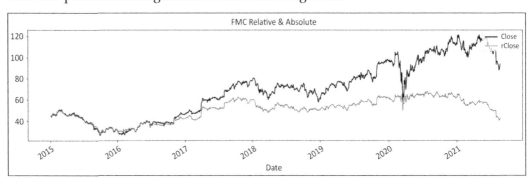

Figure 4: FMC closing price in absolute and relative series

The following section plots the data in three charts:

```
# CHAPTER 5: Regime Definition
plot_abs_cols = ['Close','Hi'+str(lvl), 'clg','flr','rg_ch','rg']
# plot_abs_cols = ['Close','Hi2', 'Lo2','clg','flr','rg_ch','rg']
plot_abs_style = ['k', 'ro', 'go', 'kv', 'k^','b:','b--']
y2_abs = ['rg']
plot_rel_cols = ['rClose','rH'+str(lvl), 'rL'+str(lvl),
'rclg','rflr','rrg_ch','rrg']
# plot_rel_cols = ['rClose','rH2', 'rL2','rclg','rflr','rrg_ch','rrg']
plot_rel_style = ['grey', 'ro', 'go', 'kv', 'k^','m:','m--']
y2_rel = ['rrg']
df[plot_abs_cols].plot(secondary_y= y2_abs,figsize=(20,8),
            title = str.upper(ticker)+ ' Absolute',# grid=True,
            style=plot_abs_style)

df[plot_rel_cols].plot(secondary_y=y2_rel,figsize=(20,8),
            title = str.upper(ticker)+ ' Relative',# grid=True,
            style=plot_rel_style)

df[plot_rel_cols + plot_abs_cols].plot(secondary_y=y2_rel + y2_abs,
    figsize=(20,8), title = str.upper(ticker)+ ' Relative & Absolute',
    # grid=True,
    style=plot_rel_style + plot_abs_style)
```

This creates three charts: absolute, relative, and absolute and relative combined. The red/green dots are swings. The horizontal lines are regime change swings. Note that the following charts are produced with lvl set to 2 on both absolute and relative series. You can increase or decrease or increase the sensitivity on either series by changing this value in the `df = regime(df,lvl = 2,rel = False)` line for absolute, and the `df = regime(df,lvl = 2,rel = True)` for relative.

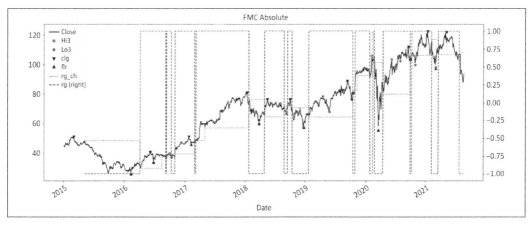

Figure 5: Absolute chart with floor/ceiling regime shown with a dashed line

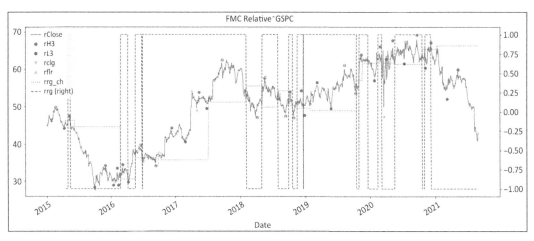

Figure 6: Relative chart with floor/ceiling regime shown with a dashed line. Red/green dots are swings

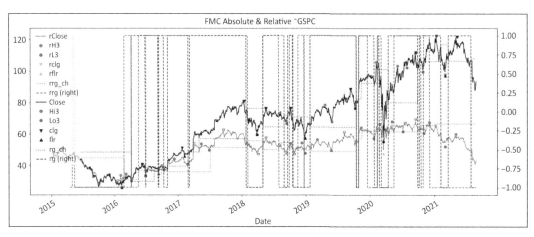

Figure 7: Absolute and relative chart with floor/ceiling regimes

The next block of code uses the graph_regime_combo() for a nice visual rendition. First, this absolute series comes out, then the relative series:

```
# CHAPTER 5: Regime Definition

ohlc = ['Open','High','Low','Close']
_o,_h,_l,_c = [ohlc[h] for h in range(len(ohlc))]
# ma_st = ma_mt = ma_lt = lt_lo = lt_hi = st_lo = st_hi = 0

mav = [fast, slow, 200]
ma_st,ma_mt,ma_lt = [df[_c].rolling(mav[t]).mean() for t in
range(len(mav))]
```

```
bo = [fast, slow]
st_lo,lt_lo = [df[_l].rolling(bo[t]).min() for t in range(len(bo))]
st_hi,lt_hi = [df[_h].rolling(bo[t]).max() for t in range(len(bo))]

rg_combo = ['Close','rg','Lo3','Hi3','Lo3','Hi3','clg','flr','rg_ch']
_c,rg,lo,hi,slo,shi,clg,flr,rg_ch =[rg_combo[r] for r in
range(len(rg_combo)) ]
graph_regime_combo(ticker,df,_c,rg,lo,hi,slo,shi,clg,flr,rg_ch,ma_
st,ma_mt,ma_lt,lt_lo,lt_hi,st_lo,st_hi)

rohlc = ['rOpen','rHigh','rLow','rClose']
_o,_h,_l,_c = [rohlc[h] for h in range(len(rohlc)) ]

mav = [fast, slow, 200]
ma_st,ma_mt,ma_lt = [df[_c].rolling(mav[t]).mean() for t in
range(len(mav))]

bo = [fast, slow]
st_lo,lt_lo = [df[_l].rolling(bo[t]).min() for t in range(len(bo))]
st_hi,lt_hi = [df[_h].rolling(bo[t]).max() for t in range(len(bo))]

rrg_combo = ['rClose','rrg','rL3','rH3','rL3','rH3','rclg','rflr','r
rg_ch']
_c,rg,lo,hi,slo,shi,clg,flr,rg_ch =[rrg_combo[r] for r in
range(len(rrg_combo)) ]
graph_regime_combo(ticker,df,_c,rg,lo,hi,slo,shi,clg,flr,rg_ch,ma_
st,ma_mt,ma_lt,lt_lo,lt_hi,st_lo,st_hi)
```

This produces the following two charts.

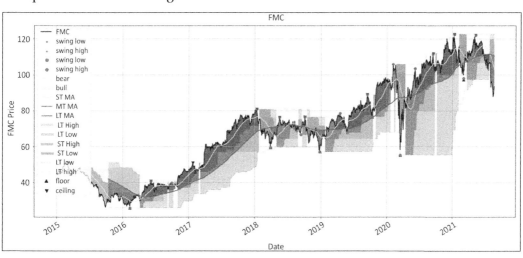

Figure 8: Absolute chart with multiple regime methodologies

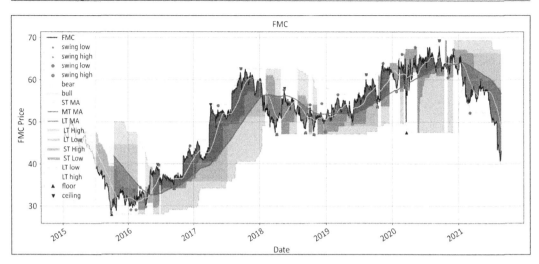

Figure 9: Relative chart with multiple regime methodologies

This is the end of this book and the beginning of your journey in the vast wilderness of short selling. You now have a map that will help you navigate the treacherous waters of the short side.

As a parting word, our ruthless industry faithfully abides by one law: supply and demand. In the long/short business, there is an ample supply of long side stock pickers and a cruel shortage of skilled short sellers.

When markets are down, those who stand up, stand out.

packt.com

Subscribe to our online digital library for full access to over 7,000 books and videos, as well as industry leading tools to help you plan your personal development and advance your career. For more information, please visit our website.

Why subscribe?

- Spend less time learning and more time coding with practical eBooks and Videos from over 4,000 industry professionals
- Learn better with Skill Plans built especially for you
- Get a free eBook or video every month
- Fully searchable for easy access to vital information
- Copy and paste, print, and bookmark content

Did you know that Packt offers eBook versions of every book published, with PDF and ePub files available? You can upgrade to the eBook version at www.Packt.com and as a print book customer, you are entitled to a discount on the eBook copy. Get in touch with us at customercare@packtpub.com for more details.

At www.Packt.com, you can also read a collection of free technical articles, sign up for a range of free newsletters, and receive exclusive discounts and offers on Packt books and eBooks.

Other Books You May Enjoy

If you enjoyed this book, you may be interested in these other books by Packt:

Machine Learning for Algorithmic Trading – Second Edition

Stefan Jansen

ISBN: 978-1-83921-771-5

- Leverage market, fundamental, and alternative text and image data
- Research and evaluate alpha factors using statistics, Alphalens, and SHAP values
- Implement machine learning techniques to solve investment and trading problems
- Backtest and evaluate trading strategies based on machine learning using Zipline and Backtrader

- Optimize portfolio risk and performance analysis using pandas, NumPy, and pyfolio
- Create a pairs trading strategy based on cointegration for US equities and ETFs
- Train a gradient boosting model to predict intraday returns using AlgoSeek's high-quality trades and quotes data

Expert Python Programming – Fourth Edition

Michał Jaworski

Tarek Ziadé

ISBN: 978-1-80107-110-9

- Explore modern ways of setting up repeatable and consistent Python development environments
- Effectively package Python code for community and production use
- Learn modern syntax elements of Python programming, such as f-strings, enums, and lambda functions
- Demystify metaprogramming in Python with metaclasses
- Write concurrent code in Python
- Extend and integrate Python with code written in C and C++

Packt is searching for authors like you

If you're interested in becoming an author for Packt, please visit authors.packtpub.com and apply today. We have worked with thousands of developers and tech professionals, just like you, to help them share their insight with the global tech community. You can make a general application, apply for a specific hot topic that we are recruiting an author for, or submit your own idea.

Share your thoughts

Now you've finished *Algorithmic Short Selling with Python*, we'd love to hear your thoughts! Scan the QR code below to go straight to the Amazon review page for this book and share your feedback or leave a review on the site that you purchased it from.

https://packt.link/r/1801815194

Your review is important to us and the tech community and will help us make sure we're delivering excellent quality content.

Index

Made in United States
North Haven, CT
23 January 2023